Yale Historical Publications

Miscellany, 96

Szechwan and the Chinese Republic

Provincial Militarism and Central Power, 1911–1938

Robert A. Kapp

New Haven and London, Yale University Press

1973

Published with assistance from the foundation
established in memory of Philip Hamilton McMillan
of the Class of 1894, Yale College.

Library of Congress catalog card number: 73-77155
International standard book number: 0-300-01604-2

Designed by John O. C. McCrillis
and set in Baskerville type.
Printed in the United States of America by
The Murray Printing Company, Forge Village, Massachusetts.

Published in Great Britain, Europe, and Africa by
Yale University Press, Ltd., London.
Distributed in Latin America by Kaiman & Polon,
Inc., New York City; in Australasia and Southeast
Asia by John Wiley & Sons Australasia Pty. Ltd.,
Sydney; in India by UBS Publishers' Distributors Pvt.,
Ltd., Delhi; in Japan by John Weatherhill, Inc., Tokyo.

To the Memory of
Mary Clabaugh Wright

Contents

Illustrations

Between pages 86 and 87

Liu Hsiang, late December 1934
Liu Wen-hui, 1935
Chungking, ca. 1910
Yang Sen, 1924
T'ien Sung-yao, 1934
Teng Hsi-hou, probably early 1930s
A Szechwanese army unit, ca. 1922
Local militia in Szechwan, probably 1939

Maps

Acknowledgments

Knowing how much I have benefited from the aid and advice of others in preparing this study makes it all the more important to express my thanks and to emphasize that the shortcomings in what follows are among my own personal contributions.

Mary Clabaugh Wright was the patient yet rigorous director of the dissertation from which this study is drawn. She died shortly after the dissertation was finished, and I soon moved far from New Haven, where we had worked together. Perhaps it is my own distance from Yale and the constant reminders of her absence that accounts for the power of her continued presence in my mind; it is as though she were not gone. Alone with my work, it is still possible to consult her, ask what she thinks or would do, and find answers in the memory of her mind and her conversation.

Professor Jonathan D. Spence of Yale was on hand to launch me into this project and to meet me with valuable advice as I completed the dissertation; I am very grateful to him.

Among the many people who have contributed their ideas and memories or their bibliographic knowledge are Professor Jerome Ch'en, Mr. Chou K'ai-ch'ing, Professor Parker Po-fei Huang, Mr. Liu Hang-shen, Professor Hung-mao T'ien, Mr. David Tseng, and Mr. Weiying Wan.

I also appreciate the cooperation of the following institutions: The Church Mission Society Library (London), The Hoover Institution (Stanford, California), The Institute of Modern History, Academia Sinica (Taipei), the Jimbun Kagaku Kenkyusho (Kyoto), The Kuomintang Archives (Taiwan), The Library of Congress, Orientalia Division (Washington), The National Diet Library (Tokyo), The Public Record Office (London), The United States National Archives (Washington), and the Yale University Library, particularly the East Asian Collection and the China Records Project of the Divinity School Library.

Financial support for this work has come from several NDEA fellowships, a Lewis-Farmington Fellowship at Yale University, a summer study grant from the International Relations Council at Yale, and summer research grants from Rice University. Special thanks must go to Edward Tripp and Cynthia Brodhead of the Yale University Press for patience and editorial competence, and to Karl Rueckert for skillfully preparing the three maps.

As for my wife, Mary Catherine, let it suffice that now I know why authors grope for words in speaking of their wives in their acknowledgments.

R. A. K.

Houston, Texas
November, 1971

Introduction

This is a study of militarism and separatism in one Chinese province, and of the efforts of would-be political centralizers to integrate that province into a national political structure after decades of confusion and disunion. The province is Szechwan, huge, rich, and populous, on the upper reaches of the Yangtze River. The time is primarily the late 1920s and the 1930s, prior to the outbreak of Sino-Japanese war in 1937.

The significance of the subject is actually twofold. Szechwanese provincial militarism in Republican China was on the one hand a symptom of the times, a manifestation of specific conditions after the fall of the Ch'ing dynasty. On the other hand, however, provincial separatism in Szechwan was a manifestation of political tendencies and dilemmas as old as the Chinese Empire. Indeed, the conflict between mechanisms of political integration and tendencies toward disintegration has characterized Chinese history ever since the destruction of feudal independence by the Ch'in dynasty in the third century B.C.

To start with the more immediate sense, twentieth-century militarism and regional separatism emerged in a dark period of intellectual and political disorganization, as ancient institutions and ideologies crumbled and collapsed. As many scholars have noted, no plans or prefabricated political and ideological structures stood waiting for China when the imperial form of government vanished in 1912. The twentieth century has seen the piecemeal and painful transformation of the Chinese Empire into the Chinese state, the clash of tradition and innovation, the failure of many experiments. In the nineteenth century basic questions had gradually risen to the surface: how was China to defend itself against predatory Western nations? Was China a "nation," or how could it become one? How could a modern Chinese government be organized, operated, and above all justified? How should such a government relate to a populace whose traditional contact with formal government had been confined to a few spheres of life and whose

1

political consciousness was underdeveloped? Workable solutions to such colossal problems were slow to emerge, and China passed through a long season of instability and disorganization following the destruction of the Empire.

One symptom of this unhappy condition during the Republican period was the failure of repeated efforts to create a genuinely national government and the dissolution of China into numerous independent areas, each under the control of an individual militarist or a militarist faction. Twentieth-century subnational militarism, or "warlordism," as it is usually called, fed on the fundamental uncertainty over what should take its place. Western-style constitutionalism failed from the start as a meaningful alternative to imperial government, while lingering and ill-founded dreams of a return to imperial forms were shattered in 1916 and 1917. A particularly twentieth-century quality of Republican militarism was thus a lack of widely recognized alternatives to fragmentation, a lack of a sense of system from which subnational militarism was somehow a deviation.

Still, Republican militarism cannot be viewed solely within its postimperial context. It was at the same time a new expression of the ancient problem of local differentiation and local autonomy. The roots of powerful anticentralism lie in China's geographic enormity, in the varieties of climate and terrain within China, in the difficulties of communication over long distances in pre-modern China, and in the regional variations in historical experience arising from these other factors.

Furthermore, local autonomy, within limits, had been an essential ingredient in the political formula of imperial Chinese government. The effectiveness and viability of a central regime staffed by a tiny corps of bureaucrats depended on the minimization of formal governmental intervention in the affairs of local communities. It was a matter of proper balance between central and local control. If it became too virulent, local particularism threatened the existence of central power. Inability to gather revenues or maintain order in a region or province was both a sign of Imperial weakness and the cause of further decline. If the elusive harmonious balance between legitimate central authority and persistent localism were too severely upset, central authority became untenable. Once the political–administrative center collapsed, the enhanced strength of local separatism made reunification of the Chinese polity all the more arduous.

Not all of the militarism which devoured postimperial China derived from such historic, geographically based localism, but much of it did. The survival or demise of many Republican militarists depended on the same factors which underlay a region's sense of its own peculiarity. Political units whose boundaries had long reflected the influences of geography became even more distinctly separate from the larger polity after 1911 than they had been under the Empire. Moreover, resurgent localism was not confined to a single level of administrative organization. China did not dissolve after the 1911 Revolution into a set of equally independent provinces, or a mass of equally autarkical districts, or a labyrinth of equally autonomous subdistrict units.

One level of particularly powerful, persistent, and conspicuous localism was the province. Despite the collapse of regularized administrative procedures with the fall of the Ch'ing, the province as a political unit endured throughout the Republican period. During the so-called warlord era, individual provinces like Kwangsi, Kwangtung, Shansi, Yunnan, and Szechwan provided the long-term bases of support for military leaders whose interests were in turn defined above all in terms of provincial power.

Szechwan Province in West China was a case in point. For most of the period between 1912 and 1937, the year in which the Chinese National Government migrated to Szechwan, the province as a whole lay beyond the reach of outside political authority and military power. Central government efforts to weave Szechwan into the shaky national political structure in the mid-1930s provided ample evidence of the Chinese Nationalists' approach to national integration and revealed many of the obstacles that the centralizers had to overcome.

Szechwan's political position after 1912 rested on the province's geographic isolation from the rest of China and on its great wealth and population. The central, heavily settled portion of Szechwan, known as the Red Basin because of the characteristic color of the soil, is cut off from the outside world by a variety of natural barriers. Along the northern frontier with Shensi and Hupei, the Ta Pa Shan range forms a wall through which only a few ancient and treacherous paths reach to connect Szechwan with the Wei Valley and the North China Plain. Szechwan's eastern borders with Hupei and Hunan are also mountainous; though the Yangtze River, Szechwan's principal link with the outside, leads directly to central and East China, the upriver passage through the rapids and the Yangtze Gorges along the Szechwan–Hupei border is slow and easily obstructed. More mountains line the southern borders with Kweichow and Yunnan, while in the west and northwest

Szechwan faces the inhospitable and thinly populated plateaus and mountains of Sikang, Tsinghai, and Kansu.

Geographically, Szechwan was thus a world of its own, easily cut off from outside control when the integrating mechanisms of imperial government lost their force. The province's economic self-sufficiency also contributed to its isolation. From the first Chinese settlement in Szechwan in the third century B.C., the area was renowned for its productivity. The term "Treasure Vault" (*T'ien-fu chih kuo*) has stood for Szechwan since the third century A.D. Szechwan was as famous for the variety of its products as for the quantity it produced.[1] Not only in the Chengtu Plain, where three crops can be raised each year, but in the hillier sections of the Basin, intensive agriculture thrives. Szechwan traditionally supplied surplus grain to poorer provinces, and the province customarily provided large quantities of sugar and silk. Salt was produced in many places, including the vast Tzuliuching well complex in the southwest. In the nineteenth century, Szechwan became one of China's principal opium-growing regions as well. Such enormous productivity supported a vast population in the twentieth century; by the mid-1930s, there were nearly fifty million Szechwanese.[2]

From the Three Kingdoms period, when Liu Pei and Chu-ko Liang had established their power in Shu, to the creation of the Great Western Kingdom by the rebel Chang Hsien-chung at the end of the Ming, Szechwan showed a tendency to become separated from the political life of the rest of China. History provided numerous cases of separatist leaders establishing themselves in Szechwan during times of weakened central authority. Yet the cultural assets of the region which became Szechwan Province left no doubt that Szechwan was an integral part of China proper. Repeated waves of immigration and colonization, such as that which followed the depopulation of Szechwan at the end of the Ming, brought people from other provinces into Szechwan and helped to strengthen the cultural links with more central regions of the country.

Among Szechwan's most renowned assets were Mount Omei, sacred in Chinese Buddhism; the magnificent water control system on the Chengtu Plain, first constructed by Li Ping in the third century B.C.; and the huge salt-producing complex at Tzuliuching, where natural gas from the salt wells was brought up thousands of feet and used to boil brine. Wood-block printing also originated in Szechwan, and the province produced some of China's most famous literary figures. The Han poet Ssu-ma Hsiang-ju, the T'ang poet Li Po, and the Sung

SZECHWAN PROVINCE

master Su Tung-p'o all were Szechwanese. In the Ming and Ch'ing periods, despite its distance from the political centers in Peking and the lower Yangtze region, Szechwan retained its reputation for cultural refinement and regional cultural leadership. Chengtu, the provincial capital known as "the Peking of the West," was famous for its elegance and grace. The German geographer von Richthofen, who visited Szechwan in 1870, wrote:

> [Chengtu] is among the largest cities of China, and of all the finest and most refined. . . . The streets are broad, most of them straight, and cross each other at right angles. . . . All teahouses, inns, shops, private dwellings have their walls covered with pictures, many of which remind one of the Japanese ink and watercolor drawings in point of artistic touch. . . . This artistic taste is perceptible throughout the surrounding country, every smaller city being in that respect like a piece of Ching-tu [*sic*]. No traveller can help being struck with the great artistic perfection of the triumphal arches worked in red sandstone which abound in the country. They are covered with sculptures in *haut* and *bas* relief representing scenes of mythical or everyday life, mostly with a tinge of the humorous; some of them are masterpieces of Chinese art. In no respect is the refinement more perceptible than in the polished manners and gentle behavior of the people, in regard to which the inhabitants of Ching-tu-fu [*sic*] are far ahead of the rest of China.[3]

Szechwan was a Chinese province, not only because of its ethnic composition and cultural history, but because of its very uniqueness. Underlying resurgent localism and the long struggle for political unification after 1912 was the paradox that particularity was itself universal. The provincial dialect, Szechwanese cuisine, the atypical settlement pattern in which peasant homes lay scattered across the land rather than clustered in villages: these peculiarly Szechwanese characteristics made the province distinctive but no less Chinese. In the Republican period, Szechwan shared with other regions the miseries of rampant militarism and economic distress, but it continued to display its particularities of custom and consciousness. Thus the province was neither wholly representative of China's condition in the "warlord era" nor wholly atypical. Would-be unifiers in Szechwan and elsewhere had to strike the proper balance between essential national standardization and an equally essential recognition of the many levels and implications of powerful anticentralism.

In an important sense, the story of Szechwanese military separatism in Republican China is the story of Szechwan's ruling militarists themselves. Szechwan offers neither the attraction of outstanding heroes, rising inspired above the turmoil and agony of their age, nor the promise of a satisfying and conclusive resolution of the struggle between central and subnational power. Instead of "the Model Governor" or "the Christian General," Szechwan gives us "the Stubby Melon," "the Rotten Pig," "the Two-Headed Snake," "the Yes-Man," "Laughing Boy," and, at best, "the Indestructible."[4] Most of the study which follows deals with the decade from 1927 to 1937, during which Szechwanese militarists were strongest and most independent. It concludes with the death of the foremost provincial militarist early in 1938, because his passing coincided with the arrival of the Chinese central government in Szechwan and the modification of Szechwan's relationship to central authority.

The coming of China's highest political leaders to Szechwanese soil did not eliminate the problem of provincialism, however, let alone the larger problem of localist opposition to Chinese political integration. That situation far predated Szechwan's military leaders and the Chinese Nationalists, and it endures even as the last of these figures disappear from sight.

1 The Evolution of Provincial Politics, 1911–1926

The "warlord era" in twentieth-century Chinese history began, it is generally acknowledged, with the fall of Yüan Shih-k'ai in 1916. Yüan's unsuccessful attempt to re-establish imperial government opened the floodgates to militarist opposition and provincial secession, while his own death in June 1916 removed the one figure who had proved capable of maintaining a degree of centralized control over China after the fall of the Ch'ing.

There is less agreement as to how long the "warlord era" lasted. It is axiomatic, in some circles, that Chiang Kai-shek's triumph over the Peking militarists in 1928 ended the warlord period.[1] A recent study of one Chinese militarist has rightly noted that subnational militarism continued after 1928 and has used the term "residual warlordism" to describe it.[2] Both of these views imply that the era of such powerful northern militarists as Tuan Ch'i-jui, Chang Tso-lin, and Wu P'ei-fu was the period in which Chinese warlordism arose, flourished in its disorderly way, and declined.

Provincial militarism in Szechwan did not conform to such an interpretation. Far from signaling the end of warlordism in Szechwan, the "unification" of China under Chiang Kai-shek in 1927 and 1928 left Szechwanese leaders stronger and freer from outside interference than they had been before. Perhaps militarism in Szechwan after 1927 was "residual" in the sense that the whole phenomenon of autonomous provincial militarism eventually receded after 1949, but it gave no sign at the time of being merely a leftover from a bygone age.

The strength and independence of Szechwanese commanders after 1927 was rooted in the first fifteen years of the Republican period. Before examining in detail the flourishing Szechwanese localism and militarism of the late 1920s and the 1930s, it is essential to consider Szechwan's experiences between the Revolution of 1911 and the Nationalists' Northern Expedition of 1926.

During this period of preparation, four particularly significant processes went forward in the province. First, militarization engulfed provincial government and society. Second, unified provincial political authority gave way to geopolitical fragmentation of the province. Third, Szechwan's involvement in national affairs and its relation to outside political leadership passed through a series of stages. Fourth, a generation of early Republican militarists rose to power in the province after the 1911 Revolution, only to lose their positions and give way to a younger generation of commanders by the mid-1920s. This second generation constituted the ruling military elite in Szechwan during the later 1920s, the 1930s, and even the 1940s.

These developments filled a dismal period of Szechwanese history. Especially after the fall of Yüan Shih-k'ai in 1916, Szechwan suffered from nearly uninterrupted war, burgeoning opium addiction, economic disruption, and ineffectual or nonexistent provincial government. Constantly shifting military alliances, frequent military conflicts, and the spread of social disorder make the chronicle of events bewildering. Even after 1927, Szechwan could hardly boast of long-lasting and all-pervasive tranquillity, but at least by then a stable military elite had emerged and a rough solution to the problem of territorial distribution within the province had evolved. The question of political legitimacy which underlay the chaos of the early Republican years had been partially resolved. After 1927 the province's relations with the rest of China were simpler if not more intimate. For these reasons, the first fifteen years of the Republican era form a single, discernible phase in the province's political development.

The Militarization of Szechwan

The militarization of Szechwan—that is, the spread of armed forces throughout the province and the substitution of territorial control based on armed force for legitimate civil government—began almost as soon as Szechwan severed its ties with the Ch'ing government late in 1911. Even before the Wuchang uprising of October 10, 1911, Szechwan had been the scene of a major confrontation between provincial and imperial interests. At stake was the right to finance and build the proposed railway from Szechwan to Hupei. Led by active and influential Szechwanese merchants and gentry figures, provincial protests against the Ch'ing government's decision to build the road itself had led to violence during the fall. Armed bands, formed by secret societies and the Railway Protection League (*Pao-lu t'ung-chih hui)*, appeared in many parts of the province. After the Wuchang uprising and the outbreak of opposition to Ch'ing authority in other areas of China, Szechwan moved toward provincial independence. As the situation in central China crumbled, the governor-general of Szechwan released the provincial leaders whom he had earlier imprisoned, and on November 27, 1911, he declared Szechwan independent. The leaders of the Railway Protection Movement and the Provincial Assembly in Chengtu formed the "Szechwan Great Han Military Government," its name signifying the destruction of alien Manchu rule.[3]

Since the prerevolutionary Provincial Assembly had emerged as the most vigorous champion of Szechwanese provincial interests in the waning days of the Ch'ing, the government created by its leaders had a reasonable claim to the legitimate authority formerly exercised by the dynasty. By virtue of its location, its composition, and the manner in which it was born, the Chengtu government was clearly the heir to the Ch'ing in Szechwan. Yet in less than two weeks, this successor government collapsed amid military disorders in the capital. P'u Tien-chün, the gentry leader of the Railway Protection struggle who had become the head of the Chengtu government, was unable to control the horde of unpaid soldiers who flocked into the city. On December 7, 1911, which became known as the "Day of the Great Looting," the soldiers mutinied and P'u resigned. Yin Ch'ang-heng, an army officer with extensive contacts in the Railway Protection League and the powerful *Ko-lao hui* secret society, became the leader of the Chengtu government.[4]

The demise of P'u Tien-chün's government marked the disintegration of the revolutionary movement which had been centered in the Provincial Assembly and focused on the railway issue. With the collapse of both Ch'ing hegemony and the political movement which had brought revolution to Szechwan in the first place, both claimants to legitimate provincial power disappeared from the scene. Furthermore, the departure of Ch'ing officials left an administrative vacuum in the province.[5] The looting of the provincial treasury during the December disorders in Chengtu deprived future provincial administrators of the financial wherewithal that might have helped to bring stability to the province.[6]

Yin Ch'ang-heng did not last long in power in Chengtu; by 1913 he was in prison in Peking at Yüan Shih-k'ai's order. His removal did not indicate a return to civilian-based government in Szechwan, however.

On the contrary, the militarization of Szechwan continued with only temporary interruptions during Yüan Shih-k'ai's tenure in Peking. At the heart of the militarization of Szechwan was the rapid spread of arms and armed forces throughout the province. As one foreign observer mused,

> It was all so simple in the old days of the Empire. Then there were few weapons of precision in private hands, and law and order were maintained with a relatively inconsiderable number of troops. . . . But the Revolution scattered arms throughout the province, and individual and conflicting ambitions recruited troops by the thousands; the able-bodied of the erstwhile underworld were absorbed into the armies, and there they stayed, so that there were now more troops in the province than it could support. Send them off to other provinces? But the other provinces are in like plight.[7]

In the absence of recognized criteria of political legitimacy and mechanisms for their fulfillment, military commanders rose to occupy the openings in the ranks of political leadership. From 1916 to 1927, militarists held the two highest provincial offices, the military and civil governorships, almost without interruption.* Military forces proliferated, and with them a pattern of decentralized military control emerged. Even when a high-ranking commander claimed control of wide territories, individual units of his armies drew their sustenance from the lands they occupied.[8] Local occupying forces appointed civil administrators such as district magistrates and circuit intendants, who were often military officers themselves.[9]

While the trappings of political authority came to rest in the hands of military commanders, the size of the more or less formally designated armies in Szechwan rapidly increased. On the eve of the 1911 Revolution, Imperial army troops in Szechwan totaled slightly more than 53,000, of whom just over 16,000 belonged to the modernized New Army division organized in the province and about 10,500 to the Banners and the Army of the Green Standard.[10] Comprehensive and reliable figures on the growth of armed forces in Szechwan from 1911 to 1927 are not available. By 1919, however, the number of soldiers in formally designated units exceeded 300,000.[11] Szechwan's provincial armies in the mid-1930s were larger than the entire New Army had

---

*An exception was Chang Lan, civil governor of Szechwan in 1917, who had been a leader of the prerevolutionary Provincial Assembly and who went on to a distinguished career as an educator and liberal political leader.

been at the time of the Revolution. Coincident with the vast increase in army enrollments, a heavy buildup of locally supported militia forces took place. Much of the increase in the strength of Szechwanese militia occurred in the early years of the Republican period. By the early thirties, estimates of militia size ran as high as more than half a million men.[12]

The First Generation of Republican Militarists in Szechwan

Among the hundreds of military officers who commanded brigades or higher-level military units between 1911 and 1926, some played more important roles, and for longer periods, than others. A finite and gradually diminishing corps of militarists commanded the largest forces in the province for most of these fifteen years. Within this group, men might be allies one week and enemies the next. Together, though, they formed a distinct generation of Szechwanese military leaders. Having risen to high rank and military power in the earliest years of the Republic, the commanders of the first generation fell from power before 1927. In fact, one of the defining characteristics of this militarist generation was that most of its members had dropped into obscurity by 1927.

From limited available information about these provincial militarists, a modest profile can be drawn.[13] First, the great majority of them were born between 1875 and 1880. Hsiung K'o-wu and Tan Mou-hsin, two of the province's most influential commanders prior to 1926, were born in 1881 and 1879 respectively. Hu Ching-i, who engineered the downfall of Yin Ch'ang-heng and succeeded Yin as military governor of Szechwan, was born in 1877. Chou Tao-kang, military governor in 1917, was born in 1875. Liu Ch'eng-hsün, commander-in-chief of Szechwanese armies in 1922, was born in 1879. Among the Szechwanese generals closely associated with the Kuomintang (Nationalist Party), Shih Ch'ing-yang was born in 1879, Yang Shu-k'an in 1880, and Huang Fu-sheng in 1875. There were, of course, exceptions to the rule. Yin Ch'ang-heng was born in 1886, and Liu Ts'un-hou, who had a long and checkered military career before his final defeat in 1933, was born in 1884.

All of these men were natives of Szechwan. Many of them were graduates of the first modern military school established in the province during the last years of the Ch'ing, the Szechwan Military Preparatory School *(Ssu-ch'uan wu-pei hsüeh-t'ang)*. The Military Preparatory School was founded in 1902 by the Szechwanese governor-general and it operated until 1906. Its curriculum was based on Japanese

military academy models and Japanese teachers and drill instructors
were employed. Four of the five divisions into which Yin Ch'ang-heng
organized Szechwan's armies in 1912 were commanded by graduates
of this school. Yin himself, Liu Ch'eng-hsün, Liu Ts'un-hou and others
who had attended the Military Preparatory School began their careers
in the newly created modern army of the late Ch'ing. Several, including
Yin, Hu Ching-i, Chou Tao-kang, and Liu Ch'eng-hsün, served under
Szechwan's former Governor-General Hsi-liang in other provinces.[14]

Not all of the first-generation militarists had attended this particular
school. Another group of Szechwanese commanders gained prominence
through their association with the anti-Manchu revolutionary movement in the early 1900s. Hsiung K'o-wu and Tan Mou-hsin, the two
most powerful men in this group, had long records of revolutionary
activity in Japan, Canton, and Szechwan before 1911. Others in this
category included Lu Shih-t'i, Shih Ch'ing-yang, Huang Fu-sheng, and
Yang Shu-k'an.

Whether or not they had trained at the Szechwan Military Preparatory School, the great majority of Szechwan's first-generation
militarists had gone abroad for military education. Like students from
other provinces at this time, most Szechwanese cadets went to Japan,
where the Japanese Cadet Academy *(Nihon Shikan Gakko)* trained
hundreds of Chinese in the first years of the twentieth century. The
revolutionary activities of Hsiung K'o-wu, Tan Mou-hsin, and other
anti-Manchu Szechwanese officers dated from their student days in
Japan and their early contact with Sun Yat-sen's Revolutionary
Alliance *(T'ung-meng hui)*.

Stepping after 1912 into positions which were at least nominally
equivalent to the highest posts in the Ch'ing provincial political structure, the members of Szechwan's first militarist generation rose to the
height of their careers early in life and were still young when they fell
from power. Yin Ch'ang-heng had come and gone by the age of thirty.
Hsiung K'o-wu was military governor at age thirty-seven and fled
Szechwan for the last time at forty-three. Hu Ching-i's military career
ended when he was thirty-nine, while Liu Ts'un-hou was reduced to
military insignificance by the time he was forty-one. In retirement,
many of these figures became respected members of gentry society,
retaining a degree of prestige that testified to their respectable origins.*

*Yin Ch'ang-heng, for example, spent his retirement writing and studying, and he main-
tained enormous prestige among the students of Chengtu. As a British diplomat noted, "He
is the only man to whom students and others will listen hour after hour with rapt attention,

All in all, this first group of prominent Republican militarists were indeed well-educated, even cosmopolitan products of the shifting educational and social milieu of the very late Ch'ing.

By 1926, however, military power in Szechwan had passed from the hands of these commanders into those of younger leaders whose age, education, military experience, and outlook distinguished them from their predecessors. The flight of Hsiung K'o-wu and the elimination of Liu Ts'un-hou as an important figure in provincial politics were the clearest signs that the first generation was passing from the scene. The line between the two generations was not absolutely clear; some of the younger men held high military posts in Szechwan well before 1926. But the general distinction between the two groups is clear enough, and the military ruling group of post-1927 Szechwan deserves separate treatment in the next chapter.

Fragmentation of the Province

With the removal of Ch'ing administration and the ensuing militarization of Szechwan, unified control of the entire province ceased to exist. In Szechwan, as in China as a whole, geography made the maintenance of effective centralized control difficult, once the norms and institutions of structured bureaucratic administration failed to function properly. The mountainous areas surrounding the Szechwan Basin were hard to reach and hold. Within the Basin the richness of the territory, the scattering of major cities in many sections of the province, and the primitive state of communications in the hilly terrain promoted the fragmentation of territorial control in the first years of the Chinese Republic.

Szechwan began to break apart in the very first days of the Revolution. Even before the declaration of provincial independence in 1911, uprisings against Ch'ing authority had taken place in numerous districts all over Szechwan under the leadership of the decentralized Railway Protection League. With the Revolution, district after district declared its own independence. In addition to the Chengtu regime

---

and his power over them is enormous" (Hewlett [Chengtu] to Peking, December 5, 1921, F.O. 371/8027). For a character sketch of Yin in retirement see King, *China in Turmoil*, pp. 223–29. Chou Tao-kang, driven from his position in 1918, reappeared as vice-chairman of the Chengtu Rehabilitation Conference of 1925, a post indicative of his high social standing. Hu Ching-i was one of the provincial dignitaries selected to welcome Chiang Kai-shek on his arrival in Szechwan in 1935. See *Ssu-ch'uan shan-hou hui-i lu* [Proceedings of the Szechwan Rehabilitation Conference] ([Chengtu] [1926]), pt. 1, p. 9; *KWCP*, May 20, 1935; and Davidson (Chungking) to Peiping, February 11, 1935, F.O. 371/19307.

formed by leaders of the old Provincial Assembly in late November, three other notable governments emerged, one in the great Yangtze port of Chungking, another in Luchou farther up the Yangtze, and yet another in Kuangyüan, on the Chialing River near the Shensi border.[15] The two main centers of power, Chungking and Chengtu, reached a merger agreement in March 1912, but by permitting military authority to remain in Chungking while administrative authority stayed in Chengtu the agreement failed to re-establish effective unified provincial government.

Particularly after the fall of Yüan Shih-k'ai, as the growth of Szechwanese armies accelerated, provincial government for all practical purposes vanished. The functions of government—revenue collection, appointment of officials, maintenance of order, administration of justice, and public works—fell into the hands of military commanders in the territories held by their forces. This geopolitical fragmentation persisted in Szechwan throughout the 1920s and most of the 1930s.

Occasionally in the early years of the Republic an individual commander or a coalition of provincial militarists would claim control of all the territory of the province. Invariably, however, the pattern of alliances would soon shift, and these leaders would be driven from their cities and their titles. Furthermore, it soon became clear that the real test of a high-ranking militarist's power was his control over his own subordinates; in the disorders of postrevolutionary Szechwan, even the claim to regional territorial control carried little weight, since local power frequently resided in the hands of lower-level commanders. In its confusion as to what constituted acceptable forms of political power, and in its fragmentation into numerous unstable military domains, Szechwan was in fact a microcosm of China's national condition after the destruction of Ch'ing authority.

Szechwan and the Outside World, 1911–26

In 1911 Szechwan was an integral, if distant, element in a centrally dominated imperial political structure. In 1927 the province was an isolated, independent militarist region with virtually no substantive ties to external political authority. This change in Szechwan's relation to the outside world did not happen overnight. Instead, the province passed through stages of growing disengagement and diminishing external influence which culminated in the nearly total autonomy characteristic of the years after 1927.

Though this process was gradual, one feature stood out from the beginning of the Republican period. With the exception of a brief period in 1914 when Yüan Shih-k'ai's forces maintained a semblance of coordinated control over the entire province, no outside military or political force was able to govern all of Szechwan after 1911. Nevertheless, the province was enmeshed time after time in the political affairs of other areas during the 1911–26 period. Recurrent outside interference in Szechwan was as characteristic of the times as was the inability of outsiders to gain control of the province. Szechwan's wealth and great population made it a natural target for predatory neighbors. Over and over, the province was a battleground for conflicting external interests and the prize for competing outside forces. Only in 1926 did the Szechwanese manage to drive non-Szechwanese troops from their province for an extended length of time.

There is a well-known saying in Chinese, "When the Empire is peaceful, Szechwan is the first to have disorders; after peace is restored, Szechwan is the last to be stabilized." It is a revealing expression, because it indicates both Szechwan's integration into the larger Chinese whole and its peculiar position in relation to political conditions elsewhere. At the end of the Ch'ing, the outbreak of the Railway Protection Movement in Szechwan presaged the revolution against Manchu rule. After the Revolution, Szechwan continued for a while to play an active role in national politics, particularly in the conflict between Sun Yat-sen's adherents and the Peking militarists. Szechwanese forces joined the opposition to Yüan Shih-k'ai in the "Second Revolution" of 1913, but the movement failed elsewhere before the Szechwanese dissidents reached Chengtu; the leaders of the rebellion fled the province.[16]

In 1915 and 1916, Szechwan became the principal battleground in the war against Yüan Shih-k'ai that brought about his downfall. Numerous Szechwanese militarists, including Hsiung K'o-wu and Liu Ts'un-hou, joined with the so-called Army to Protect the Nation led by the Yunnanese Ts'ai O when it invaded Szechwan in December 1915. By the spring of 1916, Yüan's governor in Szechwan, Ch'en I, realized that Yüan's cause was lost. When Yüan refused to relinquish the presidency, Ch'en declared Szechwan independent. By the end of June 1916, both Ch'en and the Northern forces of Ts'ao K'un and Chang Ching-yao had withdrawn from Szechwan.[17]

The war against Yüan Shih-k'ai was the last time that Szechwan played a decisive part in China's national politics until 1937, when the National Government migrated to the province. This did not shield

Szechwan from further outside interference, however. Starting with the movement of troops from Yunnan and Kweichow into Szechwan at the moment of independence in 1911, Szechwan endured repeated invasions and occupations by outside armies until 1926. At times, individual Szechwanese militarists invited the "guest armies" into the province in order to combat their Szechwanese rivals more effectively. At other times, broad coalitions of Szechwanese generals cooperated to drive intruding forces out.

Invasion and occupation by external forces occurred in many Chinese provinces after 1911; Szechwan was not unique in facing uninvited "guest armies." Militarization of Szechwanese politics after the Revolution coincided with the expansion of armed forces elsewhere. The fluctuations of warlord politics and civil wars often tempted successful commanders into invading new territories and compelled defeated militarists to flee into areas beyond their original bases. Szechwan did suffer more heavily from outside invasion than did many other provinces, but in the decade from 1916 to 1926 such provinces as Hunan, Kwangtung, Kwangsi, and Fukien also endured repeated and prolonged "guest army" occupations. In central and northern China, territorial control shifted back and forth among the armies of Yüan Shih-k'ai's former disciples, whose forces carried national instead of provincial titles and seldom identified with the provinces they occupied, while the Fengtien forces of Chang Tso-lin identified closely with Chang's Manchurian base.

Generalizations about local response to the presence of "guest armies" are hazardous both for Szechwan and for China as a whole. Evidence of nativist hostility to the outsiders simply as outsiders can be found, but it fails to cover all instances of guest army occupation. The Northern armies, not representing specific provinces as did the Yunnan, Szechwan, or Kwangtung forces, usually did not provoke sustained, provincially defined opposition. On the other hand, in his specific denunciation of the Kwangsi occupation of Kwangtung, the influential Cantonese politician Tsou Lu emphasized the misdeeds of the Kwangsi armies, rather than their provincial origins, as the cause of Cantonese resentment. Another Cantonese writer noted that the Yunnanese occupation of Kwangtung had been far less repugnant than the subsequent Kwangsi occupation.[18]

The behavior of any army, native or "guest," strongly affected its local reception. Even in Hunan, where provincial antipathy toward outside armies was pronounced in the early 1920s, local and provincial leaders were sorry to see Feng Yü-hsiang's well-disciplined and popular armies end their two-year occupation of Ch'angte.[19] And in Kwangtung, local goodwill toward the Cantonese militarist Ch'en Chiung-ming in his native region during the early twenties stemmed not only from his local ties but also from the concrete reform policies that he carried out.[20]

In Szechwan itself, evidence of highly vocal resentment against the "guest armies" must be weighed against the provincial militarists' demonstrated willingness to entertain outside armies on Szechwanese soil, share occupation of vital centers, and even allot some sections of the province to the sole control of non-Szechwanese armies on several occasions. Moreover, violent local opposition to occupying armed forces was not directed only at troops from other provinces; in the twenties and early thirties, conflicts between Szechwanese provincial military units and local armed bands in the province occurred frequently.*

Nonetheless, in Szechwan as in Hunan and Kwangtung, restoration of provincial control to provincial natives became a rallying cry for provincial militarists and civilian politicians, particularly during the early twenties. Resentment against "guest armies" and outside interference proved to be a useful political instrument in those provinces, like Szechwan, which were subject to intensive invasion and civil war after 1911. Maximization of provincial power in provincial hands offered a legitimizing rationale for warding off Northern military pressure.[21] It expressed both the genuine sense of provincial loyalty which could be found in areas like Szechwan, Kwangtung, and Hunan, and the conscious aims of ambitious militarists in early Republican China.

Prior to 1920, the most serious intervention in Szechwan came from Yunnan and Kweichow.[22] This was a by-product of the war against Yüan Shih-k'ai, during which large numbers of troops from these provinces poured into Szechwan. Even Chungking and Chengtu were occupied by non-Szechwanese troops for extended periods. After 1920, when Liu Ts'un-hou and Hsiung K'o-wu joined forces under the slogan "Szechwan for the Szechwanese" to expel the Yunnanese, outside invasions were smaller and less frequent. In 1924, for example, Wu P'ei-fu sent forces into Szechwan from Hupei in cooperation with the Szechwanese Yang Sen, only to withdraw them soon after when his fortunes in North China shifted. Kweichow forces under Yüan Tsu-ming also entered Szechwan in 1924, taking partial control of

*See below, chap. 3.

Chungking and occupying some of the surrounding territory.[23] Yüan stayed on in Szechwan until 1926, when Szechwanese forces blocked his attempt to seize full control of Chungking and drove him out of the province.[24]

Thus, for most of the period between 1911 and 1926, outside military presence in Szechwan was a sign of Szechwan's continued involvement in external political conflicts. But it was not the only indicator; even the purely internal struggles of native militarists revealed the continuing concern among first-generation militarists for the broader currents of Chinese politics. Although the endlessly shifting alliances among provincial generals seemed to rule out any consistent adherence to outside causes, Szechwan's civil wars prior to 1926 often corresponded to developments in the struggle between the Kuomintang in the south and the Peking militarists.

Several important Szechwanese military leaders, such as Lu Shih-t'i, Huang Fu-sheng, and Shih Ch'ing-yang, commuted between Canton and Szechwan, returning to the province on critical Kuomintang assignments and fleeing downriver when defeated by opposing provincial militarists. In the "Second Revolution" of 1913, and again in 1918 and 1924, these leaders came to Szechwan, organized armies, and fought against the Kuomintang's alleged enemies in Szechwan, even though their opponents were also Szechwanese.

Here again, the distinction between purely provincial or personal military interests and larger commitments to outside political causes was not black and white; no doubt there were elements of both in most of the squabbling that took place in the name of the Kuomintang or the Peking government. Yet the leading militarists of the first generation had been raised in a national, not merely a provincial, milieu. They maintained personal contacts with militarists and politicians in the vital political centers of China even though their own province lay on the periphery. They retained some of the concern for larger Chinese political problems that they had gained in Japan, in Chinese military academies, and in the Revolutionary Alliance. Even though Szechwan rested beyond the comprehensive control of outside authority after 1915, developments within the province responded to outside pressures as long as the first militarist generation retained the principal positions of power in Szechwan.

Yet in this period Szechwanese forces rarely campaigned outside of Szechwan itself. Liu Ts'un-hou fled on several occasions across the border into Shensi, but he stuck close to the provincial boundary and did not attempt to create a permanent base there. The only real Szechwanese campaign into another province took place in August 1921, when rival Szechwanese militarists drove together into western Hupei in conjunction with a similar thrust into Hupei by the Hunanese Chao Heng-t'i. The ostensible purpose of this expedition was to "save" Hupei from the embraces of Wu P'ei-fu. The operation failed immediately and dismally, however, and Szechwanese forces fled up the Yangtze to Szechwan, where they resumed fighting among themselves. After having antagonized the powerful Wu P'ei-fu with this ill-fated Hupei maneuver, one of the Szechwanese leaders reached an amicable agreement with Wu and forestalled Wu's invasion of Szechwan.[25] Later in the 1920s, Szechwanese forces occasionally marauded in western Hupei, but these excursions did not last long, and the interest of Szechwan's principal commanders remained concentrated on the home front.

With the passage of time, the reluctance of Szechwanese commanders to venture beyond the borders of their province was reinforced by a rising tide of provincial separatist sentiment. The growth of this exclusive provincialism coincided with the emergence of a younger generation of Szechwanese military leaders from within the ranks of the older commanders' armies. In Szechwan's interminable military wrangling, these younger men advanced rapidly to high rank and even to independent command, and as the older leaders eliminated one another, the younger officers assumed the principal military roles in Szechwan. As a result of differences in their backgrounds and experiences, the second-generation leaders' views of outside entanglements differed markedly from those of the older militarists. Less deeply rooted in the political environment of the 1911 Revolution and the clash of North and South, the younger commanders cared more exclusively for their personal interests within Szechwan and were less concerned about conditions on the outside.

Provincialism itself was nothing new to Szechwan, but the provincialism of the rising militarists was a new departure, the product of the failure of national political development in the postrevolutionary period. Second-generation militarists were franker in acknowledging the inability of both North and South to acquire political legitimacy. Within Szechwan, their narrow provincialism accompanied their aggressive pursuit of personal advancement. Their perception of their own interests in exclusively provincial terms was symptomatic of Szechwan's detachment from external political structures in the wake of the Ch'ing collapse and the demise of Yüan Shih-k'ai.

Thus it should not be surprising that Szechwan's younger militarists took the lead in promoting Szechwanese provincial autonomy during the short-lived federalist movement that flourished in several provinces in 1921 and 1922.[26] On December 20, 1920, after Yunnanese armies had been expelled from Szechwan, a group of officers in Chungking sent a telegram to Hsiung K'o-wu and Liu Ts'un-hou, Szechwan's two foremost commanders. The officers advocated provincial autonomy on two basic grounds. First, they maintained that autonomy would free Szechwan from the buffeting it was taking in the conflict between North and South. Second, they enunciated the principle, "First improve the governance of the people, then improve the government," an expression of their idea that local government had to be developed before central authority could be established. Among the signers of the telegram were Liu Hsiang, Yang Sen, Teng Hsi-hou, and T'ien Sung-yao, four of the five most powerful militarists in Szechwan after 1927.[27]

The provincial autonomy movement in Szechwan moved forward speedily. Early in 1921, the Provincial Assembly proclaimed Szechwan's independence and pledged that the province would take no further part in the North–South controversy. The autonomy movement found support among Szechwanese living outside the province, as students in Peking and Szechwanese in Shanghai organized associations and published journals to promote Szechwanese self-government.[28]

The campaign continued throughout 1921 and into 1922. To some foreign observers, at least, it looked promising. General Liu Hsiang in particular emerged as the champion of provincial self-rule. The American consul in Chungking reported in June 1921 that

> the chief point of interest [was] his reiteration of the statement that Szechwan is a self-governing province and has no connection with either the Peking or the Canton Government. He enlarged on the theme that self-government is in accord with the practice of the day all over the world, and stated that the constitution of China should be changed giving the provinces more authority, something after the style of the German Confederation.[29]

In the spring of 1922, another American official observed that

> the Szechwanese appear determined not to go back into any national government that does not provide a maximum of provincial autonomy. They also believe that due to the geographical

situation it will be very nearly impossible for the National Government to force them back against their will. The Generalissimo [Liu Hsiang] has stated a number of times that Szechwan would be glad to enter a federal form of government whereby the provinces were practically autonomous, and that a form of government like that of the United States would probably be best for China.[30]

In the end, despite formation of two separate committees to work on a provincial constitution, nothing came of the campaign for formal provincial autonomy. Internal war and shortages of funds ended the committees' work in 1923.[31] Moreover, the abortive expedition to Hupei and Wu P'ei-fu's later intervention by proxy in Szechwan undermined the rhetoric of provincial noninvolvement in outside politics. The goal of a provincial constitution persisted for years, but the vitality of the independence movement waned in Szechwan, as in other provinces, after 1922.

By 1926, the "Szechwan for the Szechwanese" slogan of the younger militarists and intellectual supporters of provincial autonomy had been realized. The people of Szechwan could hardly be said to govern their province, but at least those who did govern were natives. Separatism had become a reality, not in the sense that Szechwan formally withdrew from the Chinese polity, but in the sense that Szechwan-born leaders had gained practically complete control over the affairs of the province and would exercise it for nearly a decade.

The Chengtu Conference of 1925–26

In the first fifteen years of the Republican period, the militarization of Szechwan, the rise of two militarist generations, the geopolitical disintegration of the province, and the evolution of Szechwan's approach to external affairs laid the bases for provincial political life in the ensuing Nationalist decade, 1927–37. Late in 1925, a conference in Chengtu brought all of these processes into the limelight. Originally proposed by Liu Hsiang in October 1925, the Szechwan Rehabilitation Conference *(Ssu-ch'uan shan-hou hui-i)* opened on December 26 and closed on February 11, 1926. The conference went far beyond the ordinary meetings called by provincial militarists to discuss the division of a defeated opponent's armies and territories. Delegates to the Chengtu Conference came from both military and civilian circles: in attendance were commanders or their representatives from thirty-five divisions, twenty-nine mixed brigades, and nineteen independent brigades, plus sixteen other military leaders.[32] Elaborate conference regulations also provided for one civilian delegate from each of Szechwan's 148 districts, plus representatives of the provincial educational and agricultural associations and the Chungking and Chengtu chambers of commerce.[33]

The conference was extraordinary, therefore, in that it was composed of the most powerful military and the most prestigious civilian figures in provincial life. The chairman was Shao Ming-shu, a veteran of the Railway Protection crisis in Chengtu, who enjoyed immense prestige among Szechwanese gentry leaders. Chou Tao-kang, the vice-chairman, was a first-generation militarist who had lived in honorable retirement in Chengtu since his defeat in 1918. Lo Lun, a leader of the prerevolutionary Provincial Assembly and the Railway Protection Movement in 1911, reappeared as chairman of one of the conference's principal committees. Yin Ch'ang-ling, another leading member of the Chengtu gentry, was head of the civil government section of the conference. Chang Lan, a leader of the old Provincial Assembly and former civil governor of Szechwan, directed another important committee. Hsiang Ch'uan-i, head of the military affairs section, was also a first-generation militarist, who had been educated in Japan and enjoyed close connections with the Kuomintang movement.[34]

Weeks of discussion finally produced a document embodying and generalizing the main resolutions introduced by the delegates. Like the conference itself, this covenant sought to reestablish a locus of legitimate authority in Szechwan and to restore stability to Szechwan's disrupted political and social affairs.[35] The Szechwanese armies renounced civil war in the preamble to the covenant. Military and civilian affairs were to be legally separated, so that military leaders could not interfere in civil administration. The document went on to provide for the "rights of the people," most of which were freedoms from various forms of military abuse; for reversal of the trend toward ever larger and more expensive military forces; for improvement of Szechwan's disorganized currency and tax systems; and for the elimination of such militia abuses as cooperation with bandit gangs and affiliation with "regular" provincial armies.

Halting the provincial militarists' arbitrary misuse of power and curbing the militarization of Szechwan were the primary themes of the covenant and the conference. Yet the conference itself offered the clearest proof of the triumph of military power in Szechwan by 1926.

Each resolution passed by the delegates had to be submitted to the militarists Liu Hsiang and Lai Hsin-hui, as rehabilitation commissioner and civil governor respectively, for consideration and implementation. Even the draft covenant had to go to Liu Hsiang first, and the emasculation of five of the original articles to suit the tastes of provincial militarists underlined the impotence of Szechwan's civilian dignitaries, however much they might resent the conduct of newly powerful military commanders. The outbreak of war between Liu Hsiang, sponsor of the conference, and the Kweichow militarist Yüan Tsu-ming while the conference was in session contradicted the covenant and the purpose of the meeting itself.

Yüan Tsu-ming's flight back to Kweichow ended an era of outside military interference in Szechwan and opened a decade of conspicuous provincial isolation. In part, this isolation reflected the narrow provincialist separatism of the new rulers of Szechwan. With separation, the quest for legitimacy became less urgent, even irrelevant to them. The defeat of the Peking militarists and the emergence of a National Government too weak to interfere in Szechwan were fitting complements to their own provincialism, and they threw their allegiance to Nanking with great, albeit hollow, ceremony.

2 The Rulers of Szechwan

In the decade of reform preceding the 1911 Revolution, no development was more significant than the undermining of traditional status determinants and the modification of established paths to recognized forms of prestige, social influence, and political power. Abolition of the imperial bureaucratic examination system in 1905 was particularly important, since it severed the bond between classical education and the civil service career which for centuries had led to the highest layers of status and power. No new, ready-made career patterns lay at hand to fill the void once the examination system was invalidated.*

Developments in the military field, however, laid the groundwork for the emergence of a new power elite after 1911. Creation of the modern "New Army" and of military schools for the training of New Army officers engendered a new kind of status and a new path to its achievement. Before 1911, the power of the New Army was subordinated to Ch'ing authority. But when the dynasty fell, the first products of its modernized military education set out on their own. Deprived of a national institutional framework in which to make their way, they forged a new route to power based on personal military strength. From this standpoint, the great result of the Republican Revolution was the launching of these new leaders on the uncertain pursuit of power in postimperial China. This was certainly the case in Szechwan Province. Most of the men who rose to the highest positions of power in the province between 1911 and 1949 were alumni of late Ch'ing military academies whose careers bounded ahead in the wake of the dynasty's demise.

In the decade between the establishment of the National Government at Nanking and the outbreak of war with Japan in 1937, Szechwan was in the hands of five supreme militarists: Liu Hsiang, Liu

*Michel Oksenberg has asserted that the re-establishment of institutionalized paths to institutionalized forms of political and social power did not occur until well after 1949 (see Michel Oksenberg, "The Institutionalisation of the Chinese Communist Revolution: The Ladder of Success on the Eve of the Cultural Revolution," *China Quarterly* 36 [October–December 1968]: 61–92).

Wen-hui, Teng Hsi-hou, T'ien Sung-yao, and Yang Sen.* Unlike some other Chinese militarists of the Nationalist period, most of the Szechwanese have not left extensive information about their backgrounds, their careers, or their personalities. Even less is known about their high-ranking subordinates. Still, it is possible to draw a rough sketch of the military leaders of this remote and populous province during the early years of Kuomintang national leadership.[1]

These were the most powerful members of the second militarist generation in Szechwan. All were native Szechwanese. Members of the earlier group had been born around 1880; the younger leaders were born around 1890. Liu Hsiang was born in 1889, Liu Wen-hui in 1894, Teng Hsi-hou in 1889, T'ien Sung-yao in 1888, and Yang Sen in 1887.[2] The family backgrounds of these militarists are obscure. Liu Hsiang, born in Tayi district on the western edge of the Chengtu Plain, is said to have come from a "bankrupt old family," while Liu Wen-hui, his uncle, came from the richer branch of the family in the same district.[3] One who knew both Liu Hsiang and Yang Sen suggests that they both came from "small landlord" backgrounds,[4] but Yang's parents may have been more well-to-do than Liu's. Yang's native district was Kuangan on the Chü River north of Chungking.[5] Other than the fact that Teng was a native of Yingshan district in north central Szechwan and T'ien a native of Chienyang district near Chengtu, nothing has come to light about the origins of these two militarists.[6]

The educational credentials of Szechwan's ruling militarists reflected the turmoil and change characteristic of Chinese education in the last years of the Ch'ing. None of the five held any traditional degrees. Their education generally included primary and middle school in their native areas, followed by training at one of the modern military schools in Szechwan.† Some continued their military education at

---

*Liu Ts'un-hou, a prominent militarist from the early years of the Republic, maintained himself and a small army in a few districts of Szechwan until 1933. T'ien Sung-yao was removed from command of his army in 1935, but the army remained intact under his former chief subordinate. See below, chap. 5.

†A sympathetic English-language biography of Yang issued in 1924 states that he received the *hsiu-ts'ai* degree, but since Yang does not mention the *hsiu-ts'ai* in his personal recollections he presumably did not obtain it (see Spiker [Chungking] to Peking, July 28, 1924, S.D. 893.00/5510). Liu Hsiang attended only a local traditional school *(ssu-shu)* before embarking on his military education (see Shu, "Liu Hsiang fa-ta," p. 17). It can be assumed that the five foremost commanders and other militarists with some formal military education did not come from impoverished families, since only families with some means could afford to send a son to school (see Yoshihiro Hatano, "The New Armies," in *China in Revolution: The First Phase 1900–1913*, ed. Mary Clabaugh Wright [New Haven, 1968], pp. 365–82).

academies in other provinces, but Szechwanese military schools gave others their last formal education, military or otherwise.

In conspicuous contrast to the pre-1927 generation of militarists, the later group did not go abroad for training. The ten-year age differential between the two was responsible; the younger men were just too young to be sent overseas by the Ch'ing authorities before the Revolution, and after 1911 their own province offered the most immediate and attractive career possibilities. Liu Hsiang, the most powerful commander in Szechwan after 1927, did not cross Szechwan's borders until 1934.

Though they had had some formal education, Liu Hsiang and his fellow militarists were not particularly highly educated when compared with their first-generation predecessors.* Of the five foremost generals, only Liu Wen-hui completed the full course of training at an outside academy. For the other four, and for most of their highest subordinates, military education was limited to a short period before the outbreak of the 1911 Revolution interrupted their schooling and cast them loose on active military careers.

The vast majority of Szechwanese militarists prominent after 1927, including not only the top five army commanders *(chün-chang)* but also the many division and brigade commanders in the provincial armies, attended one of two military academies in the province. One was the Szechwan Army Rapid Course School *(Ssu-ch'uan lu-chün su-ch'eng hsüeh-hsiao)* and the other was the Szechwan Army Primary School *(Ssu-ch'uan lu-chün hsiao-hsüeh)*. The Rapid Course School was founded by Governor-General Chao Erh-sun in 1908 at Chengtu. The sudden creation of a modern army division in Szechwan caused a serious shortage of officers with modern-style military training, and the purpose of the Rapid Course School was to provide lower-level officers for the new division as quickly as possible. Only two classes graduated from the school, which closed in 1910. Like the earlier Military Preparatory School which many members of the first generation had attended, the Rapid Course School at first employed Japanese teachers, but Chinese students back from military school in Japan subsequently took over some of the teaching. The curriculum of the Rapid Course School was exclusively military; there were departments of infantry, cavalry, artillery, engineering, and transport.[7]

*The most notable military figures who lacked formal education were Fan Shao-tseng and Yang Ch'un-fang. Both were "graduates of the forest," bandit leaders who entered the army of a provincial commander (Yang Sen) with their forces under a special amnesty.

The Army Primary School also opened in 1908, but this academy was part of the tiered system of modern military schools that the Ch'ing was setting up throughout China. Under the Ch'ing plan, each province was to have a military primary school, while middle schools would be established at four locations in the country. At the top of this educational structure, the Army Officers School at Paoting in Chihli Province would train selected graduates of the regional middle schools. Students entered the provincial primary schools between the ages of fifteen and eighteen. Unlike the Rapid Course School, the primary schools included in their curriculum foreign language and Western science courses in addition to military subjects. Five classes convened at the Szechwan Army Primary School, though the fourth and fifth classes had not graduated when the Revolution of 1911 interrupted their training. Because the middle school at Sian was not ready when the first class of the Szechwan Army Primary School graduated in 1909, students from this class continued their training at the Nanking Middle School. Subsequent Primary School graduates went off to Sian.[8]

The significance of these two military academies lay in their impact on the militarists' personal associations in later years.[9] Relations among Szechwanese officers were influenced by many special bonds, including family ties, common native places, and shared military mentors, but the school ties formed in the late Ch'ing were especially important. By 1927, two cliques—the "Rapid Course Clique" and the "Paoting Clique"—included most of Szechwan's high-ranking officers. In the armies of the Rapid Course Clique, notably those of Liu Hsiang and Yang Sen, almost all ranking subordinate officers had attended the Rapid Course School. Similarly, in the armies of Liu Wen-hui, Teng Hsi-hou, and T'ien Sung-yao, all of whom attended the Army Primary and Middle Schools, subordinate officers and advisors were drawn from among former students of the two schools or the Paoting Academy itself.[10] Exclusion of Rapid Course graduates from Paoting Clique armies was as complete as was the exclusion of Paoting graduates from the Rapid Course armies.*

In Szechwan and throughout China after 1927 the reputation of Szechwan's military rulers was not good. As one Chinese writer put it:

---

*This is less true in Liu Wen-hui's army after its defeat and reorganization in 1933. Although no Rapid Course graduates joined Liu Wen-hui's forces, the supremacy of Paoting Clique officers within Liu's army was weakened by Liu's increasing reliance on members of his own family.

Liu Wen-hui's oppression of the people is heavier than that of
the other militarists. Teng Hsi-hou is crafty and cowardly besides.
T'ien Sung-yao is base and decadent. Liu Hsiang has the appearance of a gentleman, but he is as ruthless as a hawk. Yang Sen is a
coarse person still trying to establish himself.[11]

Of the leading generals it was said, "The chief regret of the people was
that so few of them died in the battles they fought." Another Chinese
writer called them "blood-breathing monsters."[12] A Japanese writer
found merely a collection of mediocrities:

Although some of them have better credentials than others, as far
as their talent goes it is neither particularly low nor exceptionally
high. If they were all lined up together, no one would stand out
especially eminent above the rest. Continuous war in Szechwan
has been the womb in which they have developed, and this is the
reason why Szechwan has lacked one pre-eminent general among
them.[13]

Except for Yang Sen, whose public career far outlasted the others',
the personal characteristics of the principal commanders are obscure.
Unlike such notable militarists of the time as Feng Yü-hsiang or Yen
Hsi-shan, the Szechwanese were not prolific writers. During their
heyday and since that time, moreover, few writers have turned their
attention to these dim figures. Szechwan itself in the 1920s and 1930s
was so remote and so isolated that little was known about its rulers and
still less recorded.[14]

The three Paoting Clique generals, Liu Wen-hui, Teng Hsi-hou, and
T'ien Sung-yao, were least well known. Teng was called "the crystal
monkey" *(shui-ching hou-tzu)* ; the nickname was both a play on one of
the characters in his name and a reference to the special cleverness he
allegedly displayed. Observers remarked on his "slippery" behavior
and his tendency to wait on the sidelines while other generals fought, so
as to profit from their difficulties.[15] T'ien Sung-yao, whose derisive
nickname "rotten melon" reflected his squat physical appearance, was
known for his military incompetence and for the low quality of his
troops.[16]

Of the five leading militarists, Yang Sen was by far the most flam-
boyant. More than any other provincial commander, Yang was known
for his "modern" attitudes and accomplishments.[17] As early as 1920,
when he was circuit intendant for southern Szechwan, Yang supported

the development of modern middle schools and promoted overseas study for promising students in his region. He also gained fame by widening streets and building roads and parks in the towns occupied by his forces.[18] His efforts to stamp out footbinding and to eradicate gambling brought him renown.[19] To modernize the dress habits of his people, Yang at one time stationed soldiers at the gates of Chengtu with instructions to apprehend wearers of traditional long gowns and shorten their garments with the huge shears he provided for the purpose. Yang also developed a passion for physical fitness and athletics that he maintained throughout his life.[20]

Yang's chief shortcoming was "singlemindedness and failure to see whether people can bear the burden of carrying out his plans."[21] Thus his attempts to change social attitudes or customs were often spectacular but usually superficial. At one point, during a campaign to emancipate women, he declared that women ought to learn to swim; when his wife bashfully refused his order to set the proper example, he dressed her in peasant clothes and forced her at gunpoint to splash in a river before 15,000 onlookers.[22] After prohibiting the raising of pigs in the streets of Luchou, he had the city's police chief, holder of a *hsiu-ts'ai* degree, publicly beaten when he discovered hogs rooting in the road.[23] When he was able to exercise it, Yang was equally direct in the matter of army discipline: "Once he found a soldier catching a hen in a cottage and he had him shot immediately on the spot."[24]

All in all, despite his reputation for progressive ideas, Yang's efforts in the direction of social progress were sporadic and shallow. That he was more progressive than his fellow militarists reflected more on their conservatism than it did on Yang's modernity. While he made significant improvements in the streets and roads of Chengtu, he was not above executing a convicted murderess by the *kua,* or slicing method, almost unknown in Szechwan in the twentieth century, or maintaining a huge stable of wives and concubines.* Yang shared with his militarist colleagues and rivals the primary task of military survival. Lasting social or economic reform played little part in his efforts to preserve his position in Szechwan.

Liu Hsiang was the most powerful provincial military leader after 1927. To outside observers, Liu displayed a singular colorlessness, even slothfulness: "[Liu] did not strike us as an impressive personality. . . .

---

*The list of Yang's wives has lengthened steadily over the years. By 1968 he was said to have had more than thirty and to have lost count of his children. Yang's use of the *kua* is mentioned in a letter from Jerome Ch'en to the author, December 3, 1968.

While he appeared good-natured and reasonable, he gave no signs of either character or intelligence," reported two Englishmen.[25]

However, another foreigner perceived early in Liu's career that there was more to the man than met the eye; his perception was borne out by Liu's subsequent success in Szechwan:

> [Liu] does not strike one as being a brilliant intellect—it is hardly an exaggeration to say that in conversation he appears stupid but his record leaves no question as to his ability. His Machiavellian diplomacy in May last will be recalled. . . . His latest coup has already been referred to; he is a man who knows his own mind.[26]

The same seasoned observer remarked a decade later that Liu "has shown himself to be of a cautious, far-seeing disposition, not given to dramatic politics and anxious to take no step until he sees clearly where it will land him."[27]

Liu's educational background further suggests that his intellectual and military abilities in the most obvious sense were limited. In his first attempt to secure a modern military education, he failed the entrance examination for the Army Primary School. Enrolling instead in a New Army Petty Officers Detachment *(Lu-chün pien-mu tui)*, he placed last on the final examination for the Army Rapid Course School and was admitted in the end only because his examiner, Wang Ling-chi, had been one of his teachers in the Petty Officers Detachment.* At the completion of his training course in the Rapid Course School, Liu again graduated last in his class. Later, when he had risen to great power in Szechwan, school children in the province would point to Liu's early difficulties when their parents chided them for laziness or stupidity.[28]

Liu's lackluster image also stemmed in part from ill health. From the mid-1920s on, Liu suffered from a stomach disorder which periodically incapacitated him and supposedly caused his death. The ailment, which an intimate associate maintained was the result of too much "drinking and gambling" with Yüan Tsu-ming in Chungking, was probably gastric ulcers.[29] Especially as the 1930s wore on, his activities were often curtailed because of the illness, which was common knowledge in China at the time. An American reporter noted in 1937:

---

*Wang, a member of the first militarist generation, became one of Liu Hsiang's principal subordinates. He was known for his exceptional integrity. In the 1940s he served as governor of Kiangsi and, briefly, as governor of Szechwan.

He is a very sick man, and many of the deeds attributed to him are the orders of underlings employing his seal. I have been told by one of General Liu's doctors, an American, that the old warlord, now forty-seven years old, does not have over two more years to live.[30]

The salient feature of Liu Hsiang's personality, as observers remarked and as his career demonstrated, was the quality of calculating shrewdness undiluted by any governing idealism or breadth of vision. Liu, who looked like a plump and placid merchant, often voiced in public the highest ideals and purest purposes. In fact, as a perceptive Englishman said:

> He was a cool-headed opportunist, easy-going in nonessentials, supple, imperturbable, irrepressible, strictly limited to the world of reality. He did not seem to have any particular ideals; no picture in his mind, for instance, of a regenerated China speaking with authority in the councils of the nations. He often gave vent to the noblest sentiments; indeed, almost invariably when he spoke in public, and no action of his ever lacked the support of some motive impeccably platitudinous. But this was all policy with him, a protective covering, a concession to the herd.[31]

Of course, Liu Hsiang was not alone in divorcing his rhetoric from his behavior; the habit was characteristic of the second-generation militarists of Szechwan. While their ascent through the ranks of the older commanders' armies was made possible by the 1911 Revolution and the ensuing conflicts in Szechwan, the younger militarists were a step removed from the national struggle, and the challenges they faced in the early years were fundamentally different from those of their superiors. To these aspiring officers, the main problem was not so much how to eliminate opposing armies as how to rise within one's own. Thus in the pre-1926 period Szechwan was the stage on which they had to rise to greater power or drop into obscurity. With career advancement as their primary goal, the junior militarists placed a premium on maneuverability, a sense of timing, and the ability to guard against the maneuvers of others. Coherent ideologies were of little concern; as one Chinese writer remarked in 1934, "Most Szechwanese militarists do not believe in any isms; in fact, they don't understand any isms either."[32]

In the chaotic world of Szechwanese military politics after the

Revolution, when a plethora of independent military leaders rose and fell, the ambitious officers of the younger generation concentrated on means, not ends, in order to advance their fortunes. Very early, each of the principal post-1927 leaders began to form an independent power base. Teng and T'ien made their first serious move in 1921, when they declined to follow their defeated commander Liu Ts'un-hou into exile in Shensi, making instead a separate peace with Liu's adversaries.[33] Yang Sen's independent career dated from 1920, when on the eve of war between the Yunnanese and Szechwanese armies he deserted his Yunnanese superior in favor of a partnership with his old schoolmate Liu Hsiang under the overall command of Hsiung K'o-wu.[34] Liu Hsiang, having survived the defeat of his superior Chou Chun in 1916, enlarged his own unit with some of Chou's troops and became a division commander soon after.[35] Liu Wen-hui, last of the five to reach a powerful independent command, worked quietly but effectively to build a solid base in southwestern Szechwan during the wars against Yunnan.[36] From these early bases each man gathered troops and territory as older militarists met defeat, until by 1926 the second generation had displaced the first altogether.

Several factors therefore combined to narrow the vision of the post-1927 military rulers of Szechwan: their comparative youth, lack of foreign experience and exposure to the Chinese revolutionary centers, and early careers in provincial armies where they scrambled for advancement rather than for principles. One result of this narrowed vision was their rigid provincialism. Their unshakable preoccupation with provincial issues, both before and after 1927, made hollow their rhetoric of revolutionary nationalism.[37] Often their concern for their personal armies and territories even outweighed their concern for the welfare of the entire province of Szechwan.

Of the five leading lights, Liu Hsiang was the least cultivated. He did not even go to middle school. In the low-level academy he attended, he did very badly. Unlike Teng, T'ien, and Liu Wen-hui, who had gone to military schools in other provinces, or Yang Sen, who had served in Yunnan in the early years of the Republic, Liu Hsiang had never been out of Szechwan. Unlike Yang, who made a great show of attacking popular superstitions, Liu Hsiang displayed in the early 1930s an astonishing and nearly disastrous credulousness.[38] Yet by 1927 Liu had the strongest army in Szechwan, and by 1933 he had gained a degree of power within the province unknown since the days of Yüan Shih-k'ai.

Even with Yang Sen's superficial modernity, the rulers of Szechwan seldom displayed the qualities of dynamic leadership, intellectual brilliance, battlefield skill, personal charisma, or social progressivism. Although literate, they had enjoyed only limited education. Reaching the top of the provincial ladder by the age of forty, they held on, keeping the highest positions for themselves or passing them on to ranking subordinates who had shared the same background and were usually the same age, until the Chinese Communists took Szechwan in 1950.

Were Liu Hsiang and his fellow militarists "warlords"? Liu Hsiang, for one, would certainly never admit that he was one of the *"chün-fa* who kill and burn."[39] One thoughtful scholar has suggested that a warlord was anyone who was "lord of a particular area by virtue of his capacity to wage war."[40] By this definition, Szechwan's five supreme militarists could broadly qualify as warlords. Indeed, writers commonly called them *chün-fa* during their tenure in power. But thus to classify them reveals little, because the meaning of the crucial term "lord" remains unclear. In fact, the connotation of the term would probably vary from militarist to militarist, and from area to area, in Republican China. The term "warlord," a translation of a Chinese term of broad and unspecific meaning, obscures as much as it clarifies in English. It is a convenient and vivid term, but it is a kind of slang. What matters about the two Lius, Teng, T'ien, and Yang is that they were provincial —and provincialist—militarists, army officers whose careers developed within the confines of their native province.

3 Szechwanese Militarism and Provincial Society after 1927

Szechwanese provincial independence and military power rose to their highest levels during the Nationalist decade from 1927 to 1937. By looking closely at the mechanics of provincial militarism in Szechwan in this period it is possible to define more clearly the nature of the provincial militarists' control over their domains. To put it another way, it becomes possible to probe the meaning of "lord" as it appears in the familiar term "warlord" from the standpoint of Szechwanese experience.

The Garrison Area System

The most conspicuous feature of the Szechwanese military and political scene after 1927 was the division of Szechwan's territories among the armies of the five militarists discussed in chapter 2. Forces professing loyalty to each of these five army commanders (*chün-chang*) occupied a number of contiguous districts which together formed a "garrison area" (*fang-ch'ü*). From the standpoint of their independence from one another and from higher, external authority, the army commanders were supreme within their garrison areas. The major qualification to this supremacy lay in the practical application of their power.

The size of the garrison areas as measured in numbers of districts varied greatly at any one time and the dimensions of the garrison areas changed over time. Generally, these changes were marginal. Major alterations of garrison area boundaries occurred in 1929, when Yang Sen lost heavily to Liu Hsiang, and again in 1932, when Liu Wen-hui abandoned most of his territories in Szechwan proper to a victorious coalition of provincial militarists also led by Liu Hsiang. More often, a district would pass from the hands of one army to another, as the result of either a minor military encounter or a prearranged agreement.

Through most of the decade after 1927, the location of the militarists' central bases remained stable. Yang Sen shifted his headquarters from Wanhsien on the lower Yangtze to his native Kuangan north of

34

Garrison Areas on the Eve of the Two-Liu War, 1932

Chungking in 1929, and Liu Wen-hui transferred his headquarters from Chengtu into Sikang in 1933. But Liu Hsiang maintained his headquarters in Chungking throughout the period; Teng Hsi-hou did the same in Chengtu, while T'ien Sung-yao's headquarters lay in T'ungch'uan (Sant'ai), east of Chengtu on the Fou River.

Similarly, despite changes in garrison areas sizes and shapes, the militarists maintained themselves in the same general areas of Szechwan throughout the decade. Liu Hsiang began with several districts in south-central Szechwan and after 1929 controlled most of eastern Szechwan south of the Yangtze down to the Hupei border. Liu Wen-hui controlled vast areas of western and southwestern Szechwan until 1932, when he retreated with his surviving forces to Sikang on the western periphery of Szechwan itself. Teng Hsi-hou held many districts north and west of Chengtu, while T'ien Sung-yao's garrison area lay in north-central and northeastern Szechwan. For a time Yang Sen held the lower Yangtze region, but after his defeat in 1929 his territory was confined to the few districts that he managed to retain around Kuangan. Liu Ts'un-hou, a first-generation militarist, occupied a few districts in northeastern Szechwan above Yang Sen's garrison area, and maintained his head-quarters at Suiting (Tahsien), but he remained aloof from the military and political maneuverings of the other military leaders.[1]

Leaving aside Yang Sen's and Liu Ts'un-hou's shrunken territories, the garrison areas of Szechwan were large and populous domains. At its largest, Liu Wen-hui's area contained more than eighty districts; at the same time, Liu Hsiang, Teng Hsi-hou, and T'ien Sung-yao claimed control of from fourteen to twenty-eight districts each.[2] Each militarist maintained his own arsenals, most of them primitive, and minted currency for circulation within his garrison area.[3] The functions of government within the garrison area belonged to the army commander, his subordinates, and his appointees, and not to any other Szechwanese army or outside authority. In this sense, each of the garrison areas was like an autonomous province; indeed, the larger areas held as many districts as some other, more unified provinces contained. Yet there was no sign that the rulers of Szechwan ever contemplated formal autonomy for their personal territories, or that they ceased to regard themselves and their provincial rivals as Szechwanese. On the contrary, even during their most severe clashes they retained and shared the sense of their Szechwanese identity. This was to have significant effects on their relations with central political authority in China during the Nationalist decade.

This sense of shared identity did not, however, prevent friction and conflict among the Szechwanese army commanders. Through most of the decade, a rough balance of military power prevailed, but it was shaken by numerous skirmishes. Both Liu Wen-hui and Liu Hsiang were for most of the period far stronger than the other principal commanders, but no one militarist attained sufficient power to risk the opposition of all the others at once. A kind of stable instability reigned for most of the late twenties and early thirties, shattered by the "Two-Liu War" of 1932–33 and then partially resurrected until the advent of central government power in Szechwan after 1935. While province-wide conflicts thus seldom developed, plotting and skirmishing characterized the Szechwanese political scene, and ephemeral coalitions and countercoalitions emerged and vanished with astonishing swiftness.

Two instances of cooperation among provincial army commanders were especially helpful in preserving the overall peace of Szechwan during the late twenties and early thirties. In Chengtu, the three Paoting Clique leaders—Liu Wen-hui, Teng Hsi-hou, and T'ien Sung-yao—shared control of the city and its resources for years prior to the "Two-Liu War" and avoided serious military conflicts among themselves.[4] In 1928, Liu Hsiang and Liu Wen-hui also agreed to cooperate on matters of common interest, including military finance, and thereby implicitly warned other provincial militarists not to tamper with the military and economic status quo in the province. Cooperation between the two Lius was never comprehensive, and it began to deteriorate almost at once. For a time, however, it did help to freeze the military situation in central Szechwan.[5] Above and beyond these two relatively durable and effective coalitions, the army commanders kept representatives in one another's headquarters cities both to communicate with their rivals and to learn more about their potential opponents' strengths and weaknesses.

Within the army commanders' world, circumscribed by the boundaries of their own province, the militarists' overriding concern was survival in the face of constant threats from their military rivals. In the most immediate sense, each army commander's control over his garrison area depended on his army. After 1926, the Szechwanese armies went by the designations provided by the Nationalist government. Yang Sen's army was known as the Twentieth National Revolutionary Army, Liu Hsiang's as the Twenty-first, Liu Wen-hui's as the Twenty-fourth, Teng Hsi-hou's as the Twenty-eighth, and T'ien Sung-yao's as the Twenty-ninth. Until early 1929, the veteran militarist Lai Hsin-hui maintained a small force called the Twenty-second Army in one or two districts of southern Szechwan, but when Lai was eliminated the Twenty-second Army ceased to exist. The combined armies of Szechwan by the early 1930s outnumbered the forces of any other Chinese province. Liu Wen-hui and Liu Hsiang in 1932 each maintained armies of around one hundred thousand men; Teng and T'ien each claimed more than forty thousand at that time. Yang Sen, with about thirty thousand troops, was weaker than his colleagues, but he managed to play a major role in provincial politics by aligning carefully with one or another coalition of generals at crucial and advantageous moments.[6]

The fighting ability of the Szechwanese forces varied from army to army and from unit to unit, but the overall quality of the provincial forces was low by comparison with China's best. In one army, it was said in 1934, wives outnumbered officers, officers outnumbered soldiers, and soldiers outnumbered guns.[7] An American diplomat reported late in 1929 that only half of Szechwan's quarter of a million troops had usable rifles.[8] Opium smoking was widespread among officers and troops alike.[9] Pay was frequently in arrears, though this problem was more severe in some armies than in others, and officers commonly kept part of their soldiers' pay for themselves.[10] Even when paid in full, the ordinary soldier received little, and low pay frequently caused morale problems in the provincial forces. The status of the common soldier emerges vividly from the casual remark of one of Liu Hsiang's agents, when asked about protection of the bodyguard contingent in Liu's new limousine. "Never mind about that," he replied. "Soldiers cost only eight dollars a month apiece, and we can easily find some more if these get killed."[11] To an American observer in 1937, the sight of a Szechwanese army on the march was both fascinating and hilarious:

> They swarmed along the road and through the adjoining country without any sort of order. Some wore uniform coats or hats, but the remainder of their costumes was dictated by individual tastes and means. All were armed with the traditional umbrellas and carried as well numerous washbowls, teakettles, flashlights, towels, uncooked vegetables, and extra sandals—these were slung over their shoulders or tied to their clothes with twine. Many who had guns swung their smaller effects in cloths tied to the gun barrels in Dick Whittington style. Those who could afford to rode in sedan-chairs or rickshaws, and those who had pets—dogs, birds, monkeys—carried them or led them on strings.
>
> I understand that by now such musical-comedy Chinese troops belong entirely to legend. . . .[12]

Motley though the provincial armies may have appeared, they were the tools with which each of the principal militarists maintained his position in Szechwan. Loss of armed strength meant loss of territory and revenue—and eventual destruction. Each of Szechwan's army commanders faced the constant problem of preserving and augmenting his forces. This lowly goal dominated the lives of Szechwan's military rulers during the garrison area period.

Of course, maintaining an army sufficient to preserve its commander and perhaps even take advantage of rival militarists depended in turn on other factors. One of these was an adequate garrison area. Another, separable from the first only for purposes of discussion, was the army commander's ability to control potentially destructive forces within his own army and within the communities which his army occupied.

Maintaining a Garrison Area

Under militarist rule in the twenties and thirties, armies and territorial bases were mutually dependent; the army commanders held their garrison areas with their armed forces and they maintained their forces almost exclusively from what their garrison areas could provide. But more than simple military presence in a set of districts was required if the garrison area was to supply the necessary sustenance. Effective mechanisms had to be devised to put the resources of the area to work for the armies, while at the same time assuring the continued supremacy of the army commander over army and territory alike. Thus the garrison areas possessed civil administrative structures which, at least in Liu Hsiang's relatively well-documented case, attained considerable complexity.

Responsibility for civil administration of each garrison area rested with an Administrative Affairs Bureau (Cheng-wu ch'u) or Committee (Cheng-wu wei-yüan hui), chaired by the army commander himself, within Army Headquarters.[13] Below this committee or bureau were separate functional departments dealing with such matters as finance, education, administrative affairs, or public works and reconstruction, as well as numerous specialized agencies such as mining bureaus and industrial experimentation institutes.[14]

The Administrative Affairs Bureau and thus the army commander himself retained the power to appoint district magistrates and chiefs of the various sections within the district governments.[15] This was one important method by which Army Headquarters extended its power into lower levels of organization within the garrison area. District governments themselves tended to be highly elaborate and heavily overstaffed. In addition to the general affairs, education, finance, reconstruction, and secretariat sections, numerous "legal bodies" *(fa-t'uan)* such as labor and merchants' associations, and various district-level committees such as the militia or relief committees were a part of the formal district administrative apparatus. District assemblies composed of high district officials and local leaders met semiannually, and a smaller group of officials known as the District Government Conference met every week or two in many districts to discuss outstanding problems. Below the district level lay several additional layers of quasi-administrative organization, the so-called self-governing organizations *(tzu-chih chi-kuan)*, including the *hsiang*, the *chen*, the *lü*, and the *lin*, delineated either by number of households or by economic function.[16]

Among other things, this complex structure of bureaus, departments, and powerless committees served to provide employment for thousands of civilian hangers-on of the principal military leaders and to absorb many underemployed graduates of Szechwan's inadequate schools into petty officialdom.[17] As such, the bureaucratic maze of Army Head-quarters and local administration had a stabilizing influence beyond the immediate business of handling garrison area finance and administration. At the same time, the ornate edifice of civil administration could not conceal the fact that control of the territory in Liu Hsiang's or anyone else's garrison area rested firmly in the hands of military personnel.

Selection of officials for the nominally civilian bureaucracy made this abundantly clear. A well-informed Szechwanese writer estimated in 1935 that more than half of the administrative officeholders in the garrison areas got their jobs because of special relations with someone in the army. Relatives or former schoolmates of brigade or division commanders or of the army commander himself were especially favored, as were longtime civilian members of the army headquarters staffs.[18] District magistrates generally fell into two categories: civil officials who had served a particular militarist for years at low pay and received a magistracy as a financial reward, and men with personal ties to some high-ranking officer. In either case, administrative talent was less important than the special relationship itself.[19] Many district officials, moreover, were active military officers at the same time.[20] Military control over appointments to civilian governmental office was partly responsible for the enormous turnover of personnel in district government during the twenties and thirties.[21] It typified the interference of the military in civilian affairs against which delegates to the Chengtu Conference in 1926 had railed so ineffectually, and it bespoke the extent to which military power had come to dominate the pathways to influence, status, and wealth in postimperial Szechwanese society.

The purpose of the garrison areas, toward which the operations of civilian administration were directed, was to enable the army commanders to maintain their armies and better their positions in Szechwan at the expense of their fellow militarists. Thus the principal function of militarist government in Szechwan was the extraction of the wealth and resources of local society for military use. While tax collection had historically been one of the chief functions of Chinese provincial and local government, it became the primary and even the exclusive activity of lower level formal administration in the strife and disorder of the early Republic. The modest welfare and service functions which had once accompanied tax collection were neglected. Though official corruption and "squeeze" were prevalent in provincial and local government before 1911, the ascendancy of the extractive process had profound effects on Chinese society in the Republican period. Inherited structures of authority and civil administration degenerated into networks of profiteering, bribery, and extortion scarcely disguised by the vestiges of regular governmental procedure.

In Szechwan, the different resources of each garrison area determined the relative importance of various categories of revenue in the occupying army's overall income. The principal categories of revenue were the land tax, taxes on production and sale of salt, opium-related taxes such as "opium-prohibition fees," taxes on trade and commerce, so-called surcharges *(fu-chia)* to the land tax, traditional taxes on land deeds, alcoholic beverages, and tobacco, "miscellaneous levies" on virtually any product or commodity under an endless variety of names, and various forms of loans.[22] While the land tax remained an important component in garrison area revenues, other categories provided high percentages of the armies' total intake. Systematic figures are lacking for most of the armies, but in Liu Hsiang's case, grain taxes accounted for roughly 19 percent of itemized income, miscellaneous taxes for 18 percent, opium taxes for about 12.5 percent, and salt taxes for over 11 percent in 1934.[23]

Taxes on trade provided funds to local commanders along Szechwan's busy interior commercial routes. Likin stations dotted the riverbanks and major land arteries throughout the province. Between Chengtu and the treaty port of Wanhsien below Chungking, there were 280 riverine tax stations in 1933; 134 were reported between Chungking and Lu-hsien alone in 1933.[24] The effects on internal commerce in Szechwan can be imagined. A missionary's account of the shipment of paper for printing gospels from Chungking to Chengtu gives an idea of what traders had to cope with in the province:

> We left Chungking in the second week of July. . . . The taxes from Chungking to La Ch'i [sic] were a fixed quantity and were paid to the motorboat company in Chungking, who assumed responsibility for the transit of the goods. These military taxes amounted to $1000. But at Suifu there is no fixed rate. A relative of Liu Tze-chien [sic—Liu Wen-hui] holds the fort and gets every cent he can. We talked price for some hours and were supposed to be let off easy by the payment of approximately $500. At Kiating we escaped with $300-odd, Wang Tu Ri [sic] $200-odd. But Kiangkeou [sic] was a bad place, and we had great difficulty in getting away under $500. Hwanglongch'i [sic] was almost as bad. At Chonghochang [sic] we paid over $350 and about $150 at the East Gate of Chengtu. Excluding Chungking taxes, which were heavy in themselves, the cost of shipment was about $6000 from Chungking to Chengtu, of which about $2500 may be reckoned as freight and $3500 as taxes.[25]

In addition, important revenues were derived from taxes on specific commodities, the list of which was practically limitless. There were, for example, taxes on the sale of sugar, rice, paper, pigs, and illuminating oil. Additional taxes on trade were named for their alleged uses: "bullet taxes," "winter defense funds taxes," "Northern Expedition fees," or, after 1931, "national defense funds," plus dozens of others.[26] In raising money from the opium trade, militarists not only taxed production and consumption of the drug, but frequently levied a "lazy tax" on farmers who failed to obey orders to grow the profitable crop.[27]

Thus for Szechwanese military leaders, control of grain-producing territory was one prerequisite for maintaining a strong army, but it was by no means the only one. The wide range of opportunities for wealth and profit which the military life offered after 1911 laid the bases for Szechwan's garrison area system and the growth of its enormous armies. Even in Szechwan, which by coastal Chinese or foreign standards was monumentally underdeveloped and technologically primitive, much of the wealth on which provincial militarism fed came from commerce, business, and certain forms of industrial enterprise.

The vital importance of nonagricultural economic activity pointed up the special advantages that Liu Hsiang gained by controlling Chungking. Liu's garrison area contained other important nonagricultural resources, notably the opium-exporting city of Fouling on the lower Yangtze, the salt fields at Yünan *ch'ang,* the port of Wanhsien and, after 1933, the great Tzuliuching salt facilities in southwestern Szechwan. Nevertheless, Chungking was the key to Liu's strength and to the gradual expansion of his power within Szechwan. First opened as a treaty port in 1890, Chungking was the greatest commercial center on the Yangtze above Hankow, and the principal market center for a vast area of western China.[28] Goods from all parts of Szechwan and from areas of Kweichow, Yunnan, Shensi, Kansu, Tsinghai, and Sikang converged on Chungking for sale and shipment down the Yangtze, or passed through the city on their way down the river to outside markets. Chungking thus acted as a huge funnel for virtually all of Szechwan's external trade. For this reason, and because imports destined for central and western Szechwan could scarcely avoid Chungking, the militarist who held the city was able to tax or cut off major sources of his rivals' revenue.

Chungking's greatest value, however, was the enormous opportunity it provided for increasing military revenue and accumulating personal wealth. Liu Hsiang's Twenty-first Army taxed the internal and external trade of the city, and especially in the 1930s raised additional funds from the city's powerful merchant community through bond issues and "voluntary" contributions. Despite occasional disputes with Chungking's mercantile associations over taxation policies, Liu Hsiang carefully and successfully cultivated his ties with the city's businessmen and financiers through his policies and through close personal contacts.[29] Merchant goodwill toward Liu was in turn based on the relative stability that he brought to eastern Szechwan and on the realization that if Liu Hsiang were to fall and his currency become useless, the merchants would suffer most of all.[30]

Chungking thus gave Liu Hsiang a strong advantage over other Szechwanese militarists in his efforts to maintain a well-equipped, large, and, by provincial standards, effective army. In the early 1930s, Liu even managed to purchase a small number of French biplanes, which proved useful in his conflict with Liu Wen-hui in 1932.[31] But Chungking was also vital to Liu from the standpoint of his own supremacy within the Twenty-first Army. To maintain their personal leadership within their army establishments, the army commanders needed to have key centers of concentrated wealth which they could control with their own forces, single localities at which they and their closest associates could collect large amounts of revenue without dispersing their personal military strength over too great an area. The Tzuliuching salt fields and the Ipin opium entrepôt, both of which belonged to Liu Wen-hui before 1933, were resources of this type, as were the T'ungch'uan salt fields under T'ien Sung-yao's control.[32] But Chungking was the richest of all. For this reason, and for others to be discussed shortly, Chungking was crucial to the internal stability of the Twenty-first Army and the preservation of Liu Hsiang's influence within his own military establishment. The whole eastern region of Szechwan was in the hands of the Twenty-first Army after 1929, but the city of Chungking and its immediate environs formed the basis of Liu Hsiang's personal strength within his army and thus in all of Szechwan.

In general, revenue-raising in Szechwan during the militarist era after 1927 was an arbitrary and often cruel process, governed above all by the chronic financial ill-health of the expanding provincial armies and secondarily on estimates of what the traffic could bear. Even before the great increase in taxes that began in 1932, taxation in Szechwan reflected the armies' insatiable thirst for new and larger revenues. In the long run, the effect of unrestrained taxation told heavily on the Szechwanese economy and on the armies themselves. But Szechwan's armies in the late twenties and early thirties displayed little concern for long-range problems and made no serious attempts to confront the spiral of militarization and taxation even when the disastrous results of this combination became unmistakable.

Problems of Local Control

Both of their essential resources—the armies and the garrison areas— presented Szechwanese militarists with problems of control. More than personal charisma or battlefield brilliance, the key to survival in the menacing climate of the twenties and thirties was the army commander's ability to meet continual challenges to his personal hegemony.

Two anecdotes illustrate major aspects of the control problem which each army commander faced. The first, related by Liu Hsiang himself, concerned a general passing through the city of Chienyang on his way to Chengtu. A crowd surrounded him, saying, "Only half a month ago we paid 200,000 *yüan;* now we beseech you not to tax us again." The general was astonished. "I never saw the money," he replied, "except for a single *yüan,* which I used to buy medicine."[33]

The second story concerned Fan Shao-tseng, a former bandit leader, whom Yang Sen had granted an amnesty and commissioned as a division commander in the mid-1920s. In 1928, when Liu Hsiang and Yang Sen went to war, Fan changed his allegiance three times. Finally, attracted by an offer of 100,000 *yüan* from Liu Hsiang, Fan left Yang for good, on the condition that Liu Hsiang never compel him to fight against his former superior.[34]

The first story points up the problem of excessive independence on the part of ostensibly loyal subordinate officers within a given army hierarchy. The second raises the problem of outright subordinate disloyalty, in particular the defection of powerful officers from one army commander to another. Both these problems critically affected the strength of the highest militarists in Szechwan.

The question of vertical control over nominally loyal subordinate officers lay at the heart of what is usually called warlordism. One of the difficulties in defining "warlords" is determining what independent powers lay at what levels within a military hierarchy. If, to take an extreme hypothetical example, regimental commanders raised all their own funds, recruited their own troops, produced their own weapons, even minted their own money for the small areas they occupied, they would merit the name "warlord" just as much as their superiors at the top of the formal command structure. The distribution of powers among officers at various levels of command heavily influenced the character of military rule in Szechwan.

Although writers in the militarist period occasionally noted that in Szechwan smaller garrison areas seemed to exist within larger ones,[35] comprehensive evidence as to the centralization or decentralization of powers is not available for most of the provincial armies over extended periods. From available data, however, it is clear that Szechwan's provincial military structures were seldom rigidly controlled from the very top to the very bottom, and that a high degree of autonomy generally persisted at levels of organization below the Army Headquarters and the army commander's office. What this suggests is that the "control" which one army commander exercised over his garrison area depended heavily on the working arrangements he developed with his subordinates.

Collection of the land tax in Szechwan illustrates this point. The collection process which prevailed in most areas of Szechwan by the early 1930s had evolved in the Republican era, as traditional forms were adapted to the social conditions and military realities of the garrison area system. Two changes were particularly significant. The rural disorder and banditry which accompanied the collapse of Imperial authority and the militarization of Szechwan made it too dangerous for the peasant to take his own tax payment personally to the nearest local collection center *(fen-kuei)* established by the district government; instead, armed militia or provincial army units gained the power to extract tax revenues from individual peasant and landlord households. Simultaneously, authority to collect taxes shifted from the Imperial central and provincial governments to the headquarters of whatever army occupied a given district.

As the mechanics of tax collection changed in the early years of the Republic, districts were divided into smaller sections, each the exclusive domain of an army unit such as a battalion or a regiment. Army Headquarters issued instructions for the collection of specific revenues in each district. Within the districts, however, district governments and local military units were free to adopt any method of collection. Generally, the armies did not collect directly from the households. The armies relied either on special tax collectors, whose families had performed the function for generations and knew the financial condition of their taxpaying households in detail, or they depended upon native coercive forces—the *t'uan* or militia—to secure the revenue from the peasants of individual *hsiang* or local communities. The leaders of the *t'uan* and of the multifamily groups known as *chia* who collected taxes on behalf of the army commonly extorted extra funds for themselves from the taxpaying families, but it was generally recognized that these abuses were milder than those of the special tax collectors.[36] Regardless of who actually collected the taxes, advance collection was one of the most notorious features of Szechwanese militarism; by the early thirties, collection of annual land taxes for the 1960s and 1970s was widespread, while in some districts taxes were being collected as far ahead as the 1990s.[37]

Thus collection of the land tax, the main point of contact between government and populace both before and after the Revolution of 1911, was reserved for army subunits in conjunction with the lowest level institutions of civil administration and control in the 1920s and 1930s. The land tax system provided a high degree of financial independence for lesser units within the five principal armies. The role of Army Headquarters was confined to the issuance of vouchers authorizing collection of the tax by subordinate officers. Moreover, though the army commanders appointed district magistrates and the heads of district government revenue collection bureaus within their garrison areas, appointment of personnel for the numerous offices that handled individual local taxes was left to the lower level military officials on the scene. Thus local bureaus for collecting "commerce-protection fees" or "meat taxes" or "opium suppression levies" were frequently controlled by subordinate officers, and their revenues employed locally.[38]

The delegation of local revenue-raising functions to lower level commanders explains the army commanders' and headquarters' heavy reliance on those receipts which could be gathered at a limited number of sites, especially at or near the headquarters themselves. The lower units were not completely independent, of course; Army Headquarters sent them at least a portion of their weapons, ammunition, and uniforms. But in their daily dealings with local officials and the population of the districts they held, brigades, regiments, and battalions were free of immediate outside control, just as the Szechwanese army commanders were independent of each other and collectively independent of extraprovincial authority.

In addition to exercising considerable freedom in raising local revenues, subordinate officers frequently went into private business for themselves. This was especially true in the more developed areas of Szechwan, but private entrepreneurship among regimental, brigade, or division commanders was by no means confined to the vicinity of Chungking and Chengtu. Some ventures related directly to military strength; numerous brigade commanders, for instance, ran their own primitive arsenals, and rudimentary mints were operated even by battalion commanders.[39] Other enterprises were primarily commercial. Fan Shao-tseng manufactured morphia, for example, and Liu Hsiang's division commander Wang Ling-chi had a major share in a wood-oil export firm in the early 1930s.[40] Military funds also went into public works facilities such as water works and electric power plants.[41] Pawnshops, banks, and opium trading all offered to provincial army officers opportunities for profitable investment.[42]

Predictably, real estate was another favorite field for investment. A small clique of military and bureaucratic officials owned numerous properties in Chungking, drawing income from rents and from land sales. In Chengtu, real estate was traded through several large brokerages, but it was common knowledge that powerful militarists controlled the brokerages. In rich agricultural areas like the Chengtu Plain, military men acquired extensive new tracts of land. Liu Ts'un-hou and three of his division commanders each owned more than three thousand *mou* in Pihsien, just north of Chengtu, in the early thirties, while in the same district many brigade commanders and even regiment commanders owned more than a hundred *mou*, a considerable amount by local standards.[43] In Liu Hsiang's native Tayi district in 1935, families of militarists constituted less than 3 percent of all families but held 66 percent of all land. The largest single holding was a gigantic 30,000 *mou*, and the average holding among militarist families in the district was 3,000 *mou*.[44]

Moreover, as long as the militarists' property lay within their own armies' garrison areas or in the territory of a well-disposed commander, their families ordinarily paid no taxes on the land or its produce.[45] Thus when the district of Teyang near Chengtu belonged to T'ien Sung-yao, fifty or more of his officers owned lands in the district but none paid any taxes.[46]

There was implicit danger for the provincial army commanders in their subordinates' accumulation of wealth. One of Liu Hsiang's brigade commanders, Lan Wen-pin, maintained a force of seven regiments, even though Army Headquarters only provided for three. He financed the other four privately, selling Szechwanese opium in Shanghai and using the profits to secure arms, ammunition, and other military supplies. Lan also profited from his investments in Chungking theaters and motion picture houses, which he guarded with his own troops. His career ended abruptly in 1931 when Liu Hsiang arrested him and disarmed his forces on the grounds that Lan had been plotting with Liu Wen-hui to destroy him.[47]

As the above examples indicate, all of the army commanders faced the problem of their subordinates' establishing domains-within-domains while outwardly remaining loyal to their superiors. The case of Liu Hsiang gives some idea of how the highest military leaders handled this dilemma. Liu was aware from an early date that he lacked centralized control over his constituent forces, and superficially at least he yearned for greater power over his subordinates.[48] Yet in his relationships with the most powerful among them, Liu generally displayed a retiring, even permissive attitude. A British visitor noted in 1929, "We were told that he leaves the conduct of affairs a great deal to his subordinates and himself generally shrinks from taking any strong line of action for fear of offending one interest or another."[49] In the case of the unfortunate Lan Wen-pin, for example, Liu left Lan in the lucrative office of chief of the Bond Issuance Bureau for years, though he certainly knew of Lan's privately maintained military forces.

This seemingly pliant attitude notwithstanding, Liu Hsiang was never upset from below or defeated by external enemies after 1921. He was Szechwan's most successful militarist; paradoxically, his success and power were due in large part to the permissive stance he took toward his own generals. He preserved his position in the Twenty-first Army by carefully allowing his ranking subordinates to acquire wealth and power for themselves. The heart of Liu Hsiang's success lay in granting his chief lieutenants wide opportunities for self-enrichment, while spotting and forestalling dangerous disloyalty before it came to the surface.

Of course, Liu benefited from his long association with P'an Wen-hua and T'ang Shih-tsun, classmates at the Rapid Course School who served Liu for many years as loyal subordinates one rank below the general himself. Similarly, Wang Ling-chi, known as Szechwan's most honest and upright general, had been Liu's teacher in the early days, and he remained a loyal subordinate for a long time in the twenties and thirties.[50] But the conspicuous stability of Liu Hsiang's coterie of high-ranking officers, in contrast to the unreliability and treachery of the other army commanders' lieutenants, points to another cause. Liu Hsiang's garrison was rich enough to keep Liu's generals happy where they were. While all of his top subordinates were members of the Rapid Course Clique, it was equally significant that P'an for many years was mayor of Chungking; that T'ang was commissioner of roads; that Wang Tsuan-hsü, another division commander, was commissioner of salt transport.[51] It is not at all clear that, without these lucrative appointments, the bonds of common schooling or long service would have sufficed to keep Liu's principal subordinates from rising against him or defecting to another army commander. As it was, they fared well under Liu's indulgent leadership, as one Chinese reporter noted in 1932:

> Liu is known for his strict army discipline, but in the areas they garrison, his subordinates do as they wish. . . . The great princes of Szechwan live splendid lives and have many women. Liu's subordinates mostly have imposing houses and buy good field-lands. P'an's and Fan's houses are worth 100,000 *yüan*. T'ang's forests and fields cover several thousand *ch'ang*.[52]

Liu was able to keep his loyal officers loyal because his garrison area provided special opportunities for individual enrichment through private or semiprivate enterprise. Here again, the importance of

Chungking to Liu's overall position in the province cannot be overestimated.

Aside from Liu Hsiang, whose happy mixture of skill and good luck lessened the problem, Szechwan's ruling militarists continually confronted the danger of crippling defections by their subordinates. Aware that their shifts could cause the downfall of their superiors and thus open opportunities for personal profit and advancement, high-ranking officers changed sides in Szechwan with ease, both before and after 1927. Wang Tsuan-hsü's desertion of Yang Sen in favor of Liu Hsiang in 1925, for example, ended Yang's brief hegemony over most of the province.[53] In 1928 and 1929, Yang again lost three division commanders to Liu Hsiang. During the furious maneuvering that preceded the Two-Liu War in 1932, Liu Wen-hui lured several of Teng Hsi-hou's and T'ien Sung-yao's commanders to his side and nearly bought Lan Wen-pin away from Liu Hsiang.[54]

Officers at all levels faced the defection problem. Some attempted, through various training programs, to build cadres of devoted subordinates, as the Chinese Nationalists were doing at the Whampoa Academy near Canton. Yang Sen operated a military academy at Chengtu in the mid-twenties, where his students learned slogans like "Be Brave Toward the Enemy," "Revolutionize Thought," and "Reject Rebellion." During his tenure at Wanhsien, Yang's officers from the rank of company commander up had to attend daily sunrise lectures on topics of "spirit."[55] Liu Hsiang tinkered sporadically with political indoctrination of his officers, but there is no sign of any systematic, let alone successful, program.* Liu Wen-hui, after losing many of his ranking subordinates during the disastrous war of 1932–33, turned to members of his own family, a technique which evidently served him well in the remote reaches of Sikang until 1949.[56]

The constant undercurrent of disloyalty and potential defection

*An early "Special School" run by Liu Hsiang in 1919 produced a group of loyal officers bound to Liu in a semi-secret club. In 1926 he created the Military Political Institute to train officers from the rank of company commander to that of regiment commander. Teaching materials used in this institute closely resembled the materials in use at the Whampoa Academy. In 1927, after Liu declared his allegiance to the Nationalist cause, a political section was created for each of his divisions in accordance with Nationalist army custom. The political section attached to Liu's headquarters was abolished on September 1, 1929, and there is no evidence of the effective operation of the various divisions' political sections. See Chang Chung-lei, "Ch'ing-mo hsüeh-t'ang," p. 357; Pai Yün [pseud.], "Ssu-ch'uan chih ko tang ko p'ai" [Szechwan's cliques and factions], She-hui hsin-wen, November 15, 1932, p. 326; Liu Hang-shen, "Jung-mu pan sheng," HWTT, July 15, 1967, p. 21; and Lockhart (Hankow) to Washington, October 14, 1929, S.D. 893.00/P.R. Chungking 16.

among Szechwanese officers was a symptom of the times. It reflected both the causes and consequences of militarization. Clearly defined and recognized authority was hard to discover, nor were regular, non-military avenues to prosperity and social status available. The continual defection of lesser officers from one army to another revealed the same institutional and ideological rootlessness which Liu Hsiang and his second-generation colleagues displayed as they rose to power. Sufficient wealth was the best insurance against treachery from below. The fact that Liu Hsiang outlasted Liu Wen-hui, T'ien Sung-yao, and Yang Sen, remaining Szechwan's most powerful military leader until his death in 1938, was due above all to his possession of Chungking and the lower Yangtze region of Szechwan.

Problems of Social Control

Just as a garrison area could not save a high-ranking militarist if his subordinates turned against him, it could not sustain him if his army was unable to reduce local social disturbance and disruption to manageable levels. The responses of Szechwanese militarists to rising urban radicalism in the 1920s fall within the scope of the following chapter. But the means by which the provincial generals sought to deal with social disturbances outside of Szechwan's major cities can be examined in the present context.

The central point that emerges from such an examination is that Szechwan's "regular" armies, no matter how local they might have appeared from external vantage points, were often themselves external to the communities they occupied. Local social unrest was not necessarily an immediate and direct function of provincial military politics, though militarist conflicts often contributed to it. But the relationship of occupying provincial forces to more narrowly local groups was itself laden with potential conflicts. Minimizing these conflicts, while continuing to draw upon the resources of the garrison area, was a basic problem in the militarists' dealings with the populace of their territories.

Two manifestations of social unrest that aroused the active concern of Szechwanese military commanders were the organized peasant movement that developed during the revolutionary period from 1925 to 1927 and the sporadic hostility of local armed elements, usually called militia (t'uan or min-t'uan) and led by so-called militia lords (t'uan-fa). Generally of less concern to high-ranking officers were Szechwan's tens of thousands of bandits (t'u-fei), who preyed on commerce and on market towns, and the "sect bandits" *(chiao-fei)* who erupted violently in scattered locations throughout the province.

The history of the revolutionary peasant movement in Szechwan was short; in restrospect the movement had barely begun when the provincial armies crushed it. The first attempts to organize the peasantry along the lines of the revolutionary movement then brewing in South and central China came in 1925, when a left-wing Kuomintang organization was established in the province. But progress was slow. Only 9 of Szechwan's 148 districts had peasant associations by October 1926.[57] Organizational work was hampered by the low level of existing Kuomintang development in the province and by the lack of trained rural political workers.[58]

Twenty new organizers arrived in Szechwan in October 1926. This was the first group to come from the Peasant Movement Training Institute operated by the Kuomintang near Canton, which was dominated by Communist elements within the Kuomintang-Communist coalition. Nonetheless, the Kuomintang Left had made only the tiniest beginning among Szechwan's peasants by the following spring. Only a few districts were well organized; isolated uprisings against local authorities in which the peasant associations played a role ended quickly in bloody defeat. Moreover, some peasant associations were infiltrated by agents of the militarists, the conservative wing of the Kuomintang, or local militia.[59]

When Liu Hsiang and then the other militarists turned irrevocably against the revolutionary movement in the cities and the countryside after March 31, 1927, the hopes of the revolutionary peasant movement were destroyed. It was hard for promoters of the movement to maintain their optimism in the wake of militarist counterattack and the flight of surviving Communists from the province. They wrote almost wistfully, "Early this year, risings of peasants everywhere in Szechwan could be foreseen. Unfortunately, the March 31 Incident occurred. The evil gentry . . . counterattacked. Lately, the news is that the local peasants are struggling openly and secretly against them."[60]

The collapse of the revolutionary peasant movement in the spring of 1927 marked the end of coordinated, multidistrict peasant unrest in Szechwan, except in those parts of the northeast where invading Red Army forces established a soviet in 1933. After the demise of the peasant associations, agrarian protests were confined to occasional uprisings against local or district authorities, usually over tax grievances. Although these demonstrations could be violent and destructive, they usually brought at least part of the desired response from military authorities. A hated magistrate would be replaced, or a particularly odious tax temporarily abolished or reduced. While such protests sometimes spread across district borders, their aims were local and specific, and they often enjoyed the support of members of the local elite. Fundamentally different from the nascent revolutionary peasant movement of 1926 and 1927, they evoked a much more flexible reaction from provincial militarists.[61]

The revolutionary peasant movement was externally inspired, and it did not last. On the other hand, armed opposition from locally supported militia forces was unequivocally domestic, and it persisted throughout the twenties and thirties. Conflict between provincial armies and local armed forces was a revealing indicator of the very delicate relationship between the Szechwanese armies and the local communities into which they intruded. Like the expansion of more formally constituted armies, the growth of Szechwan's militia forces after 1911 was an important characteristic of the militarization process.[62] Militia growth accelerated after the Revolution, along with other interrelated social changes including the impoverishment of former landholding families, the enrichment of military officers and their bureaucratic retainers, and the emergence of a cycle of increasing rural usury, spreading tenancy, and agrarian unemployment.[63]

Growing quickly in response to the insecurity and disorder that followed the collapse of Ch'ing authority, local militia forces were usually organized in and supported by the market towns (chen and hsiang) which comprised each district.[64] As the power and authority of civil administration declined in the confusion of the early militarist period, militia forces came to enjoy enormous power in their local communities. Militia units collected their own revenues, erected their own customs barriers on trade routes, and inflicted their own penalties on delinquent taxpayers or their leaders' enemies. "Militia lords" (t'uan-fa) engaged heavily in rural usury and in opium trading.[65]

As more and more landowners moved to the towns and cities or sold their property to absentee militarists and bureaucrats, and as regular civil administration continued to deteriorate, the militia of Szechwan became a kind of sub-government capable of exercising extensive control over the inhabitants of their communities. The strength of the local militia was common knowledge by the 1920s. Organizers of the abortive peasant movement, recognizing the militia's power, asserted that district magistrates in Szechwan had in effect lost the power to govern.[66] Liu Hsiang himself noted the power of the militia at about the same time, claiming that a popular instrument of local self-defense had been converted to a "villain's tool" by the "evil gentry" who had seized control of local armed forces.[67]

Holding so much power, the militia elite thus played a pivotal role between the provincial armies and the Szechwanese populace. Ordinarily, army and militia acted as partners in the extractive process. A popular provincial adage of the time held that "the army takes the skin, and the militia extracts the sinews."[68] Militia units often served as the occupying armies' agents in collecting the revenues that the military establishment required from local society. At the same time, militia forces continued to raise their own funds independently of the armies, often using the opportunities provided by tax farming to reap their separate harvests. On the other hand, this essential cooperation of armies and local militia was not indestructible, and it sometimes broke down. Frequently, the schisms between army and local leadership led to violent conflict.

The immediate origins of hostilities between militia and armies varied from case to case.[69] The magistrate of Pahsien joined with one of Liu Hsiang's battalion commanders to destroy the militia organization in two sectors of his district in 1929 because, in the words of the district gazetteer, "the arrogance and power of the militia had gone beyond the pale, often intruding into legal and administrative matters."[70] Some of Liu Wen-hui's forces fought a pitched battle with militia elements in the southwestern district of Meishan when the local militia set up independent taxation stations on roads in the district.[71] A foreign report from 1934 saw another factor in the conflict between armies and militia:

> [The militia] have been able to expand their forces by intercepting small bodies of stragglers of the army. For this reason they have contracted the enmity of the militarists and brought untold suffering to the localities. In many instances whole villages have been razed to the ground by the troops who return with large forces to avenge their comrades.[72]

In still other cases, the militia joined local uprisings against excessive taxation by occupying army units. Most of the members of the "tax-resistance army" which rose against Liu Wen-hui's exorbitant taxation in 1932 and 1933 were members of local militia forces.[73] Trouble also arose when army units attempted to seize militia weapons for themselves.[74]

The army commanders of Szechwan made periodic attempts to gain control of local militia forces, but they never fully succeeded in doing so. Liu Hsiang tried to master the militia by appointing the chiefs of all District Government Militia Bureaus and by adopting a plan for the phased consolidation of militia control and the elimination of the militia's independent fund-raising, but the problem of autonomous *hsiang* and *chen* militia units was as vexatious in 1935 as it had been in 1925.[75] The cooperation of local militia was vital to each of the provincial armies. When there seemed to be adequate resources for both, the two sides were able to maintain a fragile cooperation. The outbreak of repeated conflicts between army and militia, however, clearly revealed that the provincial forces were not at the same time local forces. The impact of localism on Szechwanese politics was complex. While provincial army commanders sought to protect the province from outside interference and to maintain the integrity of their respective garrison areas, they also faced difficulties at an even more local level, where from time to time they found themselves treated as meddling and unwelcome outsiders.

Banditry and brigandage generally caused the major militarists of Szechwan less alarm, though there was plenty of it. Particularly in the first few years of the Republic and again in the early twenties, Szechwan was beset by brigands. The principal sources of bandit manpower were the increasing numbers of impoverished and landless peasants and the growing pool of active or former soldiers, themselves drawn mostly from the peasantry. Along the Yangtze, thousands of junkmen turned to banditry as steam navigation cut into the upper river junk trade and threatened their livelihood.[76]

Bandit activities included the robbery of traveling merchants or men of wealth, kidnapping for ransom, and raids in force on market towns or administrative centers. The level of bandit disturbance tended to rise and fall with the level of militarist conflict, reflecting the social dislocation which attended provincial warfare. Toward the most prevalent form of banditry, highway robbery by small bands of desperadoes *(t'u-fei)*, local military authorities and civil officials were often tolerant, even nonchalant. It was widely acknowledged that the evening's bandits were the next morning's provincial soldiers. Local army officers often maintained communication with local bandit gangs and reached arrangements with the bandits. Only if bandit activity brought local commanders trouble from their military superiors would such arrangements be violated.* Bandit predations against foreigners were especially likely to bring military reaction, since the protests of foreign consuls required some sort of response by higher military authorities.

"Sect banditry" was also common in Szechwan. There were numerous uprisings by groups with names like the "Red Turbans" or the "Red Spears," each believing itself to have special powers or a special destiny. The targets of such attacks were often tax collection offices or other official places in the towns. Assaults of this type continued throughout the twenties and thirties. Usually local militia forces were left to handle the problem. One group that drew the attention of provincial militarists in eastern Szechwan was called "The Celestial Soldiers" (Shen-ping). Known to Westerners in the province as Joss Troops, the Celestial Soldiers were well organized; they had an elaborate system of signs and symbols, a leader called the Great Jade Emperor, and a rude doctrine based on resistance to overtaxation and hostility toward the provincial armies and foreign missionaries. After kneeling to pray, the Celestial Soldiers would charge at units of terrified soldiers, waving tiny flags and chanting to make themselves invulnerable to bullets.[77]

The Celestial Soldiers appeared in the Yangtze region below Chungking around 1920, and their activities were reported intermittently into the early thirties.[78] Because they interfered with foreign shipping on the river and menaced regular army units, Liu Hsiang occasionally sent strong forces to wipe them out. No decisive battles developed, however, and the Celestial Soldiers surfaced and vanished with little discernible relation to the activity of nearby provincial forces.

In general, outbreaks of sect banditry in Szechwan lacked size, organization, and staying power. For these reasons, local militia forces or small army units coped with them, when they had to face them at all. Prolonged and serious depredations against a single area by a single group of marauders were rare.

Unexpected Strengths and Ultimate Weaknesses of Szechwanese Militarism

The garrison area system in Szechwan during the late 1920s and early 1930s grew out of the simultaneous collapse of standardized

*This was especially true where bandit leaders and local authorities were fellow members of the ubiquitous and powerful Ko-lao hui secret society (see Sung Chung-k'an and Fu Kuang-lin, Ssu-ch'uan ko-lao hui kai-shan chih shang-chüeh [A viewpoint on the reform of the Ko-lao hui in Szechwan] [Chengtu, 1940], p. 9).

Imperial administrative mechanisms and the militarization of provincial life following the fall of the Ch'ing. Administration of Szechwan's affairs by Liu Hsiang and his fellow army commanders illustrated the two dominant phenomena of postimperial Szechwanese society: the substitution of the military career for the civil–bureaucratic career as the principal avenue to social and political power, and the ascendancy of the extractive function of government to the exclusion of traditional, limited service and welfare functions.

The effects of militarism and the garrison area system on provincial life were strangely mixed. The system was heavily, though not exclusively, responsible for Szechwan's growing economic difficulties. The rapid spread of opium cultivation, for example, brought huge profits to the militarists who could tax or sell opium, but it cut down the amount of land devoted to food crops and raised food prices, while subjecting millions of Szechwanese to the ravages of opium addiction.[79] Excessive military and militia taxation slashed what little purchasing power the peasants had, while uncontrolled taxation of commerce increasingly stifled Szechwan's internal and export–import trade. And circulation of separate currencies in various garrison areas, sometimes within various sections of a single area, played havoc with provincial commerce.

There is little doubt that during the militarist period Szechwanese society underwent significant and sometimes damaging changes. With the passage of time, the insatiable demands of occupying armies and local militia forces pushed many smaller landowners into tenancy and many tenants into banditry or vagrancy, while landed wealth accumulated in the hands of an elite which was at least partly new: military officers, militia strongmen, and civilian hangers-on connected with the military bureaucracies. Most of these "new landlords" were absentee landlords and many were usurers as well. One perceptive writer remarked bitterly in 1934 that the "four great powers" in Szechwan were the ruined and the unemployed, the demoralized "intellectuals" who turned to petty-bureaucratic careers under the militarists, the militia and army forces, and finally, the opium addicts and fortune tellers of the province.[80] Undoubtedly, militarist rule during the garrison area period contributed to a growing social and economic crisis which eventually undermined the militarists themselves.

On the other hand, as disordered and frequently violent as life in Szechwan had become by the 1920s, the province was hardly in a state of perpetual and total anarchy. The surprising thing about Szechwan, which was notorious for its bad government and the backwardness of its leading militarists, was that it suffered less from social disorders in the late twenties and early thirties than did allegedly more progressive provinces. Szechwan's remoteness from the revolutionary centers in eastern and south-central China partially accounted for the weakness of professionally organized agrarian revolutionary activity, for example. As for banditry and other forms of traditional rural disturbance, Szechwan seems to have enjoyed greater tranquillity than many downriver provinces despite the absence of centralized provincial control and the impotence of national authority in the province. A group of British missionaries and a British diplomat agreed in November 1930 that Szechwan was "still one of the safest provinces in China."[81] Sir Miles Lampson, the British minister to China, came to substantially the same conclusion as late as 1933. Despite high taxation and the "frankly military character" of local government in Szechwan, he observed,

> the results are not entirely bad, and while there are soldiers everywhere there are few bandits, so that travel in most parts of Szechwan is reasonably safe, in marked contrast to conditions in the middle river provinces. This change for the better has been effected during recent years, Szechwan having been at one time after the Revolution one of the most bandit-ridden provinces of China.[82]

Nor was Szechwan totally devoid of economic development and physical modernization during the garrison area period. The degree of change should not be overestimated, but noticeable beginnings were made, particularly (and predictably) in the construction of modern roads and the improvement of public works in the larger cities. Another report by a British diplomat in 1930 conveys a sense of the situation:

> A striking feature of present-day Szechwan is the surprisingly modern and up-to-date appearance of many of the large towns. Under the leadership of Chengtu, the majority of the towns in the northern part of the province appear to have undergone a wholesale reconstruction within the past few years, and are now conspicuous for their wide streets, rows of clean and uniform houses and shops, and good sanitation. In one instance—that of Tungan —the craze for modernity has even been extended to the construction of tennis and basketball courts in the middle of the city square. The capital itself compares favorably in these respects with

any Chinese city of similar size, and the spectacle of a Chinese military patrol in Chengtu inflicting corporal punishment on householders for leaving refuse outside their front doors is an eloquent enough testimony to the revolutionary changes which have taken place.[83]

Modern roads capable of handling the motor traffic that sprouted within Szechwan during this period generally followed established commercial routes which formerly had carried only human porters and wheelbarrows. The traditional provincial capital, Chengtu, was the hub of the expanding road network: the principal arteries constructed by 1935 were the Chengtu–Chungking highway and the roads from Chengtu to Chühsien in northeastern Szechwan, Loshan in the southwest, and Langchung near the Shensi border in north-central Szechwan. The total length of modernized roads constructed by 1935 was only slightly more than 1,600 miles, in a territory almost as large as France. Moreover, even after they were built, Szechwan's highways were often allowed to fall into disrepair. Nonetheless, the introduction of motor travel on such important routes as the Chengtu–Chungking line drastically shortened the time required for journeys from vital points in the province to other centers.[84]

Other constructive developments took place in Chungking and the Yangtze area. Under the protection of Liu Hsiang, a native shipping firm known as the Min Sheng Industrial Company gradually expanded its operations on the upper Yangtze, absorbing other tiny lines and recovering a large share of the Szechwan steamer trade for Chinese owners after years of foreign domination. The Min Sheng Company also ventured into modern industrial development in Chungking and in the Chialing River area north of Chungking where the company had first been formed. Min Sheng capital went into a shipyard, coal mines, Szechwan's first and only railway (a small narrow-gauge line for transporting coal), electric power and waterworks in several cities, and other enterprises as the company gained financial strength.[85] In the early thirties, Liu Hsiang and the Twenty-first Army also promoted the formation of the West China Development Corporation, which undertook to develop basic industries in and around Chungking including waterworks, a cement plant, and machine shops which could double as arsenals.[86] In absolute terms, modern industrial development in Szechwan during the garrison area period was minuscule, but it was not completely lacking and it was conspicuous precisely because Szechwan had so little to begin with.

Thus from certain standpoints the effects of the garrison area system of military administration were not entirely negative. One can even perceive, in the eight years between the Nationalist triumph of 1927 and central government penetration of Szechwan in 1935, the beginnings of a new structure of status and power in the province, and the appearance of tentative, de facto answers to the problems of political and social organization which arose with the decline of Ch'ing authority and administrative potency.

The garrison areas themselves were an essential part of this emergent structure. Their boundaries at any given moment were not necessarily "natural"; relative military power and not physical or economic geography determined the exact composition of the garrison areas, and so their configurations were not stable. But breaking Szechwan into several sizable component parts made sense, given the difficulties of communicating with all parts of the province at once and the obvious inability of any successor authority after 1911 to implant its power throughout the province. With economic resources, including major trading centers, spread out in most areas of the province, the garrison areas formed more manageable blocks of territory than the entire province did.[87]

Furthermore, the collapse of Ch'ing authority and the militarization of Szechwan did not obliterate all preexisting social and economic structures. Other than the elimination of the five circuits (tao) which had formed a part of the Ch'ing administrative network, the units of community and political organization in Szechwan underwent no basic changes after 1912. Districts retained their identities and their boundaries. If anything, the hsiang and chen, local communities organized around their market functions within the districts, enhanced their vitality as formal higher level bureaucratic administration lost effectiveness. It is important to see that the administrative confusion which followed the Revolution and the eruption of warfare and endemic banditry in Szechwan did not produce the total disintegration of earlier social and political forms.

What had changed in postimperial society was the source of social power and to some extent the notion of social and political power itself. Here again, militarization began to provide a tentative substitute for the forms and concepts prevalent in late imperial society. Coercive power, always latent in legitimate Imperial authority, became the primary, visible determinant of local power, whether in the hands of army personnel or militia lords. Although the provincial militarists did not manage to create institutions comparable to the Imperial

examination system to support it, the military career had clearly become the new ladder of success by the time of Liu Hsiang. This was
recognized at the time; interestingly enough, it was not until economic
conditions deteriorated so badly after 1933 that the ever-expanding
provincial armies had to rely on forced conscription to fill their
ranks.

Even if one did not become a soldier or an officer oneself, it was
necessary to adjust to the predominant influence of coercive power in
the province. The supremacy of coercive force was as universal and
undeniable as the primacy of the civil–bureaucratic elite had been in
prerevolutionary provincial life. Thus provincial "intellectuals,"
graduates of middle schools or even of universities in Szechwan, were
fortunate to find jobs within the armies' bureaucracies where they
might make powerful connections and achieve wealth instead of lan-
guishing in some city or town as lowly schoolteachers.[88] Landowners,
if they wished to escape the ruinous demands of bandits, militia, and
occupying armies, had to be on good terms with the predators and be
able to buy their good will with flattery, gifts, and lavish entertain-
ments.[89] Bankers and traders in such centers as Chungking and Chengtu
also needed to maintain cordial relations with the holders of armed power, in order to forestall destructive taxation or expropriation. Banks in
particular depended on the patronage of the military establishment,
though in return they enjoyed some power over the armies whose funds
they held.

The point, then, is that Szechwan under the garrison area system did
not totally lack a sense of where power—and wealth—lay, and how they
were to be gained. Nor did all existing social and political institutions
vanish with the disappearance of the Imperial system of government.
By the time that military control had become concentrated in a hand-
ful of armies and the power of the militia had matured in Szechwan's
myriad local communities, the bases of a successor system to the imperial–bureaucratic pattern existed. The influence of the late Ch'ing
military academy and Whampoa Academy models on provincial
commanders even suggested that, with time, adequate training institutions for a new provincial elite, primarily defined by its control of
the instruments of violence, might have emerged.

This nascent system of provincial power had, however, two crucial
and obvious flaws. In the first place, because of the very fact that social
power had come to rest more and more on overt coercive potential, the
garrison area pattern of territorial distribution was inherently trans-

itory. Reduction of the corps of principal powerholders in Szechwan to five or six brought temporary stability, at least by comparison with the preceding decade, but it was only a stage in the gradual centralization of provincial control in fewer and fewer hands. The militarists of Szechwan were content for a time with the basic allotment of power that persisted through the late twenties and early thirties, but the goal of eliminating rival commanders and increasing one's own territory and wealth remained. Thus, pending the future resolution of this issue, territorial control lacked the quality of permanence on which viable institutions might have been built, standardized, and extended throughout the province.

Second, with the triumph of coercion as the principal means of achieving social power, wealth became the principal end for which social power and coercion were employed, and the extractive process permeated all levels of government and society. Thus by the heyday of Liu Hsiang and the other militarists of the early Nationalist period, the practice of forcing all available wealth from less powerful groups in society had become the basis of social and political advancement. Szechwan was a rich province in which prerevolutionary tax levels had been particularly moderate; there was some room for additional extraction and expropriation of wealth during the early Republic. As late as 1934, when the tempo of military activity had risen and financial exactions had seriously worsened, a critical Chinese observer had to admit that the Szechwanese seemed to enjoy better lives than the people of provinces like Hupei, Hunan, or Hopei.[90]

But a society in which overt armed power and the unregulated extraction of wealth determined the nature and distribution of status and influence sooner or later had to bump against the limits of its economic resources. The continual need of the armies to preserve and expand their strength doomed Szechwan to increasing economic pressures without foreseeable end. Eventually, the economic bases of provincial militarism itself had to suffer. Signs of Szechwan's economic crisis, acutely aggravated by external factors, appeared in the mid-1930s.

The rule of Liu Hsiang, Liu Wen-hui, and the other army commanders brought Szechwan the reputation of the worst-governed province in China. Yet in the relatively peaceful and prosperous years from 1927 through 1932, the armies seemed to have created at least a partial substitute for the lost norms and forms of Imperial government and society, all within a single province of the old Empire.

4 Szechwan and the Center

In 1927 triumphant Nationalist armies swept down the Yangtze from Wuhan to the sea, and a new National Government was established at Nanking. In 1928, after the collapse of Kuomintang–Communist collaboration, the campaign against the northern militarists resumed, and by midyear Peking had fallen into Nationalist hands. Long years of conflict between the Kuomintang in the south and the Peiyang militarists in Peking finally came to an end. The two contestants for national power clashed and only one survived. The Nationalist Government established in Nanking remained the recognized central government of China for more than two decades.

But the Nationalists' proclamation of national reunification in 1928 was a gesture of optimism, not a recognition of reality. The end of the Peking regime left only the Nationalists with the trappings of central authority, but their control over many of China's provinces was weak, sometimes nonexistent. Indeed, the very meaning of the term "control" was unclear, because the functions of a modern Chinese central government had still to be worked out.

For some parts of China, Chiang Kai-shek's victory in 1927 and 1928 opened a new era of participation in the political life of an emerging nation and subjection to the power of central authority. As a result of the Nationalist success, some Chinese militarists were brought into the movement, integrated into the Kuomintang power structure, where reactionary militarists increasingly supplanted political revolutionaries after 1927.*

In Szechwan, however, the Nationalist victory opened a period of more complete provincial independence and isolation from outside affairs than Szechwan had previously known. Provincial independence between 1927 and 1934 rested on the National Government's inability

---

*James Sheridan makes this point about bringing militarists into the movement, and he is correct in saying that many militarists kept their "armies intact and their attitudes and goals fundamentally unchanged" (*Chinese Warlord*, p. 240). But even this fails to cover the case of Szechwan's militarists, who had no wish to be brought into the movement and who stayed aloof from national affairs.

to intrude into Szechwan's internal affairs, and on the determination of Szechwanese provincial militarists to pursue their fortunes within their own province. Their primary interests lay inside Szechwan itself. Only an intrusion by some external force which they could not handle might pierce their provincialist outlook.

In 1934 that intrusion finally occurred, in the form of a growing Communist insurgency which weakened the militarists in their home territories. Simultaneously, the growing threat of war between China and Japan stimulated Nanking's interest in the province as a potential refuge and base of resistance. Moreover, the serious deterioration of social and economic conditions in Szechwan in the mid-1930s increasingly aroused the indignation of newspapers and magazines in central and eastern China. By the end of 1934, amid demands for the "opening" of Szechwan, the central government embarked on a major effort to bring the province under its sway, and the era of provincial independence gave way to a prolonged struggle for mastery of the province.

Szechwan's independence after 1927 did not, however, imply that the province had no contact at all with China's political center. The relationship which Szechwan maintained with Nanking and the China that lay below the Yangtze Gorges embodied a mixture of centrifugal and centripetal influences. From the standpoint of the central government between 1927 and 1937, the position of Szechwan was never ideal. But though the problem of Szechwanese autonomy still had not been fully solved when the National Government moved to Szechwan and Liu Hsiang died, the problem itself and the attempts made to solve it bear on major issues of modern Chinese government.

Szechwan and the Nationalist Triumph

In late 1926, as the armies of the Northern Expedition neared Wuhan, then took Wuhan and prepared to head down the Yangtze toward Nanking and Shanghai, the principal Szechwanese militarists renounced the titles they had received from the Peking government and declared their support of the Nationalist revolution. The Nationalists responded by naming each Szechwanese army a "National Revolutionary Army" with its own numerical designation. The decision of Liu Hsiang and the other militarists to throw their allegiance to the Kuomintang side was not made on the spur of the moment. Nor did it signify Szechwan's active participation in the Northern Expedition. On the contrary, with their declaration for the Kuomintang cause the

Szechwanese made clear their intention not to intervene on behalf of the Northern militarists to whom they had formerly professed allegiance, rather than their determination to join the Nationalist campaign against the North.

The problem of how to approach the life-and-death struggle between North and South became particularly important to the Szechwanese once the Northern Expedition got underway in 1926. In Szechwan the impact of the Nationalist campaign changed with time. At first, in some military circles, the Expedition rekindled the inclination toward complete provincial autonomy. As the success of the Northern Expedition became evident in the summer of 1926, some of the second-generation militarists who had earlier promoted the provincial independence movement again advocated explicit independence as Szechwan's best course. Their arguments recalled the debate over provincial autonomy a few years before. One of Liu Hsiang's subordinates, noting that "realistic people have long advocated autonomy" and that China clearly lacked any national government, urged Liu Hsiang, Yang Sen, and other army commanders to declare Szechwan autonomous until a legal government was established. Other generals gathered in support of what they thought was Liu Wen-hui's and Liu Hsiang's determination to steer clear of the North–South struggle.[1]

As the Nationalist campaign proceeded, however, pressure on the militarists to take a more definite position increased. Rising levels of turmoil in Chungking and other major cities gave evidence of growing public support for the Nationalists, especially in Liu Hsiang's and Liu Wen-hui's garrison areas. Moreover, the army commanders began to feel pressures from their subordinates to affiliate with the Nationalists. The wishes of these high-ranking subordinates could not be ignored, for both the army commanders and the subordinates knew that the united opposition of an army's division commanders could destroy any militarist.[2]

As the tension rose, a complicated process of negotiation began which eventually led to the militarists' declarations of support for the Kuomintang. The targets of the Kuomintang's effort at persuasion were Liu Hsiang, Yang Sen, and Liu Wen-hui.* Yang was especially

---

*The Kuomintang sent a representative to Szechwan in the spring of 1926, before the opening of the Northern Expedition, to get provincial militarist support. Teng, T'ien, and Liu Ts'un-hou demurred; Liu Hsiang later did the same (see Chang Jen-min, "Ts'e-tung Ch'uan-Ch'ien liang sheng ts'an-chia pei-fa chih hui-i" [Reminiscences of pressuring Szechwan and Kweichow to join the Northern Expedition], Ch'un-ch'iu, August 1, 1961, pp. 2–5, 8.

important because his territory at the time lay closest to Hupei, and because he had enjoyed good relations with the Northern militarist Wu P'ei-fu. The Lius were important because they had the greatest strength in Szechwan—what they decided to do, the lesser commanders would also do so as not to give them a pretext for attacking in the name of a higher cause.

The Nationalists sent Chu Te, a Szechwanese-born military leader who was destined to found the Chinese Red Army with Mao Tse-tung in the following year, to negotiate with Yang Sen. Chu and Yang were old acquaintances from their early days in Yunnan.[3] Lu Shih-t'i, a Kuomintang worker from Szechwan who had served as the South's military and political appointee in Szechwan on several occasions before 1926, was sent to deal with Liu Hsiang.[4] Negotiations went on for weeks, while news of Nationalist military successes in Hupei reached Szechwan. The collapse of Northern resistance and the obvious progress of the Nationalist campaign undoubtedly helped the Szechwanese to make up their minds.[5] Nationalist victories made it clear that it would no longer be dangerous for them to cut their former ties with Peking. Inside Szechwan, the British naval bombardment of Wanhsien in September 1926 and the ensuing surge of mass support for the Nationalists in Szechwan's major cities underscored the advantages to be gained from public affiliation with the South.

Neither the provincial militarists nor the Kuomintang leadership expected that the Szechwanese commanders' pledges of support would bring them into an integrated national political structure. The significance of the redirection of Szechwanese allegiance was essentially symbolic. To the Nationalists it meant that Szechwanese armies would not actively oppose them in Hupei, and to the Szechwanese it meant that the Kuomintang would continue to leave Szechwan alone. The Nationalists' purpose in negotiating with Liu Hsiang and other provincial commanders was not to draw them into the campaign against the North but merely to neutralize them.[6] Weaning Yang Sen from his association with Wu P'ei-fu was especially vital. The Nationalists found the prospect of active participation by the ill-paid and badly disciplined Szechwanese forces less attractive than Szechwan's simple noninvolvement.*

At the same time, the Szechwanese saw an opportunity to protect

*According to Chu Te, when Chu returned to Wuhan with Yang Sen's pledge of loyalty to the Kuomintang side, Chiang Kai-shek was too busy to see him at all (see Smedley, *The Great Road*, p. 179).

their positions inside Szechwan and their independence from outside meddling. From the outset, they had no intention of opening their province to outside control or permitting the dilution of their own authority in the garrison areas. When Chu Te returned to Yang Sen's army as the Kuomintang's official representative, he found Yang waiting for money, not political workers, from Wuhan. Moreover, Yang vigorously opposed the political education program which Chu sought to carry out in the Twentieth Army. Eventually Yang permitted Kuomintang workers to instruct his officers, but only in his own military school and only on the subject of Sun Yat-sen's Principle of Nationalism; Sun's other Principles and policies had to be avoided.[7]

Liu Hsiang's reaction was similar. Liu, whom Chiang Kai-shek's supporters at the end of 1926 had called a "shameless warlord who has no idea of what our Party's doctrine is,"[8] now paid greater lip service to the role of the Kuomintang. He established political commissariats in his Army Headquarters and set up a Political Education Institute employing materials patterned after those used in the Whampoa Academy.[9] In the winter of 1927, Liu spoke frequently and enthusiastically of the role of the Party in Szechwan and in his armed forces:

> The Party has a doctrine; it uses this doctrine. Without a doctrine, naturally there would be no Party. Without a Party there would be no ability to use a doctrine to carry out the revolution. The Party is our life; like life, we cannot do without it. The Party's power is greater than anything else.[10]

Beneath this rudimentary revolutionary rhetoric, however, Twenty-first Army and internal Szechwanese problems remained primary to Liu Hsiang in his early dealings with Nanking. In his first speech upon taking up the title of commander of the Twenty-first National Revolutionary Army, Liu voiced the blend of Kuomintang rhetoric and provincialist realism which would continue to undergird Szechwan's relations with the central government for years to come. Liu's definition of the Chinese term for "warlord" casts light on his view of Chiang Kai-shek and the National Government:

> As for the term "warlord," it means those *chün-fa* who kill and burn. It does not mean "all army officers with troops" ought to be overthrown. If it did, then Chiang himself would be in the "warlord" category. So any armies that work for and with the people we will consider military friends, and we will help them to the utmost. Those who oppose this principle we will overthrow.[11]

At the moment of his formal transfer to the Kuomintang banner, Liu Hsiang was saying in effect that he expected to be excluded from the Kuomintang's list of warlord targets, and that if he were treated as a warlord his bond of loyalty to the Nationalists would be void.

Despite his new title as commander of the Twenty-first National Revolutionary Army, Liu Hsiang's priorities in 1927 continued to place the solution of internal problems ahead of Szechwan's genuine participation in the affairs of the Chinese state. This conditioned his view of Szechwan's role in the Northern Expedition: "We must carry out the Northern Expedition, but even more urgent is internal house-cleaning. If we can complete the first step, we will be able successfully to undertake the second, and the name 'Revolutionary Army' will be at one with reality."[12]

Thus perceiving that his own primary interests continued to lie inside Szechwan, Liu was unwilling to become entangled in a close political relationship with the center. His provincialism was sustained by the realization that in spite of its victories over the Peking militarists, the National Government was unable to subject Szechwan to its wishes even if it wanted to. Conditions in China, said Liu, were in a kind of anarchy, in which national laws were ineffective, the National Government was unable to handle the situation, and "no one can govern any-one else."[13] As if to make clear to the Nationalists his conception of his new allegiance, Liu avoided sending troops against T'ang Sheng-chih in Hupei when Nanking requested him to do so in 1927, on the grounds that political conditions in Szechwan were too dangerous to allow him to send any of his forces out of the province. To Nanking, which had no way of forcing him to dispatch the troops, the message from Liu Hsiang was unmistakable.

In the realignment of Yang Sen, Liu Hsiang, and other Szechwanese army commanders in late 1926, only the names and numbers of the provincial armies changed. The militarists traded a symbolic positive favor—declarations of allegiance—for a real, negative benefit—freedom from external interference and from military obligations outside Sze-chwan. At the time, the arrangement was suitable to both the province and the center.

The Central Government in Szechwan: "The Devil's Cave"

Following the establishment of the National Government at Nanking and the Szechwanese armies' acceptance of Nationalist unit designations the central government's presence in Szechwan remained minimal, and

Nanking exercised no control over the rulers of the province. During the Northern Expedition, Szechwanese neutrality had been the chief Nationalist objective in dealing with the province; but in November 1928, after the conclusion of the Expedition, the central government adopted a formal posture toward Szechwan. Nanking appointed a Szechwan Provincial Government Committee and a Provincial Military Disbandment Committee, and it issued a document called the General Order for the Governance of Szechwan. Liu Wen-hui was named chairman of the Provincial Government Committee, which also included Liu Hsiang, Teng Hsi-hou, T'ien Sung-yao, and several veteran Kuomintang functionaries like Huang Fu-sheng and Lu Shih-t'i.[14] The Disbandment Committee, whose task was to reduce the size of Szechwan's overgrown armies, included Teng, T'ien, Liu Ts'un-hou, Lai Hsin-hui, and Yang Sen, with Liu Hsiang as its chairman.[15] The composition of the two committees denoted Nanking's recognition of existing power relations within Szechwan, and it did nothing to change them.

The General Order was more significant, not so much because of its substantive effects in Szechwan but because of its tone and flavor and because of what it symbolized. In lofty phrases it declared that the central government, hearing the appeals and supplications of the people of Szechwan, had decided to issue its mandate in order to cure the maladies of the province. It called for elimination of the garrison areas, reduction of provincial army strength, and organization of a single, unified provincial government. Tax collection was to be centralized and standardized, as was the provincial currency. All miscellaneous provincial taxation was to cease. Education in Szechwan was to be improved and the Three People's Principles were to be taught in the schools. The central government was to exercise the power to appoint judges for Szechwan without interference from the provincial armies. The General Order concluded:

> With the completion of the Northern Expedition and the beginning of stable government, the central government has received the mandate of the Party and the country. It has heard the Szechwanese people's expressions of hope and expectation that it will find a concrete solution to Szechwan's problems and carry it out conscientiously. Each part of the General Order must be implemented . . . the National Government will observe the provincial government's achievements to see if these instructions have been carried out.[16]

The General Order embodied Nanking's position toward Szechwan for the next six years. It was a substitute for active interest and interested action in Szechwan on the part of Nanking, which had toyed unsuccessfully with both in 1927 and 1928.* As far as concrete results were concerned, the General Order was ineffective from the start. Some of the newly named members of the Provincial Committee, charged with the task of organizing a government for the entire province, never returned to Szechwan from East China. The provincial government, though formally established, had no power and wrought no changes in Szechwanese military politics. The provisions of the General Order calling for full implementation of all commands and verification by the central government were ignored by all.[17]

To Chinese living outside of Szechwan during the early years of Nationalist rule, Szechwan was a mysterious, foreign, and menacing land which brought to mind the famous line from the T'ang poet Li Po, "The road to Shu is more arduous than the road to Heaven." After playing its historic role in the 1911 Revolution and the successful campaign against Yüan Shih-k'ai in 1916, the province dropped from the center of the national stage. Long years of internal disorder and warfare earned for it the name "the Devil's Cave."[18] Despite the relative stability that prevailed there in the late twenties and early thirties, outside merchants were so intimidated by the province's reputation for violence that they refused to journey to Szechwan.† Szechwan's isolation behind the Yangtze Gorges and its remoteness from the centers of political and cultural activity along the lower Yangtze and the coast undoubtedly added to the aura of mystery and backwardness that clung to the province. One outsider who did investigate the province with some care explained to his downriver readers, "If you haven't been to Szechwan, or if you take a narrow and unscientific

---

*The National Government's effort to involve Liu Hsiang in the campaign against T'ang Sheng-chih had not succeeded; Chiang Kai-shek's proposal for active intervention in Szechwan in August 1928 had gone aground because Chiang could not persuade three central provinces to provide the necessary troops; and Nanking's attempt to "punish" Yang Sen for harboring Wu P'ei-fu within his garrison area merely unified the Szechwanese militarists in opposition to any outside interference in Szechwanese affairs. See the following: *Hsin chen pao*, August 27, 1928, in Hatano, *Gendai*, August 1928 sec., p. 282; *Shun-t'ien shih pao*, August 13, 1928, ibid., August 1928 sec., p. 157; *Shun-t'ien shih pao*, August 2, 1928, ibid., August 1928 sec., p. 25.

†One Chinese writer estimated that prior to 1935, only one-tenth of all Yangtze travellers to and from Szechwan were non-Szechwanese (see Chuang Tse-hsüan, *Lung-Shu chih yu* [Travels in Shensi and Szechwan] (n.p., 1941), p. 138.

approach to it, then the world of Szechwan is not only incomprehensible; it is unimaginable."[19]

More than anything else, however, Szechwan was ignored. It barely scratched the minds of most people in the eastern, southern, and northern provinces, no matter how generally well informed they might be. Below Hankow, there was virtually no news coverage of the internal affairs of the province. Occasional articles about Szechwan in the major newspapers and magazines of Shanghai, Tientsin, or Peking were generally feature stories which treated Szechwan as an exotic foreign land. Travelogues, for example, told of the thrilling boat trip through the Gorges, of the journey to sacred Mount Omei, and perhaps of a visit to Chungking or Chengtu. Only an exceptionally serious crisis in Szechwan could produce continuing news reports about the province in the downriver press. Before the war between Liu Hsiang and Liu Wen-hui and the simultaneous Communist invasion in the winter of 1932–33 brought Szechwan into the limelight, the rest of China remained in the dark about developments there. And once the Two-Liu War and the initial shock of the Communist invasion died down, national attention once again drifted away from Szechwan.[20]

This overpowering lack of information about Szechwan's internal conditions was evident even in the statistical reports, yearbooks, almanacs, and summaries which in the Nationalist decade symbolized the Kuomintang's effort to weld China's provinces and regions into a coordinated national unit. Szechwan's name was nearly always missing from the inevitable province-by-province lists of figures which were compiled on innumerable subjects in the late twenties and early thirties: the omission betrayed Nanking's weakness there.[21]

In 1932, the only central government organs operating in Szechwan were the Bank of China, the Maritime Customs, the Post and Telegraph Administration, the Salt Inspectorate of the Finance Ministry, and occasional special missions sent by one or another Nanking ministry to observe conditions in its special field of interest.[22] In accordance with the General Order, the chief judge of the Szechwan High Court was a central government appointee, but in actual fact he had no power in the province. Legal cases were handled at the district level, and the army headquarters of each garrison area acted as the highest judicial body in that area. All other judges and court personnel were appointed by the army commanders or their headquarters, and the chief judge could not intervene.[23]

Moreover, between 1927 and 1935, no outside government troops were ever stationed in Szechwan. In 1928 Kweichow units entered the province on orders from Nanking, but they quickly pulled out in the face of the Szechwanese militarists' united opposition.[24] Again in 1933 central government forces entered Szechwan in pursuit of Chinese Communist forces under Hsü Hsiang-ch'ien, but they were not welcomed by Szechwanese military authorities and soon withdrew.[25] Until 1935, the National Government had no instruments·of coercion in the province with which to influence the conduct of Szechwan's military potentates.

Nowhere was the independence of the army commanders more obvious than in their economic autonomy. The amount of revenue raised from land taxes and miscellaneous levies in Szechwan was estimated in 1934 to equal one-third of the total annual receipts of the National Government. None went to Nanking.[26] The land tax was lawfully retained within the province. But other "national" taxes which were supposed to be forwarded to the central government never left Szechwan.* Although some revenue from salt taxes was sent to the National Government, it was a small part of the total revenue retained by provincial authorities, and the Salt Inspectorate secured it only at the pleasure of the militarists, who could cut it off at will. Thus in 1929, of the $1.8 million collected in the Northern Szechwan Salt Inspectorate district, only about $70,000 was forwarded to Nanking for National Government loan service payments. In the same year the Southern Szechwan district, which included the great salt fields at Tzuliuching and Wut'ungch'iao, yielded $10.3 million in revenue, but military authorities kept $7.5 million for their own use, and administrative expenses in Szechwan accounted for part of the remainder.[27]

Without a military presence in Szechwan, the National Government was powerless to change the taxation habits of the Szechwanese or compel them to send more revenue to Nanking. So it turned instead to proclamations and orders to the militarists to cease exorbitant and "illegal" taxation. Like the General Order for the Governance of Szechwan, the central government's commands in the area of provincial taxation and revenue submission were ineffectual.[28] On at least one

*After the National Government was established in 1927, certain categories of revenue, including income from the land tax, were legally written off to provincial authorities, in recognition of Nanking's inability to compel their remission to the central government. Certain other taxes were declared to be "national," their revenues to be used for backing National Government currency and for other uses. These taxes included levies on salt, opium, and liquor, and a stamp tax (see Chia, *Ts'ai-cheng shih*, 2:15–38).

occasion when the National Government tried to secure specific "national" tax revenues which had been usurped by provincial authorities, the effort was unsuccessful and the central ministry concerned gave up in defeat.[29]

The Szechwanese Approach to National Politics

In terms of formal regularized communication and the conduct of official business between the two, Szechwan and the central government were virtually divorced between 1927 and 1934. Szechwan was not totally cut off, however. Provincial isolation was conspicuous, but even while Szechwan remained politically and economically independent, some points of contact with other parts of China were preserved.

In the first place, the high military leaders of Szechwan maintained some interest in China's national politics and military affairs. They were not interested because they wanted to immerse themselves in national politics; on the contrary, they considered maximum awareness of national developments essential to their fundamental aim of avoiding outside interference in the internal affairs of their province. Thus from the time of the Northern Expedition, Liu Hsiang, Liu Wen-hui, and Yang Sen kept personal representatives in Peking and at Kuomintang headquarters, then in Nanking and Wuhan, and finally in Nanking alone.* The prime function of these representatives was to keep their employers informed about national politics. One might have expected those Szechwanese natives who served in high National Government or Kuomintang positions to do this. But having immersed themselves in the central hierarchy, these officials were no longer suitable to the militarists as middlemen between the province and the center. Chang Ch'ün, a Szechwanese who served as foreign minister and as governor of Hupei during the 1930s, was one of these figures. The occasional missions to Szechwan on which the central government proposed to send Chang failed to materialize because of the opposition of provincial leaders.[30] Neither Chang nor Tai Chi-t'ao, a Szechwanese who during

---

*Evidence concerning Teng and T'ien is scarcer, but presumably they behaved in the same way. Li Yün-han indicates that all the army commanders sent representatives to Chiang Kai-shek when the Northern Expedition reached Hunan, and that from this contact came their designation as National Revolutionary Army commanders (*Ts'ung jung-kung tao ch'ing-tang* [From admission of the Communists to party purification] [Taipei, 1966], p. 663). Liu Hsiang, and probably other generals as well, also kept personal representatives in Shanghai to handle commercial and financial problems in the coastal port to which most of Szechwan's external trade was directed. One of the representatives' more delicate tasks was ensuring the passage of arms purchased abroad through Shanghai and up the Yangtze to Szechwan (see *Pai-jih hsin-wen* [Chengtu], August 6, 1928, p. 6).

the thirties was president of the Examination Yüan, played the role of informant and agent which Liu Hsiang and others gave to their personal representatives in the capital.

The Szechwanese leaders perceived that the struggle for survival within Szechwan would be compromised if they let themselves be drawn into external commitments. Only once during this period did they seem to throw themselves into an external political–military conflict. This was during the so-called Reorganization Crisis of 1930. A coalition of Yen Hsi-shan, the Shansi militarist, Feng Yü-hsiang, the North China militarist known as "the Christian General," and the Kuomintang leader Wang Ching-wei declared its opposition to Chiang Kai-shek in early 1930. Because of their military strength, the Reorganizationists raised a serious challenge to Chiang's position.[31] A long period of political and military maneuvering ensued, and by autumn a final military showdown was at hand.

The Szechwanese were very much interested in this affair, but as usual they were reluctant to commit themselves to either side. Late in 1929, representatives of Feng Yü-hsiang went to Szechwan to persuade the army commanders to oppose Chiang openly, but they failed and left Szechwan "declaring that they would never again have anything to do with the Szechwanese, as they were entirely unreliable."[32] Nevertheless, as the Reorganization Crisis continued, it affected Szechwanese internal politics to an unusual degree. The problem of how to respond to the Chiang–Feng dispute became intertwined with the resentment many Szechwanese militarists had begun to nurse against the financially and militarily powerful Liu Hsiang. Both Liu and his opponents in the Szechwanese political world attempted to turn the national controversy to their own domestic advantage.

Ideology did not predetermine which provincial militarists would support Chiang and which ones would come out for the Reorganizationists. The British consul at Chungking was convinced in August 1930 that Liu Hsiang and his ranking subordinates were merely awaiting Feng's seizure of Wuhan to declare against Chiang, with Liu resigning for a while in favor of his trusted division commander Wang Ling-chi.[33] The diplomat turned out to be wrong. Eventually Liu Wen-hui, Teng, and T'ien, who were separated from Chiang's territory by Liu Hsiang's garrison area but whose own territory lay on the border of Feng's region, declared their support for the Reorganizationists, and Liu Hsiang affirmed his loyalty to Chiang and the National Government.[34]

It has been suggested that if Feng's and Yen's opposition had not completely collapsed civil war would have broken out in Szechwan as a result of the militarists' opposing stands in the Reorganization Crisis.[35] But this exaggerates Szechwan's real involvement in the affair and distorts the motives of the provincial commanders. It is unlikely that any of the militarists seriously contemplated sending their forces out of Szechwan to help Feng and Yen, since that would have meant weakening their positions at home. Moreover, the alleged crisis between Liu Wen-hui and Liu Hsiang occurred just at the high point of their limited cooperation in Szechwan. To be sure, this cooperation did gradually degenerate before the final breakdown in the Two-Liu War of 1932–33, but there is nothing to suggest that the Reorganization Crisis suddenly destroyed it. Indeed, at least one close observer on the scene was convinced throughout the crisis that there was no threat of hostilities in Szechwan, and that Liu Hsiang was confident of that at all times.[36]

The Reorganization Crisis was exceptional because most of Szechwan's top generals publicly took sides in an external dispute. But they took no action. No Szechwanese forces went to help Feng Yü-hsiang, and no Chengtu forces clashed with any Chungking armies. As soon as Chiang Kai-shek's victory over the opposition was certain, all the Szechwan militarists, including the erstwhile dissidents, loudly proclaimed their loyalty to Chiang and the National Government. In the aftermath of the crisis, it soon became clear that the relationship between Szechwan's rulers and Nanking had not changed significantly, at least in the short run. Liu Hsiang bowed out of his first scheduled meeting with Chiang at Hankow in January 1931, and in reorganizing the Provincial Government Committee that year, Nanking retained Liu Wen-hui as chairman and named two of his principal subordinates to the committee for the first time.[37]

The Szechwanese Militarists and Outside Influences

Thus Liu Hsiang and his colleagues avoided outside entanglements that might interfere with their primary provincial interests. At the same time they guarded vigilantly against externally inspired threats to their supremacy within the garrison areas. Regardless of their interest in outside developments and the formal posture of the central government, it was essential to the militarists that no outside power interfere with their actions at home or usurp any of their governing or control powers. They were highly successful in guarding against the intrusion of foreign influences. The British consul in Chungking observed as early as December 1927 that "there are no outside provincial influences at present in Szechwan."[38] It was only in 1934, with the rapid expansion of the Communist soviet in northern Szechwan, that the army commanders found themselves unable to cope with an external intrusion.

The effectiveness of the militarists' opposition to outside influence is well illustrated by the history of the Kuomintang in Szechwan. For present purposes the story begins in 1924, with Szechwan's participation in the anti-imperialist nationalist movement which gripped China during the mid-twenties. Though remote from the principal scenes of anti-imperialist conflict in the 1920s, Szechwan was not immune to the impact of downriver crises. Still, by comparison with the most active Chinese provinces, Szechwanese political activity remained limited, dominated and all too often exclusively conducted by students. Chungking, because of its treaty port status and its direct river link to East China, was the focal point of anti-Japanese activity at the time of the May 4 Movement, but the Szechwanese version never fully developed:

> Szechwan province did not witness any such tremendous awakening as appeared to have occurred among the people in the lower Yangtze River ports during May and June. . . . The Japanese boycott did not take on any serious form in this province until November and December, and although they appeared serious at the time, in a very short time indeed conditions were quite normal.[39]

In Chengtu, the academic capital of the province, nationalistic student protest movements developed during the Washington Conference of 1921.[40] Though the Chengtu situation led a nervous British diplomat to conclude that "generally speaking, the foreigner is absolutely hated," the French foreign minister assured the English with perhaps a touch of condescension that French diplomats were not alarmed.[41]

The year 1925 brought a revitalization of Szechwan's student movement and a greater degree of integration with other elements of urban society. From the time of the notorious May 30 incident in 1925, the tempo of protest against foreign exploitation increased and its scope broadened. Boycotts were better organized and more effective in smaller Yangtze ports as well as in Chungking. After the May 30 incident, an effective boycott against the British continued for more than a year; the Asiatic Petroleum Corporation, one of the largest British firms in Szechwan, reported that its July sales in the province were 10 percent of their normal level.[42] The British bombardment of Wanhsien in

September 1926 further increased the intensity of antiforeign protests and demonstrations in Szechwan's principal cities.*

As in other areas of China, this expansion of urban unrest and the growing immersion of Szechwanese cities in a national political current were the result of increased Kuomintang and Chinese Communist activity in the province, particularly among urban laborers. Prior to 1924, no labor organizations which transcended traditional craft lines or concentrated on broad social and political issues had endured in Szechwan, whose modern industrial economy was tiny by comparison with that of Shanghai, Canton, or Wuhan.[43] In the early days of the Republic, the Szechwan Provincial Assembly had legislated the establishment of a provincial labor association, but the association and its district branches were never formed.[44] A Servants' Guild and a "Labor Self-Government Association," organized by Chengtu students in the early 1920s, showed signs of spreading throughout Chengtu's laboring population for a time, but both groups expired before a broadly based and politicized movement actually took hold.[45]

In the spring of 1924, a group of Kuomintang operatives under Shih Ch'ing-yang set out to organize workers in Chungking's major industries. By summer, they had formed organizations in thirty separate fields, and Shih formed the Chungking General Labor Association.[46] In 1925, as Right and Left factions within the Kuomintang grew more hostile toward each other, the Szechwanese Wu Yü-chang returned to the province and led the formation of a leftist rival labor organization in Chungking.[47] By 1926, right- and left-wing groups were competing for influence among the laborers of Chengtu as well.[48]

The active participation of party professionals in organizing labor in the principal Szechwanese cities was a key factor in broadening the base of the old student movement and in bringing the populace of the

---

*In this affair, a British gunboat bombarded the Yangtze port of Wanhsien during a dispute with Yang Sen over shipping activity on the river. The dispute arose from the long-standing problem of foreign steamships damaging or sinking Chinese craft in their wakes. Yang's forces had boarded and seized a British vessel and detained it at Wanhsien. The captain of the British gunboat sent to the scene issued an ultimatum, which Yang ignored, and then fired on the city. Chinese and British assessments of the damage caused by the shelling differed greatly. For the British version of the incident, see the note from Minister J. W. Ronald Macleay to the Chinese Foreign Ministry, September 20, 1926, in "Exchange of Notes between the British and Chinese Governments Relative to the Bombardment of Wanhsien (Szechwan)," *Chinese Social and Political Science Review* 11 (1927), Public Documents section, pp. 68–72. An account of Szechwanese response to the Wanhsien bombardment appears in Li Pai-hung, "Ssu-ch'uan min-chung yün-tung chih fa-chan chieh-tuan" [Stages in the development of the mass movement in Szechwan], *Pei-ching ta-hsüeh Ssu-ch'uan t'ung-hsiang hui hui-k'an*, February 10, 1934, pp. 57–58.

cities into greater contact with the currents of nationalism and anti-imperialism that gripped eastern and central China. At the same time, the bitter rivalry between the two factions within the Kuomintang brought internal strife to the nascent workers' movement. The two labor organizations propagandized heavily among laborers and students in Chungking, while armed "dare-to-die" squads from each side attacked the other's propaganda teams and activists in the streets.[49]

As the face of urban unrest changed in 1924 and 1925, Szechwan's military leaders found themselves hemmed in by a combination of strictures, some old and some new. On the one hand, the advent of Kuomintang-Communist influence among students and workers had made opposition to warlords a basic rallying cry and destruction of warlords a fundamental goal of urban social movements. Moreover, the old necessity of avoiding imbroglios with foreign powers remained. These were good reasons for the generals to suppress the rising urban movement. On the other hand, the strength of nationalist sentiment made opposition to the movement even more dangerous to the militarists, and made accommodation with the movement a valuable safeguard of their own positions. As the nationalist movement gained in South China and a climactic struggle between North and South developed, the probable outcome became another key consideration in the militarists' calculations; siding with the losing party in the coming confrontation was to be avoided.

Loaded with these internal and external implications, the urban disorder that mushroomed in Chungking and other cities after 1925 held many pitfalls for Liu Hsiang and the other Szechwanese army commanders. Because he held Chungking, the center of growing tension, Liu played the leading role in determining the attitude of Szechwanese militarists. His position was made even more uncomfortable because several of his own subordinates took opposing positions in the conflict between the Kuomintang Right and Left in Chungking.[50] Liu waited until November 1926 before acting. Then, after the Nationalist capture of Wuhan and after he had received his title as commander of the Twenty-first Army, Liu inclined to the left.[51] His forces descended on the headquarters of the Kuomintang Right and its labor association, forcing most of the leaders into hiding and destroying Shih Ch'ing-yang's organization. The rightists' armed labor corps was disbanded, and Shih Ch'ing-yang fled the province.[52] The anquish and bitterness of the conservative Kuomintang organizers permeated their reports to the Party center downriver: "In the end," they reported, our Chungking Party was not destroyed directly by the Communists, it was destroyed directly by Liu Hsiang. . . . It does not make sense that a Revolutionary Army should destroy a local Kuomintang Bureau, or that Liu Hsiang, a Kuomintang member, should accuse the Party Bureau of lying. . . . Our Party Bureau concealed nothing from Liu Hsiang's investigation; suddenly we were disbanded by an armed force. We had no power, and had to obey the military. . . . Our great revolutionary task has passed to other hands; bitterness turns to hope. We still hope that Liu Hsiang may come to his senses.[53]

Another right-wing member, writing from Chungking, noted that many people assumed that Liu Hsiang had joined the Chinese Communist Party and was acting as "executioner" for the Communists.[54]

Liu Hsiang's smooth and efficient dispersal of the right-wing Kuomintang organization in Chungking, (and thus in Szechwan) turned out to be only the prelude to further action. Against the background of bitter dispute between opposing Kuomintang factions at Wuhan and Nanking, the turning point in the generals' treatment of the anti-imperialist movement occurred on March 31, 1927. Conditions in Chungking had grown increasingly violent as a result of the widening breach in the Kuomintang and the surge of anti-British feeling following the bombardment of Nanking on March 24. Giant rallies organized by the Great Anti-British Alliance got larger and more frequent. The climate became so threatening that the British and American consulates in Chungking finally closed on the morning of March 31, after directing the evacuation of all British and American citizens to gunboats lying in the Yangtze.[55]

The immediate cause of the British and American withdrawal was a huge procession and rally scheduled for the evening of the thirty-first. The character of the Chungking movement had by this time thoroughly alarmed the military authorities. Liu and his generals were fully aware of the dangers of the situation. In an interview with the British consul on the thirtieth, Liu begged the British and Americans not to evacuate the city, to leave matters to local authorities, and not to strengthen the extremists' hands by landing sailors and marines from the gunboats in Chungking. Significantly, Liu revealed that he had promised to address the rally personally, but that he had subsequently revoked his permission for the pre-rally procession.[56]

The rally began as scheduled, but the crowd of several hundred thousand had been infiltrated by troops from Wang Ling-chi's division dressed in civilian clothes and armed with concealed weapons. The audience shouted slogans against imperialism, against Chiang Kai-shek, and against warlords. As the chairman of the rally mounted the rostrum, the soldiers opened fire. The chairman and several other Communist leaders of the rally died on the speakers' platform. In the panic that followed, thirty to forty people were shot to death, about two hundred were trampled to death, and a thousand were injured. Immediately after this notorious March 31 Incident, military authorities broke up the left-wing Kuomintang organization, the Party cadre training school operated by Wu Yü-chang, and several other schools. Chungking's left-wing newspapers were also destroyed.[57]

The other important provincial militarists followed Liu Hsiang's lead shortly after the March 31 affair. On April 9, Liu Wen-hui, Teng Hsi-hou, T'ien Sung-yao, Yang Sen, Lai Hsin-hui, and Liu Ch'eng-hsün joined Liu in denouncing the Communists.[58] Communist elements in many districts were suppressed by local officers, while repression campaigns took place in other cities like Chengtu, Wanhsien, and Fouling.[59] Destruction of the revolutionary peasant movement took place at the same time. By May 1927, a Russian report placed only two hundred Chinese Communist Party members in Szechwan, and the percentage of Communists in the total population was the lowest of any of the eighteen provinces listed in the report.* The labor movement never reappeared in Szechwan, and despite occasional incidents of sabotage or clandestine pamphleteering, the militarists' policy of ruthless repression kept the student population of Szechwan generally quiet and submissive.[60]

As the Nationalist era began, Liu Hsiang's successive attacks on the Kuomintang Right and Left had effectively paralyzed the party in Szechwan. Liu's actions had corresponded roughly to developments downriver, where Chiang Kai-shek's growing hostility to the Chinese Communists climaxed with the massacres at Shanghai on April 12, 1927. There was, however, an important difference. In Szechwan Liu Hsiang used his own agents and not Chiang's to strike at the leftists.

*The figure was .005 percent. Hupei's .047 was the highest, as was the absolute figure of thirteen thousand Communist Party members said to be there. See *What One Must Know About China* (Moscow, 1927), cited in Roy Hofheinz, "The Ecology of Chinese Communist Success: Rural Influence Patterns, 1923–1945," in *Chinese Communist Politics in Action*, ed. A. Doak Barnett (Seattle, 1969), p. 48. The weakness of the CCP in Szechwan continued for many years (see Chang Kuo-t'ao, "Wo-ti hui-i" [Reminiscences], *Ming-pao yüeh-k'an*, November 1969, p. 99).

When he destroyed the Left in Chungking, Liu did not leave room for Chiang's supporters to reassert themselves. Party headquarters in Chungking were closed, and all party newspapers were destroyed. Local and district party organizations, such as they were, had been organized mainly by the Left, so they too were dispersed in the wake of the March 31 Incident.[61]

In June 1927 Nanking appointed a "Party Purification Committee" headed by two longtime party workers from Szechwan to reorganize the Kuomintang in the province, weed out deviant elements, establish new labor organizations under Kuomintang auspices, and so on. From its inception, this group was at the mercy of the provincial military authorities. It was dependent on them for funds and had to plead with them to allot 4 percent of their revenues for party purposes.[62] It respectfully requested the generals to protect party functionaries, "who are subject to danger in pressing the party's fight against corruption, illegal taxation, and the evil gentry."[63] But while all the major militarists except Yang Sen pledged 4 percent of their revenues to the party, only Liu Hsiang, Lai Hsin-hui and Liu Ch'eng-hsün actually paid anything, and their payments were small. The Party Purification Committee failed for lack of militarist support, and its plans for a provincial party conference went unrealized.[64]

Early in 1928, the central Kuomintang organization made another attempt to establish the party in Szechwan, appointing a "Party Supervisory Committee" which finally commenced operations in Chengtu in July. This committee sent representatives to numerous districts in the province to register party members and develop local party organizations.[65] Again, however, the party ran afoul of provincial military authority. One district organizer near Chengtu was also the leader of a local popular resistance movement against military over-taxation, and in this latter role he was killed by an officer in the Twenty-fourth Army. With Liu Wen-hui thus aroused against Kuomintang activities in his area, the Supervisory Committee had to flee from Chengtu, and Kuomintang activity in Szechwan ceased. At the end of 1929, the party counted 77 members in Szechwan, out of a total membership of more than 266,000. The Kuomintang had fewer members in China's most populous province than in any other.[66]

In the summer of 1930, the central party organization appointed another Supervisory Committee for Szechwan, this time under the veteran Lu Shih-t'i, and once again the effort to resurrect the Kuomintang in Szechwan began in Chengtu. During the Reorganization Crisis of late 1930, however, Liu Wen-hui's hostility toward the Nanking-oriented party bureau forced its removal to Chungking, by which time the committee had shrunk to only three men. From Chungking the organization of district party bureaus began again, with somewhat greater success. But in 1932 the center attempted to reorganize party operations in Szechwan one more time, appointing a new group of "special representatives" to take over from the old directorate and operate out of Chengtu. This divided the Szechwan Kuomintang just when its efforts were beginning to bear fruit. The members of the directorate refused to cede their powers to the new appointees, and many local chapters refused to transfer their support to the special representatives. In 1933 the center reversed itself, recalled the special representatives, and Tseng K'uo-ch'ing, a young Szechwanese graduate of the Whampoa Academy, was put in charge of party affairs in Szechwan.[67] New organizational forms followed. Tseng tried to resign early in 1934 but his resignation was rejected. The Kuomintang in Szechwan on the eve of the political changes of 1935 remained weak and small, unable to sway the provincial military chiefs or to mobilize large segments of the population.[68]

The weakness of the Kuomintang in Szechwan was the political parallel of the central government's military and economic impotence there. For the failure of the party the provincial militarists were heavily to blame. Their meager support of party activities was part of their overall resistance to the influx of external forces which might dilute their control or attempt to influence their conduct in Szechwan. Most of the central government's formal orders, which often bore little relation to Szechwanese realities, were simply ignored. Thus when the Military Disbandment Conference of 1929 ordered Szechwanese armies reduced to six divisions by April 1, 1930, the army commanders of Szechwan did nothing.[69] Nanking's prohibition on arms purchases not approved by the Ministry of War went unheeded as Liu Hsiang bought large quantities of weapons through arms dealers' agents in Chungking.[70] In 1932, when the war between Liu Hsiang and Liu Wen-hui brought Szechwan to the attention of the central government, Nanking ordered all sides to cease fire and respect the provisions of the General Order of 1928. No one listened.[71] Provincial militarists remained firmly opposed to any Nationalist military penetration of their province. As one Chinese analyst remarked after central government forces had abandoned their pursuit of the Chinese Communists into T'ien Sung-yao's garrison area, T'ien feared that "it is easier to invite the guest in than it is to send him home."[72]

Liu Hsiang's Special Relationship with Nanking

The main feature of Szechwan's relationship to central political authority between 1927 and 1934 was the lack of regular contact. The army commanders steered clear of national politics, and successfully foiled Nanking's occasional weak efforts to pry into provincial business. After 1930, however, a special relationship began to emerge between Liu Hsiang and the National Government. It was a curious mixture of surface cooperation and subsurface pursuit of divergent self-interests. Liu Hsiang's behavior toward Nanking became the model for other Szechwanese commanders after 1935, when contact with the National Government became unavoidable. As was to be expected of him, Liu sought to mold a relationship with Nanking which would work to his advantage in Szechwan without compromising his authority in any substantive way.

For Liu and the center alike, the essence of the relationship was the trading of ceremony for substance, symbolic support for real benefits. Neither side, however, cared to trade its substance for the other's symbol. As a result, after an initial period of very little contact prior to 1930, Liu and the central government embarked on a series of highly stylized maneuvers that brought few real changes in Szechwan's political position relative to Nanking.

Liu's support of Chiang during the Reorganization Crisis opened the door to further contacts. The Kuomintang Central Executive Committee responded by making Liu a member of the State Council (*Kuo-min cheng-fu wei-yüan hui*) in 1931. Liu in turn accepted the title but never went to Nanking to sit with the council. To do so would have been to concede too much, and possibly to have left himself open to forms of persuasion that Nanking could not employ while he was on native soil. At the same time, the National Government created the post of Szechwan Director for Rehabilitation and appointed Liu to the job with wide powers over Szechwanese military affairs.[73] But the post remained only a name; in itself it gave Liu no new real power over his rivals in Szechwan.

For his part Liu offered symbolic support to Nanking. After he failed to keep his appointment with Chiang in Hankow early in 1931, Liu sent a special envoy to reaffirm his loyalty to Chiang personally and to the National Government. To this ritual assertion of support Liu added a request for a large central government loan. Chiang himself approved the loan to Liu's emissary, and the terms of the generous agreement were even made public. In the end, though, the loan was never issued, ostensibly because of the opposition of Finance Minister T. V. Soong.[74] When the central government faced the disaffection of the powerful southern militarists Ch'en Chi-t'ang and Li Tsung-jen, Nanking sought tangible aid from Liu Hsiang in the form of a Szechwanese expeditionary force to Hupei. Liu demurred until Chiang Kai-shek offered him a new title (Upper Yangtze Bandit Suppression Director) and, more important, enough money to permit Liu to increase his armed strength within Szechwan by the number of men he was sending downriver.[75]

With the basic premise that Szechwan's internal problems came first, Liu Hsiang tried to convince Nanking that the National Government ought to share his own priorities. Since the early 1920s, Liu's belief that provincial problems needed to be met before Szechwan could be integrated into national affairs had been well known and remarkably consistent. After 1931 Liu used the same argument to gain the support of the National Government. Through his special emissary, Liu argued to Chiang Kai-shek in February 1931 that Nanking had two options in dealing with Szechwan. One was to try to control the province by force. The other was to turn existing conditions in Szechwan to Chiang's own advantage. According to the emissary's later account, when Chiang asked whom in Szechwan he could utilize, the envoy suggested Liu Hsiang, and pointed to his stand during the Reorganization Crisis as evidence of his dependability and loyalty.[76]

Chiang could hardly have held many delusions about Liu Hsiang's attitude toward the central government; nonetheless, he was content during the early 1930s to adopt a view of Nanking–Szechwan relations which was essentially Liu's own. Liu would bear the responsibility for pacifying and unifying Szechwan under his own control, so that at some future point Szechwan would of its own volition come under National Government control. Thus Liu's successful war against Liu Wen-hui in 1933 became known as the "War to Stabilize Szechwan" (An-Ch'uan chan). Liu's own goal of dominating Szechwan while avoiding outside interference was accepted by both sides prior to the Communist crisis of 1934.

Behind Liu's success in preserving his provincial priorities lay his accurate assessment of the central government's capabilities in Szechwan. In 1927, even as he pledged his loyalty to the Nationalists, he had noted the inability of central power to interfere in Szechwan. Over the years his estimates did not change. In 1933 Liu's chief civil administrative subordinate made clear Liu's view of Nanking's powers and its connection with Liu's own priorities:

> If it is said that Szechwan's affairs can be settled by the central government, the answer is that the political power of the center today has still not achieved success. If it is said that the central government can use force to control Szechwan, then look at the unresolved problems facing the government: Manchuria, Kiangsi, Hupei, the unresolved Communist problem. If it is said that the troops of neighboring provinces could control Szechwan, then remember that the forces of Yunnan and Kweichow have been beaten repeatedly in the past, and recognize that the past will only repeat itself. . . . The first task is to bring peace between the army and the people of the garrison area, drive out other armies, and promote the political unification of Szechwan.[77]

Such a statement reflected Liu's optimistic conviction, shared by his provincial militarist colleagues prior to 1934, that Chiang Kai-shek's government would never establish itself in Szechwan. It was this assessment that impelled Liu to pursue his traditional goals and even urge his own priorities on Nanking. Moreover, the National Government in the early thirties seemingly shared Liu Hsiang's view. Even as late as 1933, it appeared to Nanking that Liu Hsiang was correct in his estimates of the limitations on central government potential in Szechwan. The remarks of a Kuomintang supporter in Szechwan corresponded closely to the statement by Liu Hsiang's own official quoted above:

> Some of the military leaders are always trying to avoid the scrutiny of the central government, and they continue to enrich themselves. Moreover, some of them think that the central government will never have the power to come and control Szechwan, and they think that they will always have full freedom of action. . . . Szechwan is a Chinese province and the central government naturally has its responsibilities here. But at present it has many problems in North China: generals become restless, the Communists rise up, the Japanese have to be dealt with. So for the moment its power thoroughly to solve the Szechwan problem is insufficient. But then again, the people of Szechwan are not unable to solve

their own problems. . . . The central government therefore places great responsibilities on Liu Hsiang. Since he has faithfully supported the central government, we believe that he can certainly undertake these most critical tasks.[78]

As it soon turned out, the Szechwanese militarists were mistaken in their assumption that the central government and Chiang Kai-shek would never come onto their territory. Until the Communist emergency of late 1934, however, neither they nor the National Government could perceive much possibility of altering the status quo between Szechwan and the center, despite the growing recognition on both sides of Szechwan's potential value as a resistance base in the event of war with Japan.*

Szechwan and Nanking: A Limited Separatism

Defined as practical independence from higher political authority and as the maintenance of freedom from external interference, Szechwanese provincial separatism in the late 1920s and the early 1930s was very conspicuous, and in China at the time it was notorious. Nonetheless, provincial separatism was not provincial nationalism. To Liu Hsiang and the other army commanders, Szechwan remained a province, one of many which made up the larger entity, China. There were no hints, even in the argument for temporary autonomy, of establishing a Szechwanese sovereign state, no suggestions of any formal declarations of permanent secession from the Republic of China. Szechwan remained linked to the China below the Gorges by history, by culture, and not least by its vital river commerce and financial ties to Shanghai. It was in terms of political control that the separatism of Liu Hsiang and the other army commanders was so pronounced and so effective.

The essence of this separatism was the preservation of distinctions between form and substance. Provincial armies became "National Revolutionary Armies" and provincial governments were appointed by Nanking. Titles were conferred, loyalties pledged and protested, aid and support promised and proclaimed by both Szechwan and the center. Neither the Szechwanese nor the Nationalists could imagine early in

*According the the 1934 Kuomintang Yearbook, Party membership in Szechwan totalled 19,444, an increase of more than 2,000 percent over 1929 figures. Given the erratic course of Kuomintang organizational efforts in Szechwan during the early thirties, which the same Yearbook describes in detail elsewhere, this figure seems unrealistic. It may have reflected rising Kuomintang interest in the possibility of extending central political influence into the province (see *Erh-shih san nien Chung-kuo kuo-min tang nien-chien, i* sec., pp. 3, 23).

1934 that the relationship between province and center was about to be upset; that within a year Szechwan would be infested with outside armies; that the militarists' way of life and accustomed prerogatives would soon be under massive attack. With Liu Hsiang in the forefront, the militarists of Szechwan were about to wage a struggle for their survival—not among themselves, as they were wont to do from time to time—but collectively, against the menacing intrusions of their friends and allies from Nanking.

Liu Hsiang, late December 1934. Wide World Photos.

Liu Wen-hui, 1935.

T'ien Sung-yao, 1934.

Yang Sen, 1924. Photo courtesy of the
China Records Project, Yale University Divinity School Library.

Chungking, ca. 1910. The confluence of the Yangtze and the Chialing rivers lies just beyond the right-hand edge of the photo. The Yangtze appears below and the Chialing above the city in this view. Photo courtesy of the China Records Project, Yale University Divinity School Library.

Teng Hsi-hou, probably early 1930s. Photo courtesy of William G. Sewell.

A Szechwanese army unit, ca. 1922.

Local militia in Szechwan, probably 1939.

5 Collapse of the Status Quo

In December 1932 civil war again gripped Szechwan. Armed conflict between Liu Hsiang and Liu Wen-hui had commenced in October, and the battle lines had shifted steadily westward as Liu Wen-hui withdrew from his holdings in central Szechwan. In Chengtu, the outbreak of fighting between Liu Wen-hui and T'ien Sung-yao marked the disintegration of the Paoting Clique that had generally kept the peace in western Szechwan since 1927. The fighting in Chengtu, which was heavier than at any time since 1911, plus the size of the forces involved in the Two-Liu conflict, revealed that this latest war was much grander than the usual skirmishing among provincial armies.[1]

With the attention of the entire province focused on Chengtu and the rich territory to the south, it was inevitable that events in the remote northeastern section of the province should go practically unnoticed. Thus when a remnant band of Communist soldiers from the former Hupei–Honan–Anhui soviet led by Hsü Hsiang-ch'ien slipped into Szechwan on December 25, 1932, the incident caused no excitement.[2] The Communist force was known as the Fourth Front Red Army. After abandoning their base in the fall of 1932, Hsü and Chang-Kuo-t'ao, the political leader of the old soviet, moved into Hupei and then into Shensi. By late November they were just south of Sian, pursued by Hsü's former Whampoa Academy classmate Hu Tsung-nan and face to face with the Shensi militarist Yang Hu-ch'eng.[3] In December, the Communists turned directly south from Hanchung, north of the Szechwan border, waded into the Ta Pa Mountains and occupied the district capital of T'ungchiang in Szechwan on the twenty-fifth.[4] Short of ammunition and winter clothing, the Fourth Front Red Army had shrunk from 16,000 to 9,000 men during its trek from the Hupei–Honan–Anhui soviet. Starting with 20,000 rifles, it reached Szechwan with 8,000. All its field pieces and all but one of its machine guns were left behind as the army worked west and south. By the time they took T'ungchiang at the end of 1932, the Communists were weak and exhausted.[5]

For the next two years, the fortunes of the Northern Szechwan Soviet which Hsü and Chang established rose and fell with the fluctuations of Szechwanese military politics. Conditions inside Szechwan had induced Hsü and Chang to go there in the first place. They were well aware of the provincial militarists' aversion to the presence of outside forces in Szechwan, even friendly ones, and they saw an opportunity to shake off their Nationalist and Shensi pursuers by crossing into Szechwan.[6] Overtaxation and maladministration under T'ien Sung-yao in the T'ungchiang area had already spawned a resistance movement with which the Communists made contact as soon as they arrived.[7] Most important of all, the area was almost unguarded. When the Communists arrived, T'ien Sung-yao had only about one thousand troops in the three districts which the Communists quickly took over.[8] T'ien had concentrated his forces in Chengtu, where his battle with Liu Wen-hui was at its peak. T'ien's weakness in the northeastern section of his territory was an early sign of the close connection between provincial military politics and the fate of the Chinese Communists in northern Szechwan.[9]

After taking T'ungchiang, the Communists occupied the neighboring districts of Nanchiang and Pachung in January 1933.[10] In these districts and the others to which they later extended their power, the Communists worked to organize the population for production, political education, and especially for military purposes.* Youths and children, women and girls were organized into Red Vanguards, Youth Corps, propaganda units, and service brigades for laundry and sewing.[11] In the two years following entry into Szechwan, the Red Armies expanded vigorously. Hsü himself later claimed that by the end of 1933 the Fourth Front Army alone had about 60,000 men. At the peak of its military strength in 1934, the soviet maintained between 80,000 and 100,000 troops.[12]

The soviet leadership also promulgated a set of reforms designed to

---

*There is a difference of opinion as to when the soviet government was actually created. Huang Tzu-ching states that "on February 7, 1933, the Szechwan–Shensi Soviet Government was established at T'ungchiang, and a Szechwan–Shensi Communist Party was also created" ("Ch'uan-Shan ch'u," p. 105). In early August, he continues, "the Second Congress of the Szechwan–Shensi Soviet convened at Pachung with about three thousand delegates attending." Chang Kuo-t'ao takes pains in his memoirs to explain his opposition to creation of a soviet in northern Szechwan and claims that the First Soviet Congress of about one thousand delegates, held in late August 1933, created the Northern Szechwan Soviet Government (see "Hui-i," Ming-pao yüeh-k'an, October 1969, pp. 97–99, and November 1969, pp. 96–99).

heighten the political consciousness of the population, improve agricultural production in a particularly poor and backward region, and assure the economic survival of the soviet.[13] Schools and classes for workers and peasants were planned, agricultural cooperatives were promoted to provide for the sharing of scarce tools and animals, and peasant consumer cooperatives were established. Representative, elected soviets were set up at several levels below the soviet government itself. A variety of Communist newspapers and magazines appeared. A single grain tax known as the soviet public tax, which was used to feed soldiers, transport workers, and officials, replaced the host of miscellaneous taxes levied by local militarists. Opium cultivation was prohibited, and a graduated program to eliminate opium smoking was announced.

Most important, the soviet government detailed a plan for land distribution. The land law called for the expropriation of all landlord property and redistribution of land to landless tenants, poor peasants, soldiers, and unemployed people who wanted to farm. It also provided for confiscation of most land belonging to rich peasants, invalidation of all outstanding mortgages, and abolition of former rent and interest obligations. Land was promised to farmers, laborers, soldiers, and professional persons who came with their families from non-Communist areas.[14]

In their efforts to create a popular base in northern Szechwan, the Communists' most tangible and outstanding success was the expansion and improvement of their military strength. The results of their attempt to stimulate production and revolutionize agrarian society were less than they hoped for. The disciplined behavior of the Communist forces contrasted favorably with the conduct of T'ien Sungyao's and other militarists' forces and undoubtedly drew a measure of support from the people.[15] But their varying success in battle against provincial armies cut deeply into the credibility of the Communists' promises, strengthening peasants' fears of what would happen when the landlords and provincial troops returned. The land redistribution program was weakened by the unstable military situation and by the reluctance of peasants to share their land and tools. Despite great efforts to prove its worth, the Communists' currency continually depreciated. Established in a poor and inaccessible region, the soviet suffered from some severe shortages, including a shortage of salt which it never managed to alleviate despite the opening of several small wells near Nanpu.[16]

In the course of two years' struggle the Communist-controlled area expanded and shrank several times. When they first reached Szechwan, Hsü and Chang sought to avoid conflict with surrounding militarists. In a letter to T'ien Sung-yao, they offered to withdraw from Szechwan the following spring if T'ien would let them remain unmolested in their original three districts through the winter.[17] However in February 1933 T'ien turned his attention from Chengtu back to his rear areas. Living up to the new title of "Szechwan Bandit Suppression Commander" bestowed on him by Nanking, T'ien dispatched a large force against the Communists in the T'ung-Nan-Pa region. Hsü Hsiang-ch'ien abandoned Pachung and Nanchiang in mid-March, and finally quit T'ungchiang, the soviet capital, on April 29. The Communists retreated into the mountains along the Szechwan–Shensi border.[18]

Again, however, provincial politics gave the Communists an opportunity. In May 1933 fighting broke out once more in Chengtu, this time between Teng Hsi-hou, who had earlier remained neutral, and Liu Wen-hui, who had moved back into the city after T'ien turned against the Communists. T'ien hastened to support Teng against Liu, and redeployed most of his troops toward the city. Late in May the Communists counterattacked with spectacular results. The original soviet districts fell back into their hands and the Communists pushed on to the west. In ten days, T'ien's terrified army lost what it had taken four months to gain.[19] The Communists proceeded along the northern frontier all the way to the Chialing River and expanded southward into the districts of Yingshan and Chühsien, within Yang Sen's garrison area.

Late in the summer, Hsü Hsiang-ch'ien scored brilliantly in the east, taking Hsüanhan and Suiting districts from Liu Ts'un-hou. Suiting had been Liu's headquarters for a decade; with its capture, the Communists gained a vast store of arms and ammunition, military clothing, medicines, a radio transmitter, a mint, an arsenal, and a great deal of hard currency.* By September 1933 the soviet included all or parts of fourteen Szechwanese districts.[20]

---

* *Tou-cheng,* June 30, 1934, asserts that 5,000 to 6,000 firearms plus artillery and materials for 15,000 rifles and 80 million bullets were captured at Suiting. Tung Ming puts the figure at 10,000 machine guns and 3 million rounds of ammunition. In *KWCP,* March 11, 1935, the figures are 5,000 to 6,000 guns, more than a million rounds of ammunition, and more than a million Mexican dollars. This report mentions that when they captured Suiting, the Communists were so short of ammunition that many were using bullets tipped with wood.

T'ien Sung-yao was trapped between two unpalatable alternatives. Either he had to fight the Communists alone, which by summer had clearly become a losing proposition, or he had to seek aid in order to wrest his lost territories from Hsü Hsiang-ch'ien. At first, when the Communists were weak, he made no effort to get help. After his spring-time disasters, however, T'ien called for provincial militarist coopera-tion against the Communists in his garrison area.[21]

Initially the other militarists were not willing to help. Early in 1933, Liu Hsiang declared his position with the slogan, "Pacify Szechwan first, then suppress the Communists." Within the framework of his own experience it was sensible for Liu to stick to customary priorities. In the first place, he was locked in his critical struggle with Liu Wen-hui by the time the Fourth Front Red Army arrived, and he stood to benefit enormously if he could hurt his uncle badly enough. Therefore, the Communist problem had to wait until he had disposed of Liu Wen-hui and taken as much of Liu Wen-hui's territory and army as he could. Liu Hsiang's own experience suggested, moreover, that the Com-munists could be used to further his own fortunes. In 1927 he had waited until Communist rebels had crippled Lai Hsin-hui before com-ing to Lai's "aid" and incorporating most of Lai's territory into his own garrison area.[22] Nor was Liu Hsiang particularly distressed to see the Communists weakening T'ien Sung-yao and Yang Sen in 1933.

The fall of Suiting in October 1933 seemed to demonstrate the severity of the Communist threat to the provincial militarists. It un-derlined the audacity and skill of Hsü Hsiang-ch'ien's forces and the incompetence of the provincial armies. Reports seeped out that Yang Sen had lost Yingshan because his army was drunk when the Com-munists appeared.[23] Hsüanhan city was occupied by sixty Commun-ist soldiers, while Liu Ts'un-hou's troops either fled or joined the Communists.[24] When the Communists moved on Suiting, most of Liu Ts'un-hou's army was off-duty, and the detachment assigned to guard a vital position had gone off to the wrong place.[25] Liu and his family escaped to Chungking with dozens of crates of treasure, his retainers firing on fleeing refugees to clear the roads and destroying a bridge and boats loaded with refugees in order to block the pursuing Communists.[26]

The most alarming aspect of the fall of Suiting was the sudden threat posed to the whole Yangtze area of eastern Szechwan. With Suiting and Hsüanhan in Communist hands, only two districts lay between them and the Yangtze port of Wanhsien. If they could reach the Yangtze, the Communists could cut Szechwan's trade with the outside, on which Liu Hsiang depended so heavily for revenue. The danger to Wanhsien and even Chungking itself soon subsided, as the Communist attack on K'aichiang and K'aihsien districts failed. But during the short period when it looked as though they might reach the river, there was near panic in Chungking and other centers of Liu Hsiang's power. Merchants quietly shipped their stocks downriver, and some traders left the province altogether.[27]

The loss of Suiting seemed to shake Liu Hsiang out of his lethargy. Nanking took away T'ien's title of Bandit Suppression Commander and gave it to Liu. To smash the Communists, Liu gathered a huge force of more than 100,000 men and divided it into six "routes" for a coordinated attack on the Red Army forces. Teng Hsi-hou, T'ien Sung-yao, and Yang Sen each commanded a "route," as did Wang Ling-chi. Li Chia-yü and Lo Tse-chou, former subordinates of Teng Hsi-hou, commanded the "Third Route," and Liu Ts'un-hou's brother Liu Pang-chun commanded the "Sixth Route."[28] This unprecedented cooperation among Szechwan's principal militarists at first seemed to bear fruit. With almost no Communist resistance, the provincial armies reoccupied the east bank of the Chialing and recovered Yang Sen's and Liu Tsun-hou's lost territories, while the Communists concentrated their forces in the central region of T'ung-Nan-Pa.[29]

The Crisis of Szechwanese Militarism

By May 1934, though, the provincial counterattack had stalled. The Communists still held T'ung-Nan-Pa and Wanyüan, having suffered few losses. Despite the exaggerated reports of victories and valor which poured from provincial army headquarters and from Nanking, the drive against Hsü Hsiang-ch'ien had fallen prey to crippling problems.[30]

The accustomed pattern of militarist behavior reasserted itself once the drive got underway, and all semblance of coordinated action soon evaporated. Less powerful commanders realized to their dismay that only Liu Hsiang would benefit from the elimination of the Communists. Teng and T'ien were already annoyed at Liu over the distribution of spoils following the defeat of Liu Wen-hui. Now, characteristically, the weaker men saw the chance to use the Communists as a lever to destroy Liu Hsiang before he became strong enough to destroy their own power. Once the "joint attack" was launched, therefore, the other commanders held back, leaving Liu Hsiang's forces to bear the brunt of the fighting around T'ungchiang and Wanyüan.[31] Not even the expansion of Communist power in Szechwan proved strong enough to shatter the army commanders' accustomed political outlook and sense of priorities.

Liu Hsiang also faced an unprecedented crisis within the ranks of his own army. Serious dissatisfaction arose among Liu's senior subordinates over Liu Ts'ung-yün ("Liu from the Clouds"), an itinerant Taoist mystic who seemed to enthrall and control Liu Hsiang. In planning the "joint attack" of 1933, Liu Hsiang used Liu Ts'ung-yün as his intermediary with other provincial commanders. In the ensuing campaign, Liu Ts'ung-yün held the position of chief of the Communist-Suppression General Headquarters, and played a major role in setting battle tactics and strategies.[32] It was rumored that Liu consulted the spirits on every matter relating to the armies, from the order of battle down to the most auspicious hour for cooking meals. Liu Ts'ung-yün's mysterious influence over Liu Hsiang, his lack of military training and experience, and his imperious behavior toward Liu Hsiang's principal subordinates gave rise to dangerous resentments. Conflict between Liu Ts'ung-yün and Wang Ling-chi grew so severe that Wang refused to carry out orders issued by Liu Hsiang's new favorite. In April 1934 Liu Hsiang relieved Wang of his command and put him under house arrest in Chengtu.[33] This widened the split within the Twenty-first Army over Liu Ts'ung-yün. Wang was a popular commander, and many usually loyal officers supported him in the dispute, which simmered through the summer of 1934.[34]

By mid-1934, Szechwan also faced a rapidly spreading social and economic crisis. The civil war of 1932–33 and the anti-Communist campaigns had brought heavy tax increases in every garrison area.[35] Yet the financial plight of the major militarists steadily worsened. Even Liu Hsiang, whose resources far surpassed those of his colleagues, confronted a financial emergency. Twenty-first Army expenditures in 1933 were almost twice those of 1931, and 1933 deficits more than quadrupled the deficits for 1929 and 1930.[36] Higher taxation could not make up the difference, and Chungking resorted more and more to emergency measures which did more harm than good. Additional paper money was printed to cover such immediate expenses as payments to the troops, but this undermined the Twenty-first Army's currency.[37] To shore up the currency and provide for other crises, the army in 1932 began selling large bond issues which indeed raised some ready money, but which imposed a heavy burden of service payments which the army had to meet lest it alienate its subscribers and ruin the chance for further bond sales.[38]

This critical period also saw the collapse of important supplementary revenue sources under the twin burdens of provincial taxation and shrinking external markets. As Szechwanese merchants had been quick to point out in the past, the armies' quest for revenue could become self-defeating if commerce taxes drove Szechwanese commodity prices so high that exports could not be sold and imports could not be bought. After 1933, taxes on trade increased along with land taxes. This was particularly true in the case of many of Szechwan's principal exports, including sugar, salt, opium, t'ung oil, wines, and medicinal herbs. As a result of the high prices of Szechwanese exports, external Chinese demand declined or turned to other producing areas.[39] Loss of external salt markets not only caused a drop in tax revenues, but threw as many as a million salt and transport workers out of their jobs.[40]

The province had begun to suffer severely at this time from economic difficulties which the provincial militarists could not control. The world depression sharply reduced foreign demand for t'ung oil, a tree product used in the making of linseed oil and one of eastern Szechwan's most valuable exports. The value of t'ung oil exports from Szechwan dropped by nearly 50 percent in 1932, and after some recovery in 1933 collapsed again in 1934.[41] Provincial silk production, a vital source of supplementary income for hundreds of thousands of farm families, collapsed in the early 1930s under the impact of world depression and competing foreign synthetic fibers. Silk production in Nanch'ung district, one of Szechwan's three great centers of silk production, had dropped by 1935 to one-fifth of what it had been in the prosperous days of 1929 and 1930.[42]

The collapse of important sources of subsidiary agrarian income, combined with the heavy increase in military taxation, accelerated the processes of social dislocation which had affected rural Szechwan for decades. The advent of large-scale Communist activity in the north heightened the crisis facing the militarists. As the tide of battle ebbed and flowed large sections of northern Szechwan were disrupted by both the provincial armies and the Communists. Hundreds of thousands of refugees filled the Communist areas; others poured into the "white" districts, particularly Chungking.[43]

The temporary military stalemate in northeastern Szechwan ended in July 1934. With the provincial attack stalled, Hsü Hsiang-ch'ien struck back, broke through the encirclement with little difficulty, and pursued the fleeing Szechwanese armies all the way back to the Chia-ing River. Lo Tse-chou's units were nearly destroyed, and T'ien Sung-yao's remnant army was further reduced. Liu Hsiang suffered most heavily, as the Fifth Route force lost fifteen thousand men and weapons. Altogether, the Communists claimed to have taken fifty thousand guns from the demoralized provincial forces.[44]

The Communists' sudden victory brought Liu Hsiang's difficulties to a head. The treachery of the other Szechwanese commanders was clear, while within his own army the newest military disaster produced angry recriminations and threats. On August 23, 1934, Liu Hsiang slipped out of Chengtu without even notifying his chief of staff. In a brief telegram to Nanking, he requested that the National Government relieve him of his duties as Bandit Suppression Commander.[45]

It is unlikely that Liu ever intended his resignation to be permanent. The central government declined to accept it, and a flood of the customary remonstrances from Szechwanese militarists, merchants, and gentry leaders implored Liu to resume his duties.[46] By early September, Liu was touring Twenty-first Army positions as a "private citizen" and demanding assurances of financial support from the terrified Chengtu merchant community.[47] Late in October, he reassumed his Bandit Suppression Commander title.[48] His brief retirement had enabled him to solidify once again his position within the Twenty-first Army, especially since Liu Ts'ung-yün vanished just after Liu Hsiang resigned.[49]

Although Szechwan was relieved to have Liu back, and Liu had secured some money and the support of his army, his return did not improve the military situation. The Chialing River line stabilized after the Communists' summer success, but in the south a new threat emerged. Communist forces under Ho Lung and Hsiao K'o, which had long roamed the border region of Hupei, Hunan, Szechwan, and Kweichow, increased their activity in southeastern Szechwan, compelling Liu Hsiang to send reinforcements to the area in October.[50] Even more ominous was the approach of the Red Army under Chu Te and Mao Tse-tung, which left its base in Kiangsi under heavy Nationalist pressure in October and proceeded westward through Hunan and Kwangsi into Kweichow. Liu Hsiang thus faced the possibility of a two-pronged Communist threat in Szechwan, and the prospect of Nationalist military penetration of the province in order to suppress the Communist armies. This combination of unappetizing prospects finally wrought a major change in Liu Hsiang's attitude toward the Nanking government.

In November 1934 the era of rigid Szechwanese isolation came to an end. Soon after he resumed his duties in Chengtu, Liu Hsiang announced that he would meet with Chiang Kai-shek to seek instructions. On November 13, Liu departed from Chungking for Hankow with a large retinue.[51] He arrived in Nanking on November 20, to a hero's welcome. It was the first time Liu had ever left Szechwan.

Besides providing a clear indication of changes in provincial policy toward central authority, Liu's visit to Nanking symbolized Szechwan's renewed contact with the thinking of the informed public elsewhere in China. Hsü Hsiang-ch'ien's successes and the beginning of the Long March suddenly put Szechwan back in the national headlines. As interest in the province grew, the volume of news coverage and private reports on provincial conditions increased. Szechwan's new importance in the minds of government officials and the reading public after mid-1934 was another factor in the growing movement to "open" Szechwan, which emerged at the time of Liu's journey to Nanking.[52]

Liu's visit lasted from November 20 to December 10. His itinerary included five days in Shanghai, Hangchow, and Soochow, but mostly Liu stayed in Nanking, where he enjoyed an endless series of banquets and high-level discussions of Szechwanese affairs. Despite the great publicity which surrounded his trip to the capital, the substance of Liu's negotiations with the National Government has never been clearly revealed.* During his talks with Chiang Kai-shek, Wang Ching-wei, H. H. Kung, and other Nationalist leaders, Liu undoubtedly attempted to retain as much of his earlier posture toward Nanking as he could. He would trade further symbolic support—his journey itself was a major concession—for increased substantive help from Nanking. Central government support would be material and financial: Liu asked for increased military aid in the form of weapons, munitions, and supplies. At the outset, at least, he sought from Nanking a huge gold loan with which to restore a modicum of financial stability in Szechwan.† Liu almost certainly did not ask for Nationalist troops; the

*The main outlines of Liu's trip appeared in many newspapers. The *Shih pao* of Peiping provided daily front-page coverage of Liu's visit to the capital. A fascinating but unsubstantiated anecdotal account of the Nanking meetings appears in Chiang Shang-ch'ing [pseud.], *Cheng-hai mi-wen* [Inside stories of politics] (Hong Kong, 1966), pp. 95–96. According to this story, at his first meeting with Chiang Kai-shek, Liu Hsiang dressed and acted crudely and awkwardly, giving such an impression of ignorance and innocence that Yang Yung-t'ai, Chiang's secretary-general, said to Liu Hsiang's secretary-general, "This friend of yours is a veritable Liu Chang [a weak character from *The Romance of the Three Kingdoms*]; how did he ever get to bear such serious responsibilities?" This account also maintains that Chiang first proposed sending ten divisions of National Government troops to Szechwan, but dropped the idea when Liu's aides politely warned Nanking officials of the certainty of Szechwanese resistance to such a step.

†Passing through Hankow on his way to Nanking, Liu revealed his proposal to turn over all

presence of a central government army in Szechwan was the last thing he and other Szechwanese militarists wanted.

Because so many conditions had changed in recent months, Liu's attempt to strike a bargain with Chiang along the lines of their 1930–33 accommodation was not wholly successful. The results of Liu's visit reflected Nanking's new position of strength relative to the weakened Szechwanese army commanders. For the first time, the two sides traded substance for substance. Liu won two major items. A new Szechwan provincial government was to be organized to replace the long-defunct Liu Wen-hui government appointed in 1931, with Liu Hsiang as chairman of the new Government Committee. It was also agreed that no central armies would enter Szechwan. Nanking's prime achievement in the talks with Liu Hsiang was the creation of a staff corps under Chiang Kai-shek's headquarters, the purpose of which was to aid Liu Hsiang in suppressing the Communists.[53] Creation of the staff corps was a milestone; it represented the Nanking government's first institutionalized participation in Szechwanese military–political affairs. Chiang chose Ho Kuo-kuang, a native of Hupei and former classmate of Liu Hsiang and Yang Sen at the Rapid Course School, to lead the staff corps into Szechwan.[54]

The financial question, which had been uppermost in Liu's mind when he went to Nanking, proved most difficult to resolve. Liu delayed his scheduled departure from the capital in order to continue his discussions with H. H. Kung.[55] One concrete result of the Nanking meetings was the appointment of a special emissary from the central government to advise the new provincial government on financial problems.[56] Liu's request for a bullion loan of 70 million *yüan* was discarded, but the National Government probably agreed to provide Liu with a monthly sum to be used in the campaign against the Communists.[57]

When Liu returned to Szechwan in December, it remained to be seen whether a new provincial government under his direction would really make any difference to Szechwanese military politics; whether Ho Kuo-kuang and the staff corps would really have any effect on Szechwan's armies and on the anti-Communist campaign; whether the special financial commissioner from Nanking would exert a rationaliz-

Szechwan salt revenues to Nanking in return for an immediate loan of 70 million *yüan*. A newspaper headline later implied that the loan idea had been temporarily accepted, but it is unlikely that Liu's proposal for a loan of this size received serious consideration at the time of his voyage to Nanking (see *Shih pao*, November 17, 1934, p. 1, November 26, 1934, p. 1, and December 1, 1934, p. 1).

ing influence on Szechwan's disheveled economy.* Nonetheless, Liu's journey to see Chiang Kai-shek was a turning point in Szechwan's relations to central authority. From 1935 on, the National Government's presence in Szechwan was established fact. Thereafter, the central government's diligent efforts to incorporate Szechwan into a political structure controlled from the national capital became the dominant issue of Szechwanese politics.

Conclusion

Hsü Hsiang-ch'ien's intrusion into Szechwan in 1933 precipitated the crisis of Szechwanese militarism which in turn brought the central government into the province by the beginning of 1935. Hsü's rapid development of a daring, mobile, and highly effective (if ill-armed) fighting force of nearly 100,000 men presented Liu Hsiang and other leading militarists with the first real threat to their collective existence since they took power in 1925 and 1926.

But the breakdown of the political status quo that had prevailed since 1927 was rooted in the nature of provincial militarism and in the weaknesses of the militarists themselves. The incompetence of the provincial armies was revealed—not caused—by the Communists' attacks.

The generals grievously weakened their own positions by clinging to their accustomed military and political habits in the face of Hsü Hsiang-ch'ien's challenge. Each commander regarded the Communists as mere pawns in the militarists' chronic struggle for provincial power. None of the major militarists perceived that the Communists might not belong to the militarists' world, or that the Communists could become a threat to all the provincial commanders at once, until the threat became a reality. Because genuine cooperation among provincial armies had no place in provincial politics, the armies failed to cooperate against the Communists. It is difficult for anyone to free himself from the frame of reference which governs his daily conduct, and the Szechwanese army commanders were no exceptions. The years of isolated supremacy which they enjoyed prior to 1933 were a key factor in their inability to view the Communists differently from the way in which they viewed each other.

---

*The first appointee as special finance commissioner, Ch'en Shao-kuei, lasted for only three months in Szechwan before leaving "hurriedly" for Nanking, charged with embezzlement (Davidson [Chungking] to London, April 30, 1935, F.O. 371/19303).

6   The National Government and Provincial Reform

Liu Hsiang's trip to the Chinese capital in late 1934 turned out to be the beginning of a new stage in provincial political life and in Szechwan's relations with external authority. Prior to this time, the dominant features of Szechwanese military politics had been the struggle of the provincial army commanders to enhance their relative strength within Szechwan and their common resistance to incursions from beyond the borders of the province, whether political or military. From early 1935 on, however, the principal theme in Szechwanese politics was Nanking's effort to incorporate Szechwan into a unified and centrally managed political structure. With a toehold established as a result of Liu Hsiang's conversations with National Government leaders, Nanking sought to strengthen its position within Szechwan over the next few years without provoking the active resistance of the militarists whose power it sought to undermine.

As it turned out, Szechwan provided almost the last opportunity for Nanking to resolve the perennial problem of regional separatism under more or less normal conditions. With the outbreak of full-scale war with Japan in July 1937, Chiang Kai-shek's regime faced a series of special emergencies that eventually led to the flight from the mainland in 1949. The central government between 1935 and mid-1937 enjoyed a rare chance to extend its control over outlying provinces. The main forces of the Chinese Communists had been rooted out of their bases in southern and central China and were on the run or confined to the far northwest. Despite occasional crises, internal politics were reasonably stable. Although tensions with Japan were rising, particularly in North China, open war had not yet developed. Under these conditions, Chiang Kai-shek turned his attention to Szechwan.

The development of Nationalist influence in Szechwan and the delicate problem of provincial–central relations after 1935 were wrapped in a thick blanket of rhetoric. Occasional protestations of

Szechwanese allegiance or paternal central government concern, characteristic of the late 1920s and early 1930s, gave way to the propaganda of enthusiastic cooperation in reforming the day-to-day affairs of Szechwan. Once Liu Hsiang had declared in Nanking, "Szechwan is the central government's" (Ssu-ch'uan shih chung-yang chih Ssu-ch'uan),[1] the stream of cordial pronouncements from both sides was seldom interrupted. The rhetoric was particularly uninformative because most of it was neither wholly false nor wholly true. At times it served to conceal serious conflicts between provincial and central interests. But on the whole it was undeniable that cooperation and a modicum of political integration did result from Nanking's concerted efforts in Szechwan.

In some ways, the political situation after 1935 recalled earlier moments from the 1910s and early twenties, when outside forces stationed themselves on Szechwanese soil. The old dichotomy of natives and outsiders reappeared in provincial politics. Each side maintained agencies and agents to deal with those of the other side. Nanking in particular brought to bear an array of instruments, many of them developed in previous efforts to secure political control over formerly fractious or independent provinces. The principal agency used by the Nationalists in Szechwan was the staff corps of the headquarters of the chairman of the Military Affairs Committee, directed by Ho Kuo-kuang. Numbering more than a hundred, it arrived in Chungking on January 12, 1935.[2] Later, in October 1935, the staff corps was reorganized as Chiang Kai-shek's headquarters, which had formerly been at Nanchang in Kiangsi Province. When it was created in December 1934, the staff corps' tasks were to plan and direct anti-Communist campaigns in Szechwan, Kweichow, and Yunnan, and to inspect, supervise, and direct the provincial armies in their anti-Communist efforts.[3] In fact, the goal to which Ho Kuo-kuang directed himself was much broader; he set out to integrate Szechwanese politics into central government political life and to integrate Szechwan's armies into China's nationally controlled and nationally standardized military establishment.[4]

Besides the staff corps, Nanking made use of several other agents. The Special Finance Commissioner (Ts'ai-cheng t'e-p'ai yüan) was charged with planning economic reforms for Szechwan and coordinating the economic efforts of central and provincial authorities.[5] The Military Training Academy established at Mount Omei in the summer of 1935 sought to train and indoctrinate army officers from Szechwan,

Yunnan, and Kweichow provinces. Furthermore, Nationalist armies entered Szechwan in 1935 and played a major role in the effort to implant central government control.[6] Finally, Chiang Kai-shek's personal presence in the province for several months in 1935 was crucial to the extension of National Government influence there.

On the provincial side, in addition to the headquarters organizations of the various provincial armies, three agencies bore the brunt of dealing with Nanking's agents and conducting the political affairs of Szechwan. These were the new Szechwan provincial government, the Headquarters of the Commander for Bandit Suppression, and the Office of the Szechwan Director for Rehabilitation. The ability of provincial interests to meet the challenge of central government penetration might have been hampered by fragmentation of authority among three separate organizations, were it not for the fact that Liu Hsiang directed all three. Liu had long been Director for Rehabilitation. He became Bandit Suppression Commander after T'ien Sung-yao's disastrous setbacks in 1933, and chairman of the provincial government in 1935. More than ever before, Szechwanese provincial interests focused on a single militarist between 1935 and 1938, and to a large extent the delicate struggle for predominance in Szechwan during those years was the struggle of Chiang Kai-shek and Liu Hsiang.

Fighting the Communists

The National Government's chosen method for extending its influence in Szechwan was a broad program of civil, military, and economic reform. But the primary reason that Nanking was able to intrude into Szechwan at all was the menace of the Chinese Communists. The double-edged Communist threat to Szechwan was the most urgent problem facing both Liu Hsiang and the staff corps when the corps arrived in January 1935. Though the reform program initiated in 1935 was at least partially directed at defeating the Communists by strengthening provincial defenses, it is convenient to deal with the anti-Communist military effort in Szechwan before turning to the varieties and methods of reform.

At first, the more serious problem lay in the south. Chu Te and Mao Tse-tung had entered Kweichow, and the prospect of a Communist incursion into Szechwan was very real. Early in January, Liu Hsiang decided to send sizable Szechwanese forces under P'an Wen-hua to the Kweichow border and even into Kweichow to block the Communists'

advance toward Szechwan.* Early in February, the Communists'
attempt to cross into Szechwan near Hochiang failed.[7] They did not
attempt to penetrate southern Szechwan again. Chu and Mao finally
crossed into far southwestern Szechwan early in May, stealing a march
on their Nationalist pursuers in Yunnan and the Szechwanese forces
of Liu Wen-hui on the north side of the Yangtze.[8] Then they raced
north, crossed the Tatu River and headed east into the heart of Liu
Wen-hui's territory.† In the second week of June 1935 they reached
Moukung and stopped to rest. Here Hsü Hsiang-ch'ien and Chang
Kuo-t'ao joined them a week later.[9]

Meanwhile, military activity increased once again in northern
Szechwan. In January 1935 central government troops under Hu
Tsung-nan entered Szechwan in the Kuangyüan area from the north
and fought on and off against Hsü Hsiang-ch'ien before withdrawing
back into Kansu.[10] With the arrival of military advisers from the staff
corps, the provincial armies which still hemmed in the Communists in
northern Szechwan began to engage Hsü Hsiang-ch'ien more frequently in early 1935.

In March the situation burst open. Once more attacking the unfortunate T'ien Sung-yao, Hsü Hsiang-ch'ien broke across the Chialing
River, his forces advancing on a broad front into territory the Communists had never before entered. Gradually as their advance forces
moved to the west, the Communists abandoned their old bases in the
rear. Szechwanese troops captured Nanchiang on April 8, and continued to reoccupy areas of the former soviet as the Communists evacuated
them.[11]

Hsü met little opposition as he moved westward through northern

---

*A close adviser to Liu Hsiang has maintained that Liu announced this decision publicly to a
conference of merchants and gentry in the first week of January 1935—before the staff corps
arrived in Szechwan. In his memoirs, Ho Kuo-kuang states that this strategic decision was
made on his advice. The truth, whatever it may be, is less interesting than the divergence of
opinion between the provincial official and the Nationalist general thirty years after the fact
(see Liu Hang-shen, "Jung-mu pan-sheng," *HWTT*, October 14, 1967, p. 24; and Ho
Kuo-kuang, *Pa-shih tzu-shu*, p. 20).

†Nationalist Chinese writers hold that the Communists were able to cross the famous Luting
Bridge only because of the treachery or cowardice of the defending forces. Some maintain
that Liu Wen-hui, who in 1949 threw his allegiance to the Communists, was already in
league with them in 1935 and let them cross the bridge. Others hold that the battalion
charged with defending the bridge revolted and let the Communists pass. All of this con-
trasts sharply with the Communist version of the crossing, a tale of spectacular bravery by
a small band of Red Army heroes. For the Nationalist version, see Ho Kuo-kuang, *Pa-shih
tzu-shu*, p. 21; and Liu Hang-shen, "Jung-mu pan-sheng," *HWTT*, October 21, 1967, pp.
23–24. For a representative Communist account, see Snow, *Red Star*, pp. 184–88.

Szechwan. Hu Tsung-nan remained north of the border to keep the Communists from breaking into Shensi or Kansu.[12] The Communists paused north of Chengtu for nearly a month while their trailing elements caught up and Chengtu waited, terrified, for a Communist invasion. At the end of May, Hsü moved again, in the direction of Kuanhsien on the western edge of the Chengtu Plain.. Continuing southwest, Hsü's armies reached Moukung, where Mao and Chu Te were waiting, on June 16, 1935.[13] From Moukung, the united Communist forces traveled north through the inhospitable mountainous terrain of northwestern Szechwan. At Maoerhkai, the Communist armies split once more. Mao led some units toward northern Shensi, while Chang Kuo-t'ao took other elements westward into Sikang. By late 1935 the Communist military threat to Szechwan had subsided.[14]

It did not take a wizard to foresee the implications of the anti-Communist campaigns for Szechwanese politics in 1935. A critical writer concluded that spring that Chiang Kai-shek's purpose in Szechwan was not really to defeat the Communists at all but to get rid of Liu Hsiang. Chiang would let the Communists defeat lesser Szechwanese militarists. Then Hu Tsung-nan would enter from the north, not to fight the Communists but to occupy former garrison areas as the Communists moved out. Thus the anti-Communist campaign would isolate Liu Hsiang from other provincial militarist support and weaken his hold over the province.[15] Western observers also realized that Szechwanese armies were being sent off to the front lines in remote parts of the province while Nanking's troops poured into the vital economic and political centers or stayed in the rear areas of the war zone.[16] As Chu Te and Mao Tse-tung moved through Yunnan and into Sikang, Liu Hsiang transferred P'an Wen-hua to the northwest; large forces belonging to Liu Hsiang remained in remote areas of northwestern Szechwan for more than a year.[17] Yang Sen, Teng Hsi-hou, and Liu Wen-hui were also embroiled with the Communists in farthest western Szechwan during most of the spring of 1935.[18] Meantime, whether or not it had been agreed upon in Liu Hsiang's Nanking conversations, twenty thousand central government soldiers entered Szechwan via the Yangtze in the first quarter of 1935, disembarking at Wanhsien and other points below Chungking.[19] In July, National Government forces under Hsüeh Yüeh, who had pursued Chu and Mao all around the periphery of Szechwan, moved into the rich Mienyang area northeast of Chengtu; by October, Hsüeh had been ordered into Chengtu itself to guard against a belated southward thrust by the Communists.[20]

The fall of T'ien Sung-yao gave further credence to suspicions that the National Government was using the anti-Communist expeditions as a lever to undermine the provincial militarists. At the urging of Liu Hsiang and Ho Kuo-kuang, Nanking deprived T'ien of his title as commander of the Twenty-ninth National Revolutionary Army, which T'ien had held since 1926. As soon as T'ien was fired, Liu Hsiang moved to take control of T'ien's remaining forces. Having seen how Liu swallowed Liu Ts'un-hou's units after the fall of Suiting in 1933, however, T'ien's division commanders refused to cooperate with him. Finally, the central government intervened and ordered T'ien's subordinate Sun Chen to take over the army. The division commanders readily assented, and Nanking had won an early victory over Liu Hsiang in the unfolding contest for control of the Szechwanese armies.[21]

Despite the presence of staff corps advisers at all provincial Army Headquarters after March 1935, the Szechwanese forces continued to perform miserably. At crucial points where Hsü Hsiang-ch'ien's westward progress could have been blocked, the provincial armies failed to stand up. The same was true of Liu Wen-hui's army facing Mao Tsetung and Chu Te in the far west. One Nationalist general recalled entering western Szechwan on the trail of the Communists:

> When we reached Huili we found the local force, a brigade of four regiments under General Liu Yüan-t'ang, all stationed inside the city walls. They had abandoned the whole territory to the enemy. And when we got to Hsich'ang, another local brigade under General Liu Yüan-tsung hid themselves behind the city walls. . . . Both generals were nephews of Liu Wen-hui. They knew nothing of military tactics.[22]

The combined central government and provincial military operation against the Communists was successful in that it kept the Communists out of southern Szechwan and out of the Chengtu Plain. The "bandit suppression" campaign was a shunting operation in Szechwan, as it had been in Kweichow and Yunnan. It served the central government's purposes by allowing it to enter Szechwan with sizable forces while the Szechwanese armies were tied up in remote areas. It partially served the provincial militarists' interests by averting a potentially catastrophic confrontation between the provincial armies and two separate Communist forces. On the other hand, the campaign against the Communists fostered a new conflict between provincial and central authorities over who would control Szechwan. At the time, however, this seemed clearly to be the lesser of two evils.

The Tide of Reform: Changes in the Provincial Pattern

For twenty-five years after the fall of the Ch'ing, life in Szechwan had been allowed to drift. Major changes took place—militarization, territorial fragmentation, and economic decline, for example—but none of these developments after 1911 resulted from the application of positive and effective policies to existing provincial conditions. The garrison areas, for instance, evolved from the administrative deterioration of the years before 1920, when no single militarist could hope to govern the vast expanse of the province with his limited forces and the province's poorly developed communications systems. But the gradual consolidation of territorial control in fewer and fewer hands through the 1920s and 1930s indicated that even the garrison area system was an unstable phenomenon which would gradually give way to other forms of control if Szechwan continued to drift along unmolested from the outside.

This characteristic aimlessness abruptly ended with the arrival of the central government in 1935. All at once, a combination of national and provincial authorities set out to take the life of the province in hand, formalize and organize political and economic activities at all levels, and even remodel customary military and popular behavior patterns to fit a new and definite ideal. The meandering evolution of provincial conditions suddenly yielded to an onslaught of detailed plans, regulations, reforms, and reorganizations. Most of this new activism emanated from Nanking and its agencies in the province. Even though they remained in their home territory, Liu Hsiang and other provincial military leaders were thus forced onto unfamiliar ground; their problem was to preserve their own interests, as defined by their experiences over the preceding twenty-five years, in the face of a sophisticated and dynamic challenge from beyond the realm of provincial life. The National Government had definite conceptions, though they were not all well formulated, of what it sought in Szechwan, and definite programs for achieving its goals. To the extent that Nanking's plans endangered the militarists' own interests, Liu Hsiang and his colleagues had to devise means to deal with the new challenge from the outside.

The heart of Nanking's attempt to bring Szechwan under its control was the wide-ranging program of reform which it sought to implement in conjunction with provincial authorities in 1935. The component elements in this reform program, naturally, were interrelated, but for purposes of clarity the measures can be grouped in several areas for separate consideration.

The most immediate and visible area of reform was provincial-level administration. The provincial government appointed in 1928 had never operated, and after Liu Hsiang drove Liu Wen-hui into the Sikang hinterland in 1933 no one even pretended that Szechwan possessed any higher political authority than the garrison areas could provide. Therefore, when Liu Hsiang's Nanking conversations laid the basis for creation of a real Szechwan provincial government, a conspicuous first step had been taken along the road to political modification.[23]

If its composition was any indication, the new provincial government formally established at Chungking on February 2, 1935, was Liu Hsiang's creature.[24] Kan Chi-yung, head of the administrative section, had been the chief of the administrative affairs bureau in Liu's headquarters. Liu Hang-shen, director of the new finance section, had controlled Liu Hsiang's finance bureau and was Liu's foremost economic advisor. Kuo Ch'ang-ming, named to lead the reconstruction section of the provincial government, had been Liu's chief of staff. Teng Han-hsiang, the secretary-general of the new government, had been Liu's personal representative in Shanghai and Nanking. The head of the education section, Yang Ch'uan-yü, had indirect ties with Liu. Only the provincial government committee member without portfolio, Hsieh P'ei-chün, had formerly been affiliated with Teng Hsi-hou's establishment.[25] The structure of the new government, with its four sections, secretariat-general and "peace-preservation office" (*Pao-an ch'u*), followed the prescription for provincial government organization laid down by the central government in July 1934.[26]

The government's first task was the elimination of the garrison area system, which everyone agreed lay at the root of Szechwan's social and economic problems. In one sense, the system had already lost much of its vitality, as Liu Hsiang and the Communists had both weakened Szechwan's less powerful militarists and reduced their original territories. But the armies remained independent of one another, particularly in the realm of finance. Shortly after taking office, the provincial government requested the army commanders to cede their territories to provincial government control. In short order, Teng Hsi-hou, T'ien Sung-yao, Yang Sen, Li Chia-yü, and Lo Tse-chou announced the abolition of their garrison areas.* Thus, at one blow, the most striking feature of Szechwanese military politics was ostensibly eliminated, and Szechwan was declared to be unified at last.

To back up its achievement, the provincial government announced that it would assume responsibility for collecting all land taxes in Szechwan after March 1, 1935, and for paying and provisioning all Szechwanese armies. Depriving the individual armies of their freedom to tax struck at the root of the militarists' independence.† In order to weaken the bases of garrison area autonomy still further, the provincial government arranged for all district magistrates in Liu Hsiang's former garrison area to be transferred to new assignments in other parts of the province, while magistrates from other areas were brought into Liu's territory. This mass transfer of magistrates was carried out by the end of May.[27]

Declaring the abolition of the garrison area system obviously did not solve the problem of Szechwan's bloated armies, so during the first half of 1935 the provincial government and the staff corps set out to reform the armies. First it was necessary to find out how big the armies really were. Provincial officers commonly inflated the number of men in their units in order to draw extra funds and equipment from Army Headquarters for their personal enrichment.‡ To determine the real size of the armies and the state of their weaponry, registration committees were organized and sent to each of the provincial armies in August 1935.§ The ultimate aim of national authorities in Szechwan

---

*The Chinese phrase was *piao-shih chiao-huan i-ch'ieh cheng-ch'üan* (see Chou, "Chien-she").

†This order sounded good at first, but its provisions were curious. After reserving for the provincial government the right to collect all land taxes and to pay and supply all Szechwanese armies, it declared that any militarist who continued to collect his own taxes was a counterrevolutionary and a rebel, and it warned that the amount of revenue illegally collected would be deducted from the amount he was entitled to receive from the provincial government (Chiang Chung-cheng [Chiang Kai-shek], *O-mei hsün-lien chi* [Collected remarks made at the Omei Training Center] [Shanghai, 1947], p. 290). In other words, the new order warned that if the old tax system were continued, the old garrison area system would continue, too, and this would somehow constitute the punishment of the guilty militarists.

‡In an interview on Taiwan, Nationalist General Liu Chi-ming asserted that neither the Communists nor the National Government commanders knew the actual strength of the Szechwanese forces. I am grateful to Lt. Col. Harry Collier for the opportunity to see the transcript of this interview.

§Who ordained these registration committees is a matter of dispute. *SCYP*, August 1935, p. 264, says it was the headquarters of the chairman of the Military Affairs Committee—Chiang's headquarters—but the headquarters did not yet exist in Szechwan. Liu Hang-shen maintains that the task of registering all troops and weapons was undertaken by Liu Hsiang and not by the central government (see "Jung-mu pan sheng," *HWTT*, October 21, 1967, p. 23).

was to reduce the size of the provincial armies. Ho Kuo-Kuang's plan called for a first-stage reduction of two-fifths of the total number of regiments in each army, to be undertaken by the armies themselves. In the second phase, another two-fifths of the remaining regiments would be eliminated. Such a plan would inevitably throw large numbers of officers and soldiers out of work. To ease the way, the central government opened a military academy in Chengtu where discharged officers could receive vocational training.[28]

Whether or not this program stood a chance of actually reducing the number of armed soldiers in provincial armies, Liu Hsiang looked on it with favor. Early in 1935 his three top division commanders, T'ang Shih-tsun, P'an Wen-hua, and Wang Tsuan-hsü, had been elevated to the rank of army commander by Nanking. They were therefore entitled to command several divisions each. Just as the other provincial armies were being asked to cut down their own forces, Liu Hsiang was able to expand his. Thus both Nanking and Liu Hsiang himself stood to gain from Ho Kuo-kuang's plan, Liu within his accustomed world of provincial rivalries and Nanking in the larger struggle for influence in Szechwan. The center also took the symbolic step of redesignating the Szechwanese armies to bring their names into line with other centrally controlled units. Teng Hsi-hou's old Twenty-eighth Army, for example, became the Forty-fifth Army under the new system, and P'an Wen-hua's old division was renamed the Twenty-third Army. The old designation "National Revolutionary Army," which Szechwanese forces had worn since 1926, gave way to the single name "army" (lu-chün).[29]

Thus from the standpoint of massive alteration of Szechwanese provincial administrative and military organization, the complexion of Szechwanese politics seemed to have changed enormously by the end of 1935. A British observer in Chungking wrote in late October 1935:

> It may reasonably be said that the occupation and control of Szechwan has been the primary objective behind every internal military or political move made by the central government authorities during the whole of the past year. The success of this campaign, which has been carried out under the general and somewhat misleading title of "anti-communist activities in the Far West," has been very marked. To-day the rule of the formerly independent Szechwan war lords has been wholly destroyed, and

Central Government troops and officials hold every position of importance, strategic or political, throughout the province.[30]

Few sophisticated Chinese onlookers were that sanguine at the end of 1935. Announcement of basic reforms was one thing; implementation was another. Nonetheless, the evident influence of the central government in Szechwanese affairs and Liu Hsiang's apparently enthusiastic cooperation with Nanking on military and political reforms showed that the dimensions of provincial politics had been significantly altered by the arrival of central government agencies in the province.

Administrative Reform: The Special Inspectorates

Unifying Szechwanese political control at the provincial level was only one aspect of the coordinated program of reforms introduced in 1935. Nationalist influence in Szechwan led to a series of important attempts to remodel and restructure the administrative process at all levels of sub-provincial organization as well.

As the focus of Chiang Kai-shek's anti-Communist campaigns shifted to Szechwan and the National Government penetrated the province, Szechwan became a so-called Bandit Suppression Province, thus qualifying for inclusion in the program of administrative reorganization which Chiang had begun using in Kiangsi a few years before.[31] The man behind most of these reorganizational schemes was Yang Yung-t'ai, a Nationalist politician and leading member of the Political Science Clique within the central government, who enjoyed considerable influence over Chiang Kai-shek at this time. Yang developed the reform program while serving as secretary-general of Chiang's Nanchang headquarters. Early in 1935 Yang and his associates came to Szechwan to promote the program, and when Chiang's headquarters moved to Chungking later in the year Yang kept his post as secretary-general. One of the by-products of Yang's presence was the intensification of national factional politics on the Szechwanese scene after 1935. The agents whom the central government used to extend its influence tended to affiliate with one or another of the rival groups within the central Kuomintang and government hierarchies, and the success or failure of individual programs in Szechwan was directly significant to the competing cliques at Nanchang or Nanking.[32]

Leaving aside the factional aims of Yang Yung-t'ai's administrative reform package, the purpose of his program was to enable higher authorities at the provincial and ultimately the national level to exert thorough control over the population and territory of the Bandit Suppression Provinces. Yang's scheme relied on a clearly defined vertical chain of command which drew its effectiveness from the concentration of power in the fewest possible hands at any one level. This effort to extend the arm of higher political authority down into the mass of the population was an innovation. Under the imperial system, whose patterns had been weakened but not wholly destroyed, formal bureaucratic power extended no lower than the district level. Smaller quasi-political social units had generally handled their own affairs according to established custom with little interference from the centrally appointed bureaucracy.

But the lesson that emerged from China's political disintegration in the twentieth century, and especially from the Chinese Communists' experiences, was that the autonomy of local society militated against the creation of a strong, unified government and nation. The problem was expressed by the common phrase, "the whip is long but it does not reach." In Szechwan after 1935, the theme of improving the effectiveness of government—especially provincial and district administration —underlay the administrative reforms of Yang Yung-t'ai.

The most striking institutional change was the introduction to Szechwan of the special administrative inspectorate system.[33] This plan had first been applied to Hupei, Honan, and Anhui, but it was designed to work in all Bandit Suppression Provinces. Szechwan was divided into eighteen special administrative inspectorates (Hsing-cheng tu-ch'a chuan-yüan ch'ü) ranging in size from half a dozen to a dozen districts; most of the inspectorates contained from seven to nine.* A special administrative inspector was to be appointed for each of these areas, but the presence of the Communists in border sections of the province prevented the appointment of inspectors for five inspectorates.[34] On May 1, 1935 thirteen inspectors were named.[35] It was a sign of the times that Chiang Kai-shek, not Liu Hsiang, named the inspectors. Moreover, ten of the original thirteen came from Kiangsi, Anhui, or Hupei.[36] Several of the appointees were experienced inspectors who were transferred to Szechwan to set an example for the province.

The duties of the special inspectors and the aims of the special inspectorate system had been specified in elaborate central government

---

*The inspectorate with only six districts was in the farthest northwest portion of Szechwan; the one with twelve districts was in the Chengtu Plain near Chengtu (Ch'eng, Ti-fang, pp. 225–27).

Special Administrative Inspectorates and Their Headquarters, 1935.

regulations. The inspector was to serve as district magistrate in the district where his inspectorate office was situated, and to serve as a model for other magistrates in his inspectorate. He was to coordinate multidistrict efforts when a task was too great for one district to manage. Most important, the inspector was given the job of "supervising and investigating" (tu-ch'a) the other magistrates in his area, so as to root out the perennial administrative problem which the Chinese called "overt obedience and covert disobedience" (yang-feng yin-wei).[37] He was also supposed to serve as the overall commander of peace preservation forces (pao-an tui), as the local t'uan were renamed, and in certain types of cases he was empowered to represent Chiang Kai-shek's headquarters in administering military law.[38]

Despite all the detailed plans, uncertainties surrounded the new program when the inspectors went to work on June 1. The most serious ambiguity concerned the inspectors' relations with the two higher authorities in the province, the provincial government and the National Government's staff corps. Should these two authorities conflict, whose purposes would the special administrative inspectors serve?[39] The other major question at the outset was how the detailed administrative and financial programs prescribed for the inspectorates would be carried out. A wide chasm between plans and achievements still had to be bridged. Even before the new appointees took office, there were signs that neither they nor the provincial government were certain as to how they could perform effectively and avoid pitfalls that would nullify their work. At a meeting of the inspectors in May, for instance, the danger of handing over local administrative power to "bad elements" at the very outset of the reform program was brought up. The conferees' only conclusion was that there were plenty of "good gentry" left in the countryside who should receive responsible administrative posts, and that they would be easily recognizable.[40]

Administrative Reform: The Districts and Below

Concurrent with the introduction of the special inspectorate system, programs designed to reinvigorate district and local administration while establishing effective control over the smallest units of provincial society were initiated. These programs, too, emanated from the central government's coordinated scheme for administrative renovation in the provinces where it sought to establish its power. Central and provincial governments cooperated in putting these plans into effect.

According to the prescription for district government reform, the largely autonomous bureaus *(chü)* of district governments were to be formally abolished, and their functions incorporated into several departments *(k'o)*. The departments and all district government activities were to be controlled by the magistrate; no agency of the district government was to act on its own without the magistrate's permission. Concentration of power in the magistrate's hands was the most important feature of the district government reform plan. The magistrate also became commander of all district armed forces, including police and peace preservation units, and he received the power to appoint key officials in all vital areas of district and subdistrict administration.[41]

The power of appointment was important because the barrage of administrative reorganization plans in Szechwan in 1935 extended well below the district level. Faced with the problem of local insulation from the benefits and demands of formal government, Nationalist planners borrowed a leaf from the Chinese Communists' book and developed a set of organizational measures to be carried out below the district level.* Every district was divided into from three to six subdistricts *(ch'ü)*, each of which was to have its own chief. The chief was to draw a salary from the provincial government, which would also fund the administrative operations of the subdistricts.[42] The chief was responsible to the district magistrate who appointed him, and all subdistrict officials were subject to evaluation by both the magistrate and the provincial government. As in the case of the district magistrates, power in the subdistricts was concentrated in the hands of the chiefs.[43]

Below the subdistricts, the reform program called for revitalizing the traditional *pao-chia* system under which groups of several families were organized into units *(chia)* which in turn were combined into larger units *(pao)*. The plan also called for creation of a new administrative level called the *lien-pao* between the *pao* and the subdistrict. This new hierarchy of *chia*, *pao*, and *lien-pao* was supposed to replace the layered but autonomous local organizations that had hitherto characterized Szechwanese social structure.[44] The way in which leaders of the new local administrative units were chosen was also an innovation. While the traditional organizations had selected their own heads, the new chieftains were to be chosen by the head of the next higher level of administration. Thus *lien-pao* heads appointed *pao* leaders, and subdistrict heads appointed *lien-pao* leaders.[45]

With this elaborate plan, rooted in the idea of structural change and

*Yang Yung-t'ai specifically acknowledged this debt to the Chinese Communists' techniques (see *CYCL*, p. 16).

centralized vertical control, the provincial government and the central government set out to make local government effective. When the program first went into effect in the summer of 1935, the Chinese Communists were still present in force, and the prime task of the new administrative system was proclaimed to be the strengthening of the local peace preservation forces. Here the central government addressed itself to the same problem that had plagued provincial militarists for decades, the independence of local armed forces. As the militarists had tried to do before, the promoters of local reform set out to wrest militia control from the hands of "bad gentry" and return the militia to their original purpose of local defense.[46] Like Liu Hsiang, the central government had a plan for the phased consolidation of control over militia forces, first at the district level, then at the special inspectorate level, then at the provincial level, and finally at the National Government level.[47] Liu Hsiang, as provincial governor, became director of the Peace Preservation Office of the provincial government, and elaborate regulations for organizing, financing, and training the local forces were promulgated.[48] The plan for securing control over local militia units rounded out the program of local administrative reform introduced in 1935.

Financial Reform

In addition to the comprehensive plan for administrative reorganization, national and provincial authorities acted on several problems in the economic sector in 1935. In particular, they attacked the acute and accumulated problems of Szechwan's disordered currency and its taxation system. Chaos in the provincial currency had long been a baleful side-effect of militarism and the territorial fragmentation of the province. Depreciation of Szechwanese currency had reached critical proportions in late 1934, and the economic crisis that resulted had been a major factor in Liu Hsiang's decision to visit Chiang Kai-shek in Nanking.

Once it had planted its feet in Szechwan, the central government took two steps to moderate the Szechwanese currency crisis. The first was a massive gold loan to the provincial government on July 1, 1935, more than half of which was set aside for the repayment of outstanding provincial bond issues and short-term loans at 60 percent of face value. This loan was similar to the one that Liu Hsiang had sought in Nanking the previous year; the amount was seventy million *yüan*, and it was secured on Szechwan's salt revenue.[49]

The second measure aimed to stabilize Szechwanese currency while simultaneously integrating the provincial economy more closely into China's national economy. Nanking issued thirty million *yüan* in Special Currency Redemption Notes, which were to be exchanged for the various circulating provincial currencies at the rate of ten Szechwanese *yüan* for eight *yüan* of the national currency. Selected banks, including the recently established Chungking branch of the Central Bank, exchanged the currencies until September 15, 1935, after which all monetary transactions had to be made in central government currency.[50] Considering the state of the provincial currencies, these were generous terms, but in return Szechwan agreed to remit to Nanking some of the revenues which the central government had claimed as its own since 1928, and which provincial militarists had collected and withheld from the center for years.

Within Szechwan there was at first some opposition to the terms of the exchange, but monetary conditions in the province soon settled down and at least in the large cities central government money supplanted the numerous provincial varieties in September 1935.[51] Nanking benefited from the symbolic integration of Szechwan into its currency area, and Liu Hsiang profited handsomely by exchanging huge amounts of his discredited currency for the more valuable central government currency.

The year 1935 also witnessed a highly publicized assault on the confused and destructive tax system in Szechwan. Tax reforms occupied as prominent a place in the overall package of improvements as elimination of the garrison areas or reorganization of local administration. The provincial government adopted a four-point tax program to "lighten the burdens of the people." First, it ordered the cessation of multiple collections of the basic land tax which amounted to many times the annual rate in most Szechwanese districts. District governments were told to collect the land tax at the rate of one year's worth per year after June 1935. Aware of the drastic reduction in revenues this reform would cause if it were ever carried out, the provincial government further permitted the collection of "bandit suppression fees" equal to three times the annual land tax rate for the duration of Szechwan's military crisis with the Communists.* With this measure the authorities claimed to have eliminated one of the most conspicuous and repulsive features of the pre-1935 garrison area system.

*There was even more to this ostensible reduction of the land tax than has so far met the reader's eye. See below, chap. 7.

A second new policy attacked Szechwan's notorious commercial taxation, which had crippled trade within the province and contributed to the decline of Szechwan's export trade as well. On the day Chiang Kai-shek arrived in Szechwan in early March 1935, Liu Hsiang ordered that the hundreds of taxation stations along Szechwan's trade routes be shut down. In their place, a single tax on imports and exports would be levied at the point of loading or unloading in Szechwan; most often this meant Chungking. This measure, like so many others in 1935, promised to weaken the independence of provincial militarists by depriving them of another major source of revenue. At the same time, collection of the bulk of the new revenue at Chungking directly benefited Liu Hsiang, who controlled the city. Promulgation of the new measure provoked bitter resentment among the merchant communities of Chungking, Wanhsien, and Chengtu, where the new tax rate far exceeded tax rates of the garrison area period. The provincial government had to negotiate and compromise with the merchants over the exact terms of the new arrangement before the threat of merchant opposition died down.[52]

In the realm of district finance, the provincial government commanded district governments to prepare detailed budgets of their revenues and expenditures, in an effort to lay the bases for rational provincial fiscal policies. Furthermore, the provincial government ordered the abolition of the endless "miscellaneous levies" which had been another favorite source of military revenue.[53]

The fourth point in the 1935 taxation program was Szechwan's new adherence to the separation of provincial and national taxation revenues collected in Szechwan. Since Szechwan had not respected the National Government's 1928 regulations governing the distribution of revenues between the province and the center,[54] the new provincial plan to render unto Nanking that which was Nanking's apparently signified a major change in the attitudes of provincial authorities. But there were strings attached to the provincial decision. As the director of the financial section of the provincial government pointed out:

> Those taxes which are "national" ought to be collected by the central government authorities, and funds which are supposed to be disbursed by the national treasury ought to be paid completely by the treasury. At present only revenue collection is apportioned, not expenditures. Thus the salt and wine and tobacco revenue now amount to seventeen million *yüan* annually, while army and bandit

suppression costs come to more than sixty million *yüan* each year.
. . . All of this expenditure ought to be the responsibility of the
national treasury.[55]

If the four-point program of tax reform initiated in 1935 had succeeded, it would have effectively altered the pattern of independent
militarist control which had prevailed in Szechwan for decades, and fundamentally modified the financial relationship between province and
central government. Success was not a certainty, though. The most
serious potential obstacle to implementation of the tax program was
Chungking's reliance on district authorities to carry out orders issued
from above. In the final analysis, most of the provincial government's
dicta were only orders directed to the nearly 150 districts of Szechwan.
Whether the districts had the personnel, the funds, or the will to carry
out the new measures was not clear. To overcome these potential deficiencies, the tax reform program was inextricably bound to the local
administrative reorganizations propounded by the central government.
Yet the fact that each depended on the other did not ensure that either
would automatically succeed.

Other Programs in 1935

While the core of the central government blueprint for gaining
control of Szechwan consisted of the administrative and economic
programs already discussed, the range of central government activities extended far beyond these central areas. For example, a major
road-building program accompanied the arrival of central influence
in the province. Designed to improve the province's internal communications and also to integrate Szechwan into a national road
network, the program called for highways from Szechwan to Kweichow,
Hunan, Hupei, Shensi, Kansu, Tsinghai, Sikang, and Yunnan. The
underlying aim of this massive construction project was to overcome
the physical barriers which traditionally isolated Szechwan from outside
influence and control. The Kweichow road opened for auto traffic by
the summer of 1935, but other roads progressed more slowly, and even
preliminary surveys had yet to be made on large segments of the
Tsinghai, Yunnan, Kansu, and Hupei roads at the end of 1935.[56]

The central government also embarked on a highly publicized
campaign to control opium production and consumption in Szechwan,
and it attempted to promote the New Life Movement in the province.
At the urging of central government agents, the provincial government

issued a plan for the phased elimination of opium cultivation in Szechwan, under which all opium cultivation was to cease by 1939. A similar
plan for the gradual elimination of opium consumption gave old and
longer-term addicts more time to break the habit than the young and
newly addicted.[57] The New Life Movement was a campaign to reform
social customs and revitalize the spirit of the Chinese people by re-
emphasizing traditional Confucian virtues and practices, while instill-
ing a sense of military discipline in the populace. Liu Hsiang and other
provincial leaders had paid lip service to the movement prior to the
central government's arrival, but the tempo of New Life propaganda
activity increased after early 1935.[58] Like Nanking's formulas for
administrative reorganization in Bandit Suppression Provinces, the
New Life Movement sought to develop uniform standards of behavior in
different places under varying conditions. Like the plans to develop
low-level administrative institutions, it sought to reach into the daily
lives of ordinary people and to mobilize them in support of a political
power draped with the mantle of legitimate authority. Like the other
reforms instituted by central and provincial authorities in 1935, the
success of the New Life Movement in Szechwan remained to be proved.

Chiang Kai-shek in Szechwan

The very fact that such a broad range of reforms was attempted
in Szechwan indicated that provincial politics had undergone significant changes under central government influence. Much of the credit
for establishing Nanking's presence in the province belonged to Chiang
Kai-shek himself. Chiang came to Szechwan on March 2, 1935, less
than two months after Ho Kuo-kuang and the staff corps first entered
the province. Except for a trip to Kweichow and Yunnan from late
March to late May and a brief trip back to Nanking in August, Chiang
was in Szechwan until October 31, 1935.[59] While in the province, he
took part in the planning of anti-Communist operations and issued
streams of orders directly to provincial military authorities on specific
internal issues.[60] Above all, Chiang employed his prestige to provide a
lofty moral basis for political, economic, and military reform in Szechwan, and, by implication, for the establishment of central power there.

This was clear in Chiang's numerous speeches. His basic message had
two points. First, Szechwan had to become "the base for the regenera-
tion of the Chinese people" (*fu-hsing min-tsu chih ken-chü ti*). Second,
"If we want to rehabilitate Szechwan, we must start by restoring the
virtue, the spirit, the knowledge and the abilities of the Szechwanese

so that they can become a modern people."[61] Surrounded by the rhetoric of national rebirth, personal purification, and the Three People's Principles, these two points formed the crux of Chiang's ideological campaign in Szechwan.

In general, while Chiang remained in the province the results of his presence were favorable to his cause. His arrival in Szechwan stimulated provincial support for the new "foreign" presence which the staff corps alone could not have elicited. An informed and usually skeptical American observer wrote in May 1935 from Szechwan that "Chiang has really been welcomed to these provinces by the people, not merely the rich classes. His propaganda has been very successful, and due also to the fact that the Reds have been on the run and necessarily robber-like in their actions to gain supplies, he has been able to gain much control."[62]

Chiang's appearance in Chungking set off a flurry of action; 1,300 opium dens, for example, were reported shut down shortly after he arrived.[63] His reception in Chengtu, which became the seat of the provincial government in mid-1935, was equally enthusiastic. Liu Hsiang's wife became chairwoman of the local chapter of the New Life Movement. Chiang's reputation and personal influence were vital in expanding the central government's presence in Szechwan. It was no coincidence that the greatest part of the provincial government's reform program appeared in the early summer, when Chiang was on hand in Szechwan.

Uncertainties after a Year of Reform

The anti-Communist campaign of 1934–35 gave Nanking the chance to penetrate several provinces which had been beyond its reach. Szechwan, the largest and richest, was the grand prize. Once the staff corps arrived in Szechwan, the province became a laboratory in which a wide variety of central government plans and political activities could be tried out. After decades of rudderless drifting, the central government's activism in pursuing well-defined goals in Szechwan abruptly changed the pattern of provincial politics.

Bringing Nanking's plans and agents to bear on Szechwan was only a beginning, however. The introduction of central government personnel and ideas into a hitherto independent province raised several important and unsettling questions, answers to which could not be found overnight. The most immediate question was what would happen in the province once Chiang Kai-shek left. If progress was so dependent on Chiang's personal influence, would his departure halt the process of reform and political integration?

A second question was more sinister: would conflicts arise between provincial and national authorities as a result of the central government's new programs? The principal reason that Liu Hsiang cooperated with Nanking once central influences penetrated Szechwan was that he benefited materially from it. In the early months, cooperation with the center enabled Liu to gain even greater power over his fellow Szechwanese militarists than he had enjoyed after his victory over Liu Wen-hui in 1933. Most of the early reforms, especially those pertaining to establishment of a new provincial government under Liu's direction, worked far more to his advantage than to the advantage of other provincial generals.

Success or failure of the overall reform program depended on the continued cooperation of Liu Hsiang and the central government. If Liu chose to obstruct rather than to facilitate the reforms, they could collapse. Chiang Kai-shek's effort to assert his authority and his government's legitimacy in Szechwan was a thinly concealed threat to Liu Hsiang's position, especially once the Communist military threat which had brought the Nationalists to Szechwan in the first place receded in late 1935. While the Communists were close at hand and the rearrangement of responsibilities brought benefits to both Liu and Chiang Kai-shek, cooperation was relatively easy. Should Liu and Chiang begin to compete for prerogatives that could not be shared, however, the reform program would be an early casualty.

Another basic uncertainty attending the advent of central government influence in Szechwan concerned the detailed schemes for administrative reorganization promoted by Yáng Yung-t'ai. The plans for reforming and restructuring Szechwanese political administration were drawn up in distant provinces by central government officials faced with widespread Communist activities. The justification for bringing to Szechwan a program designed in Kiangsi was that all Bandit Suppression Provinces where anti-Communist campaigns were taking place could be treated in the same manner, because they faced the same problems. Such an assumption might or might not turn out to be valid. The Nationalists faced the task of building a politically unified nation out of many separate and semi-independent territorial units; with programs like Yang Yung-t'ai's, they chose to treat the component parts in the same way in order to create a standardized, centrally controlled political whole. The opposite approach would have been to treat each individual case, particularly each province, separately, at the risk of sacrificing the larger uniformity on which nationhood had to rest. Having opted for uniformity, the Nationalists increased the danger that their programs would prove irrelevant to the individual localities where they were applied.

Lurking in the documents on which the new political–administrative structure was founded were signs that the whole outlook underlying the National Government's reforms might be unsuited to the achievement of the desired ends. In the Chinese context, the vision of effective central administrative control over local society was innovative and untraditional. Yet the manner in which the various plans were articulated hinted that the thinking of central government planners had not sufficiently thrown off the influence of old-fashioned, paternalistic political custom. An illustration of this was the heavy emphasis placed on securing and training the "right" men for leadership positions and the implementation of "revolution" from above. As Madame Chiang said in a speech in Szechwan,

> What we have found wrong with China has not been with the Chinese People. It has been with our leaders. . . . Each time a revolution has come, it has not started from the top—it has started from the bottom—and so the revolution was not effective. Now the government wants to revolutionize from the very top![64]

It might be argued that such an approach to political reform was more realistic and applicable, given China's accumulated political tradition, and that the paternalism of the National Government's approach was at least comprehensible to the Szechwanese. But the kind of penetration of local life which men like Yang Yung-t'ai conceived to be necessary if the Nationalists were to build genuine national power did not necessarily result from the approach the Nationalists sought to employ in Szechwan.

Answers to these questions would emerge with time; in the short run, the most pressing issue was whether or not Liu Hsiang would resist the further progress of central government efforts in Szechwan.

7 The Struggle for Provincial Supremacy

Before the year 1935 was out, the optimism and energy of the first months of reform had subsided, giving way to a long struggle between provincial and central authorities for control of Szechwan. Over the next two years, the initial cooperation between Chiang Kai-shek and Liu Hsiang collapsed and latent conflicts emerged. At the same time, the deficiencies and impracticalities of many reform measures became obvious when the new programs were put to the test in Szechwan, further obstructing Nanking's efforts to assimilate and control the province.

The severe drought which struck most of the province between the summer of 1936 and the following summer widened the conflict between Chiang and Liu and further weakened the social and administrative programs of 1935. In the spring of 1937, Liu Hsiang's and Chiang Kai-shek's forces nearly came to blows; though Liu pulled back from the brink, and the outbreak of hostilities with Japan changed the provincial picture considerably, the National Government still had not solved the problem of controlling Szechwan when Liu Hsiang died in January 1938.

Disappointed Hopes

As soon as the wide-ranging reforms promoted by the central government were announced, discrepancies began to appear between rhetoric and provincial realities. In June 1936 the secretary-general of the provincial government painted a bleak picture of the first year's achievements:

> After a year's experience, the human and financial expenditures have been great. All the new policies are unfulfilled. . . . In general, the criticisms say that in the past only money was demanded of the people, but now they must endure nuisance and trouble as well as financial burdens. Visitors from other provinces are disappointed, and one hears often of resentment among the

masses. . . . This is because officials still maintain the traditional
passive approach to their duties. . . . The feudal idea of becoming
an official in order to get rich is not easily eradicated.[1]

Ostensible abolition of the garrison areas failed to bring the centralized control over provincial armies which Liu Hsiang sought;
provincial commanders retained the "garrison area state of mind"
despite their formal cession of political and financial power to the
provincial government. Moreover, the problem of entrenched local
powerholders continued to hold up the process of reform. "A year
after the establishment of the provincial government," said the secretary-
general, "the government is uncertain about local officialdom, and
about social conditions throughout Szechwan. Thus there are serious
obstacles to carrying out the orders of the provincial government."[2]

Every area was affected by the slowdown of reform. Plans for reorganizing and retraining the provincial armies made little progress,
as Liu Hsiang's office revealed when it called for a whole new start in
the autumn of 1936.[3] The original plan for phased consolidation of
control over local militia forces vanished at an early date, when it ran
into resistance from the very "militia lords" whose power it sought to
reduce. The deadline for consolidating control at the special inspectorate level was soon pushed back from March 1936 to June 1937, and
little more was said about the timetable.[4]

The anti-opium campaign also slacked off as soon as Chiang Kai-
shek left the province. Even at its inception, the plan had allowed the
principal opium-growing districts of Szechwan to produce opium until
all other areas had been cleaned up. A veteran missionary reported
in October 1935, "In the amount of opium grown, sold, and consumed,
Szechwan led all China in the provinces I visited. I went out on the
streets of Chengtu and bought opium, sold as freely and publicly as
bread."[5] By 1937, with the financial support of Chungking bankers,
provincial authorities and private merchants organized a monopoly
company to buy and sell all Szechwanese opium; prices were kept
high, and the monopoly brought enormous profit for its creators and
backers.[6]

Next to abolition of the garrison area system and unification of
Szechwan itself, "lightening the burdens of the people" had been
the most pressing goal of both the provincial and the National Government in Szechwan. The much-abused land tax had been ceremoniously
reduced to its annual rate. But the temporary "bandit suppression

fees" authorized for the duration of the Communist crisis raised the land tax to four times the annual rate every year. Another year's worth was taken to support the peace preservation forces, and yet another year's worth was collected as a "reconstruction loan" to the provincial government. Thus, where the new directives concerning the land tax were heeded at all, the grain tax after tax reform amounted to six times the basic annual rate.[7]

New "miscellaneous levies" replaced the numerous taxes outlawed by recent reforms. With the resurrection of the *pao-chia* system came the "*pao-chia* fee," equal to another year's land tax. Construction of blockhouses across Szechwan, a favorite project of the central government's local defense experts, accounted for another sizable payment, sometimes equal to two more years' land tax.[8]

Once the provincial government had announced the tax reforms of 1935, it could do little to enforce them in the face of lower level official apathy or the resistance of provincial military leaders. Liu Hsiang and Chiang Kai-shek tried to cajole local generals and district magistrates by mail and telegram, but they lacked effective means of forcing local authorities to comply with their rulings.[9] The provincial government never fully managed to take financial control over all provincial armed forces, least of all in the first year of Szechwan's nominal unification. Liu Hsiang himself summed up the failure of financial reform at the end of his government's first year:

> Quite unexpectedly the burden of the people has been heavier since the reorganization of the provincial government as well as the abolition of the system of garrison areas. According to the original schedule, the land tax in every district should be collected four times [per year] during the period of anti-Communist suppression. However, the land tax has been arbitrarily increased by various magistrates in various districts.[10]

In addition, the onset of central government activity in Szechwan brought with it new and regular non-monetary exactions. These were levies of labor, animals, and materials for transporting military supplies and for constructing the blockhouses and motor highways with which the center hoped to make Szechwan secure.[11] Yang Yung-t'ai's new administrative structure, installed in 1935, helped to secure the necessary labor and material for these projects. Laws providing for the adequate payment of conscripted workers and limits on how far from home they could be sent were widely ignored.[12] Huang Yen-p'ei, a widely respected educator and author who visited Szechwan in 1936, recorded the appeal of a forty-seven-year-old worker whom he met by the roadside:

> We were all poor; what we produced, we ate. Just at the busiest farming season, they would not let us plant, and took us off to labor. They give us no money and no food. We borrowed a little extra food from neighbors and went, protesting. We have come sixty *li*. Now our rice is gone, but the work is not yet finished and they will not let us go home. We will starve here! Sir! Sir! What are we to do?[13]

Liu Hsiang and Chiang Kai-shek

Programs and plans for provincial reform were all well and good, but one did not have to be especially astute to realize that central government progress in Szechwan depended to a great extent on the personalities of individual leaders and their relationships to one another. This was particularly true of Liu Hsiang and Chiang Kai-shek, who grew increasingly disenchanted with each other as the initial phase of central government activity in Szechwan passed. As Nanking implanted itself ever more firmly in the province, Liu moved quietly to counter the effects of the new reform programs and to preserve for himself as many of his former prerogatives as he could.

This quiet struggle for supremacy affected many spheres, but none more gravely than the training of Szechwan's future administrators. Given the difficulties any higher authority faced in penetrating Szechwanese local society, the key to success appeared to lie in the placing of loyal men in crucial low-level administrative positions in district government or even lower levels of administration and control. The district level was the most important of all because so much of the lower level reform laid out in the new measures was to be controlled by the district magistrates. The training of future magistrates and department heads in district governments was thus vitally important to both Liu and Chiang.

In the early months of central government activity in Szechwan, the province followed the example of Hupei and Kiangsi in establishing agencies to inspect the credentials of incumbent administrators and to train new ones in the fields of district government, district finance, and police work.[14] The District Government Personnel Training Institute

(Hsien-cheng jen-yüan hsün-lien so) received the most attention. Its aim was to turn out district magistrates, department chiefs, and subdistrict officials capable of understanding and carrying out the new tasks prescribed by central and provincial authorities.[15] Each course at the institute ran for three months, and although the theme of the instruction was "Carry out the rules and regulations of the new system," the course concentrated more on cultivating the proper "spirit" in the new officials than on the technicalities of administration.[16] Though the institute ran only three classes, in a short time it had become the key supplier of local administrative personnel in Szechwan. Of the graduates of its first two classes, 54 were district magistrates, 120 were district government department heads or secretaries-general, and 232 were subdistrict chiefs in May 1936, while many additional graduates held other posts in local or district government.[17]

Liu Hsiang had initially acquiesced in the appointment of Li Lei-fu, a Cantonese who enjoyed close ties with Yang Yung-t'ai, as head of the institute: in fact, most of the instructors at the school came from other provinces.[18] But Liu Hsiang instructed his agents among the students to inform him if the school's activities seemed designed to erode his position in Szechwan. Furthermore, he sent his trusted Secretary-General Teng Han-hsiang to represent him at the institute and influence the students in his favor.[19] In response, the National Government added civil administrators to the Omei Training Corps classes, which opened in the summer of 1935.[20] The program at Mount Omei exposed its students to a heavy diet of National Government rhetoric; one American estimated that the students endured eight hours of New Life Movement lectures daily.[21]

The Hsien Government Personnel Training Institute was a prominent, but not the only, example of growing rivalry between provincial and central interests in Szechwan. Similar conflicts arose over the training of peace preservation cadres and local-level officials as well, as provincial and national agencies set up competing organizations to train and indoctrinate local leaders and their armed units.[22]

As in the case of the Chinese Communists, Liu Hsiang's response to the challenge of National power in Szechwan derived from his own experience as a provincial commander; the points he advocated in defense of his interests in 1935 and 1936 recalled the arguments he had stressed long before Nanking's presence in Szechwan became a reality. Thus Secretary-General Teng Han-hsiang's comments in late 1936 recalled Liu Hsiang's remarks of the early 1920s:

The center seeks to handle all matters, but emphasizing external affairs it naturally has not much power to help in Szechwan. We must bear the burden of Szechwan's affairs ourselves. . . . On the larger level, love the nation and support Chiang Kai-shek; on the smaller level, love Szechwan and obey Chairman Liu.[23]

Similarly, Liu played on his old contention that support for him was synonymous with support of the central government; in 1936, however, his spokesmen directed his message downward to local government trainees instead of upward to Nanking:

Support the central government. . . . Starting with the *pao-chia* personnel, if they will first support the center, then afterward all the people can gradually be induced to do likewise. The central government is very far away; how is it to be supported? By supporting the Highest Leader of the central government, supporting the orders circulated by the center, supporting policies implemented by the center. What the provincial government carries out are the orders and policies of the center. If everyone follows all the provincial government's orders and aids the provincial government and carries out central policies, that *is* support of the central government. . . . The center is remote; [Chiang's] position is so high. The carrying out of orders and the unification of all goals depends on transmission through all levels of local government. If you say, "I only support the central government and the Highest Leader, but not all levels of local government," or if you actually oppose all levels of local government, the result will be to create confusion among the people. Is that support of the central government?[24]

The conflict between Liu Hsiang and Chiang Kai-shek emerged in more ominous terms when Liu realized that certain groups among the central government's varied forces in Szechwan were making direct efforts to undermine his power over the provincial armies and remove him altogether. As one of its tools in establishing control over Bandit Suppression Provinces like Szechwan, the central government employed a unique force of specially trained and specially armed small military units called the *pieh-tung tui*, or "Special Movement Organization," which were stationed with the provincial armies for the ostensible purpose of liaison with central government agencies.[25] In fact, the *pieh-tung tui* devoted their time to propagandizing among the provincial soldiery and among the peasants. Until their most blatant activities were checked, the *pieh-tung tui* worked openly for the overthrow of Liu Hsiang. Even their director, K'ang Tse, publicly called Liu a "local emperor" and called for his destruction.[26]

K'ang Tse's ill-advised behavior brought a major crisis in Liu Hsiang's relations with the center early in 1936. Liu let it be known that if K'ang continued to agitate for his downfall, some of Chiang Kai-shek's other supporters might call for the overthrow of Chiang himself. Ho Kuo-kuang, the principal middleman between Chiang and Liu, labored to prevent the crisis from spreading. Eventually he persuaded Chiang to admonish all central government personnel not to make a delicate situation worse, and K'ang Tse resigned in May 1936.[27] Armed conflict was thus averted, but no amount of central government politeness could erase Liu Hsiang's well-founded impression that at least some elements within the central government wished him out of the way.

The same period saw other conflicts between Liu Hsiang and Nanking. The entry of the National Government into Szechwan's affairs gradually drew the province into the tangled matrix of cliques and factions whose machinations dominated the political life of the Kuomintang and the central government. Here again, the principal connecting link was Yang Yung-t'ai, who was both a factional leader with enormous influence upon Chiang Kai-shek and the master planner for central government operations in newly penetrated provinces like Szechwan. Implementation of Yang's schemes in Szechwan inevitably embroiled provincial leaders like Liu Hsiang in a new level of factional intrigue.

The case of Wang Yu-yung was illustrative. Wang, a native of Kiangsi and member of Yang Yung-t'ai's Political Science Clique, had become head of the administrative section of the Szechwan provincial government in 1935 with Liu Hsiang's acquiescence. When Liu Hsiang was searching for a way to blunt the effectiveness of K'ang Tse and the *pieh-tung tui*, he and Wang Yu-yung devised a scheme to bring K'ang's local political activities directly under Wang's section of the provincial government. This was done, and responsibility for local propaganda work among the populace was further delegated to the district governments.

Two months later, the central government demanded that Liu Hsiang dismiss Wang and another section head in the provincial government on grounds of "improper conduct." Angry at Nanking's interference, Liu Hsiang refused to fire the two and requested instead that Nanking retract its demand. The central government responded by sending Liu incriminating photographs of the two section heads and ordering their removal once more. Through the efforts of Yang Yung-t'ai, a compromise eventually emerged. Wang Yu-yung was allowed to stay in his position for three months and then to resign voluntarily, while the other section head resigned at once. The crisis over Wang Yu-yung was the product of factional rivalries in Nanking. Because of clique conflicts at the national level and his affiliation with Yang Yung-t'ai, the case of wang Yu-yung further poisoned the air between Liu and Chiang Kai-shek.[28]

By the time the K'ang Tse and Wang Yu-yung affairs came to a head in the spring of 1936, most of the programs on which Liu Hsiang and Chiang Kai-shek had embarked together the previous year were in limbo. The lurking jurisdictional and operational problems of the provincial and district governments and the special inspectorates produced further animosities. In early 1936 Nanking introduced new regulations to strengthen central control over the inspectorates and concentrate control over the districts in the inspectorates, while reducing the size of provincial governments and the scope of their operations. This obvious attempt to bypass provincial leaders brought a bitter and sardonic response from Liu Hsiang.[29]

Signs of confusion multiplied throughout the spring. A meeting of Szechwan's special inspectors, scheduled for the week following Chiang Kai-shek's conference of special inspectors from Szechwan, Yunnan, and Kweichow, was abruptly called off by provincial authorities. The provincial government announced a fourth class at the District Government Personnel Training Institute in March, then called it off in late April. H. H. Kung and T. V. Soong, the National Government's two foremost financial officials, decided not to make a planned trip to Szechwan. Liu Hsiang went home to his native district on April 10, leaving Teng Han-hsiang in charge of the provincial government, and was thus conspicuously absent from Chengtu when Chiang Kai-shek returned there on April 17. The head of the provincial government's finance section went to Nanking twice in search of further loans and returned empty-handed. When Liu sent representatives to Nanking in June to discuss budgetary disputes with Chiang, Chiang refused to deal with the emissaries personally and offended provincial leaders by leaving Nanking just as the negotiators arrived for a final effort to settle the disagreement.[30]

Drought, the Sian Incident, and the Crisis of 1937

Adding to the central government's growing difficulties in Szechwan, an exceptionally serious drought struck the province in the summer of 1936 and continued for nearly a year. Most of Szechwan's winter food crop was lost.[31] Almost 90 percent of Szechwan's districts were affected; northern and eastern Szechwan suffered most severely. Refugees poured into Chungking, where thousands starved in the streets. Before the city built crematoria to handle the problem more effectively, police buried nearly four thousand famine victims in the city in February and March 1937 alone. Rumors of cannibalism spread. Parents were reported trading their children for other families' children so that they would not have to eat their own offspring.[32]

Predictably, the drought contributed to a sharp increase in rural social disturbance in Szechwan in 1936 and 1937. Drought was not the only factor; the new wave of taxes and requisitions that had followed the introduction of Nanking's programs and personnel into Szechwan had already begun to provoke angry peasant retaliation when the drought struck.[33] But with the famine of late 1936 and 1937, banditry became a major problem once again.[34] Re-examination of land deeds, supposedly in order to lighten the peasant's tax obligations, went forward without regard for the hardships of the drought, and peasants who could not pay the "deed examination fee" lost their lands to the tax collector. During the winter of 1936–37 famine victims rioted in city after city. In Peip'ei, the Min Sheng Company's model industrial community north of Chungking, women and children broke into the town and feasted on the bark and leaves of carefully nurtured ornamental trees.[35]

The drought and famine of 1936 might have offered a chance for Liu and Chiang Kai-shek to resolve their differences and work together in a common emergency. But their relations had already deteriorated too far, and the issue of drought relief only aggravated the tension between them. Despite the provincial government's pious promises of 1935 to improve Szechwan's defenses against natural disasters, when the rain stopped falling the existing relief systems were hopelessly inadequate. Rice dealers in the stricken areas hoarded grain and raised their prices without restraint; official apathy and corruption deepened the effects of the famine.[36] Provincial authorities turned to Nanking for financial aid and grain supplies, but the central government failed to respond to Liu Hsiang's repeated requests for help. Finally, in April 1937, the central government approved a loan to Szechwan which was only a small fraction of what Liu Hsiang had asked for. In the following month, the money disappeared, and when it finally turned up Liu Hsiang "detained" it rather than putting it to its intended uses.[37] The rains returned the same month, and the worst of the famine passed. In the context of their other difficulties, however, the famine relief issue divided the province and the center still further.

Irritation between Chiang Kai-shek and Liu Hsiang in 1936 also arose from Liu's apparent interest in other militarists' efforts to undermine Chiang's power. During the difficult spring and summer, while he was embroiled in the K'ang Tse and Wang Yu-yung disputes, Liu Hsiang carefully explored the possibilities of joint action against Chiang with the restless leaders of Kwangtung and Kwangsi provinces. The revolt of Ch'en Chi-t'ang, Li Tsung-jen, and Pai Ch'ung-hsi in June and July seemed likely to lead to civil war. A representative of Li and Pai conferred with Liu in Chengtu in June, and Liu kept special envoys in Kwangtung and Kwangsi until the spring of 1937.[38] Though Liu did not ultimately move against Chiang in connection with the Kwangsi expedition into Hunan, the central government was compelled to weaken its military presence in Szechwan temporarily by sending troops from Szechwan into Hunan.[39]

The Sian Incident of December 1936, in which the Manchurian militarist Chang Hsüeh-liang kidnapped Chiang Kai-shek and detained him for two weeks, further damaged Liu's relations with Chiang. Chiang's detention put the loyalties of semi-independent militarists like Liu to a severe test. In the aftermath of the incident, it became clear that Liu had failed. While Chiang was in captivity, Liu moved to take control of central government installations and forces in Chengtu, the provincial capital, including the military academy, the military police detachments there, and even the Chengtu branch of the Kuomintang.* Liu issued no statement supporting Chiang until five days after the kidnaping. An American diplomat alleged confidentially that during Chiang's captivity Liu advised Chang Hsüeh-liang not to hesitate to get rid of Chiang.[40] Moreover, the extraordinary vehemence with which Liu's followers proclaimed his loyalty to Chiang was difficult to

---

*One of Liu Hsiang's associates emphasized in conversations with the author that Liu Hsiang had taken these steps to "allay the fears" of the organizations concerned. The Chengtu Military Academy was the same one which the staff corps had established for the ostensible purpose of employing and retraining officers from disbanded units of the provincial armies. Liu Hsiang's action to take over this academy is also mentioned in Peck, *Through China's Wall*, p. 184. Peck says that Liu made his move on the very day that Chiang was released, and retired discreetly to his native district for a "rest" when his blunder became apparent.

accept at face value. Remarks like Teng Han-hsiang's, made during the crisis, did little to soothe central government uneasiness as to Szechwan's reliability:

> When Chairman Liu received news of the Sian Affair, he was extremely upset. . . . At this time, all of us in Szechwan must clearly recognize Chairman Liu's attitude of unswerving support for the central government. All such matters as local pacification and currency stabilization have seen the closest collaboration on what measures to take, and have not given rise to any conditions of conflict whatsoever. People should not believe rumors or become alarmed in order to avoid disgrace. . . . In sum, Chairman Liu's attitude toward the present affair is clear and frank: all elements of society should be very clear about this.[41]

Sian brought matters in Szechwan to a head. Chiang confronted evidence not only of Liu Hsiang's lukewarm support but also of his own failure to reduce Liu's armed strength.* The National Government's hardening attitude toward further Japanese aggression after Sian made it all the more urgent that the Szechwan problem be settled once and for all, before it became necessary to rely on the province in a military conflict with Japan. Early in 1937, additional large numbers of central government troops began to pour into Szechwan from Shensi and Hupei.[42] Tensions in Chengtu were so severe at the Chinese New Year that authorities prohibited fireworks lest they be mistaken for the start of hostilities between Szechwanese and central government forces.[43]

The focal point of looming confrontation between Liu Hsiang and Chiang Kai-shek was Chungking and the lower Yangtze area of Szechwan. Chungking remained Liu's principal stronghold and financial resource.[44] After Sian, more central government troops from Hupei disembarked at key Yangtze ports below Chungking. Through the spring of 1937, both sides prepared ostentatiously for war in the vicinity of the city. Provincial forces on one occasion hurled shells just outside the walls of Chiang's Chungking headquarters.[45]

---

*As late as October 1936 Liu Hsiang was augmenting his own air force independently of the central government, even though the cession of the air force to National Government control had long been one of Nanking's aims in Szechwan. Manufacture of powerful weapons was also proceeding in Liu's arsenals at this time. Machine guns and automatic rifles were produced according to the specifications of the Czechoslovakian Skoda arms works, while German-type antiaircraft guns and trench mortars were turned out at other factories near Chungking (see Mills [Chungking] to London, October 23, 1936, F.O. 371/20257).

While provincial and central forces dug earthworks and skirmished outside Chungking, the two sides dickered for terms, both in Nanking and in Szechwan. Liu's envoys and Ho Kuo-kuang journeyed back and forth between Chungking and Nanking, sounding out Chiang Kai-shek, soothing his rage, and probing for a formula that would serve Liu Hsiang's interests as well as Chiang's.[46] Ho urged Liu to turn his arsenals and his air force over to the National Government in return for a promise that he would be free to act against the center if it should misbehave in Szechwan.[47] Chiang himself made small but public gestures to ease the critical situation around Chungking without weakening the central government position. In late May he issued special orders to the Chungking headquarters:

> Central government personnel in Szechwan are overzealous and hard for the people to tolerate. All sorts of illegal activities arouse bitter hatred and resentment. From now on, Ho Kuo-kuang has full power to deal with this. All who break the law, whether they be officers or soldiers, civilians or military personnel, shall be dealt with the same way: punish them first, and report it later.[48]

The crisis passed in early June 1937 without major violence. Liu turned over his mint and ten of his planes to Nanking and moved his troops out of Chungking to Yungch'uan. At the same time, after much negotiation and delay, Liu and the central government agreed on new steps to place Szechwan's armies under effective central government control. The most significant of the new measures were the transfer of all Szechwanese armies to the direct command of the National Government's Military Affairs Committee and the transfer of financial responsibility for the provincial armies from the provincial government to Chiang's Chungking headquarters. All military training was to be controlled by central government agencies and all military schools in Szechwan were to be run by the center. All aircraft, airfields, arsenals, repair works, and all military supplies in Szechwan were also to be controlled by the National Government. Funds for Liu Hsiang's headquarters were also to be reduced.[49]

A special conference to arrange the carrying out of the new program opened in Chungking on July 6, 1937 under the National Government minister of war, Ho Ying-ch'in. Major military leaders from the central armies and all of Szechwan's leading militarists attended. To ensure that the atmosphere of patriotic dedication and cooperation would not be marred, Ho Kuo-kuang thoughtfully prohibited all demonstrations, meetings, and displays of signs in Chungking during the conference.[50] But the conference had hardly gotten underway when word arrived from North China of the Marco Polo Bridge incident and the opening of hostilities with Japan. Ho Ying-ch'in left at once, and the Szechwan–Sikang Military Reorganization Conference adjourned after approving plans for the reduction of Szechwan's armies.[51]

Szechwan and the National Government on the Eve of the Anti-Japanese War

The opening of Sino-Japanese hostilities put an end to Nanking's peacetime experiment in pacifying and controlling Szechwan. In two and a half years of intensive effort, the central government had managed to erect complex new administrative structures, gain control over certain revenues previously reserved for provincial militarists, stabilize the provincial currency, and send large numbers of troops into a province that had been off limits to national military power for nearly a decade. Yet the center's experiment was by no means a total success. For while it had managed to superimpose its own presence on Szechwanese politics, it had not managed to eliminate the rival influence of established provincial militarists, particularly Liu Hsiang and his powerful subordinates. Though Liu Hsiang retreated from Chungking in June 1937 in the face of superior central government power, his own armed forces remained intact. Indeed, so did most of the Szechwanese armies; after all the early efforts to cut down the provincial forces, the task was still to be done when the Military Reorganization Conference convened in July.

In civil administration, which Nanking had considered the most vital sphere of activity in Szechwan, the results of two and a half years' work were limited. Despite the new system of special inspectorates, districts, subdistricts, *lien-pao, pao,* and *chia,* the British ambassador to China remarked in June 1937: "The central government's influence is at present being exercised only in a military sense; it has not touched the civil administration which remains to be dealt with when military control of the province has been assured."[52]

When one remembers the size of the task Nanking faced in Szechwan and realizes that a similar process was going on in other provinces at the same time, it is not surprising that the central government could not achieve in a couple of years the degree of high-level control over Szechwanese society that its planners envisioned. Compared to its position in the province in, say, 1933, the central government enjoyed enormously increased influence in Szechwan on the eve of the Japanese war. Still, some of the reasons for Chiang Kai-shek's limited success in Szechwan went beyond the mere fact of Szechwan's size and Nanking's original weakness there.

First of all, certain aspects of the central government's operations in Szechwan were so out of tune with Szechwanese conditions that the larger effort to implant Nanking's power in the province was seriously weakened. New units of political administration, for example, were created without regard to the existing relationships among market towns and their dependent hinterlands.[53] Furthermore, Nanking's attempts to establish central government legitimacy among the populace were at times divorced from the very society at which they aimed. The Suining famine riot of 1937 illustrated this problem. Soon after the Suining district government erected a flagpole in the district capital in order to fly the national flag and cultivate patriotic feeling among the people, drought came to Suining. Because the Chinese terms for "flagpole" and "drought" are very similarly pronounced, the rumor spread that the flagpole had caused the drought. A crowd gathered to demand removal of the pole, and when the district magistrate refused, it attacked and destroyed the district government offices. Police opened fire, and many were jailed or killed.[54] Nanking faced a serious problem in making its goals and methods relevant to local conditions in Szechwan.

Second, the central government slid into much the same position that provincial militarists had occupied for years in Szechwan. After 1935, Nanking was able to fly the flag in Szechwan by virtue of its military power, but it lacked the resources to infuse its influence deep into Szechwanese society. Like the militarists of Szechwan, central power imposed itself on the province from above without melting into the texture of provincial life. Unlike the militarists, the Nationalists had coherent, even grandiose plans for reaching into provincial society. But plans, while necessary, were not enough. The thousands of new administrative posts created by central government planners were of little use without efficient and loyal administrators to fill them. Even if provincial interests had not balked at Nanking's efforts to train such administrators, the task would still have been enormous. As it was, Chiang Kai-shek fared no better than the provincial militarists in rooting out recalcitrant local elites, particularly the overly independent militia forces. In fact, the new levels of local administration which Nanking introduced to Szechwan frequently offered additional opportunities for entrenched local powerholders to extract goods and services from peasants in their neighborhoods.[55] The central government tried to use propaganda and exhortation in place of the mass of local agents which it did not have. But, obstructed by its own ignorance and outright irrelevance as well as by the shortage of personnel, Nanking remained as dependent as the provincial militarists on the cooperation of local elements who had no particular interest in cooperating.

A third factor limiting Nanking's success was the inevitable resistance of provincial leaders to continued central government encroachment on their rights and privileges. To some extent this was a problem of personal relations. Yang Yung-t'ai and Ho Kuo-kuang managed in 1935 to smooth the way for certain reform programs by their leaders. But Yang was assassinated in October 1936, and with the ever-increasing likelihood of war with Japan in 1936 and 1937, the urgency of bringing Szechwan under control permitted less and less delay and politesse. The areas of mutual benefit for both Liu and Chiang Kai-shek shrank, and areas of potential conflict grew. Liu Hsiang—and to a lesser extent, Szechwan's other remaining militarists—resisted central authority in the ways they knew best: *yang-feng yin-wei* to preserve the distinction between real and apparent concessions, quiet manipulation of personnel and interference with central government agents in the province, and threats of military resistance to back up their negotiating positions on individual issues. This kind of resistance did not completely paralyze the central government's efforts in Szechwan, but it slowed down and vitiated Nanking's thrust into the province. Combined with the inherent flaws in the Nationalists' own master plan, Liu Hsiang's growing opposition enabled him to keep his armies virtually intact, despite the loss of certain key territories. When the war with Japan finally came, the National Government still had not resolved the problem of what to do about Liu himself.

8 The End of an Era?

Unlike earlier episodes of Sino-Japanese conflict in North China, the skirmishing at the Marco Polo Bridge near Peking on July 7, 1937 led to sustained action and full-scale hostilities. War between China and Japan further increased Szechwan's importance to the National Government, which had begun to prepare for removal to Szechwan well before the Marco Polo Bridge incident occurred.[1]

The war with Japan had major consequences for Szechwan and its relationship to central political authority from the start, and particularly after the most vital elements of the National Government transferred to the province in late 1938. The shipment of sizable amounts of movable production equipment from the industrial centers of the Yangtze valley and the coastal cities transformed the face of Szechwanese manufacturing industries, at least for the duration of the war. The influx of university students and staffs and other professional people from occupied areas added another new dimension to Szechwanese life during the long conflict with Japan. As the political center of unoccupied China, and as the principal supplier of manpower and provisions for China's armies, Szechwan held a very new position in national political and economic affairs.

Yet the addition of all these new factors to the already complex relationship of Szechwanese and central authorities did not eliminate the longer-term problems which Nanking had failed to resolve on the eve of the war. To be sure, two and a half years of pressure had enabled the central government to plan and carry out its transfer to Szechwan in 1937 and 1938 without overt provincial resistance. But despite the torrent of patriotic rhetoric which poured from the pens of provincial bureaucrats and the mouths of provincial commanders after the Japanese attack, resolution of remaining tensions between central government and provincial interests was still an elusive goal. The death of Liu Hsiang on January 20, 1938 was a milestone in the evolution of relations between the two sides, but even Liu's elimination failed to put an end to the bickering and the dickering which had characterized these relations since 1935.

Amid the emergency planning for the migration of government and Kuomintang bodies, educational institutions, and industrial enterprises into Szechwan, the problem of what to do about Szechwan's armed forces continued to rankle. With the Japanese onslaught in the north, all major provincial military leaders proclaimed their desire to "*ch'u cheng*"—lead their forces out of Szechwan to the front lines. In fact, however, the departure of Szechwanese troops for several battle fronts did not begin on schedule. The Reorganization Conference of July had set an August 15 deadline for the dispatch of provincial forces, but the first units did not begin to leave Szechwan until after September 1.[2] The reasons advanced by Teng Han-hsiang for this delay were plausible: the reorganization measures provided for at the July conference had been interrupted by the outbreak of war and Liu Hsiang's subsequent visits to Nanking; primitive communications and transport facilities made it impossible to move large numbers of troops long distances, especially out of the province altogether, without adequate preparation. Most telling of all, problems arose over the financing of provincial army operations. Teng implied that provincial leaders were prepared to dawdle, unless the central government provided them with adequate funds or granted them permission to raise additional funds themselves.[3] A veteran British diplomat who had watched the maneuvering in Chungking for several years regarded the provincial armies' battle plans with skepticism. "Plans are no sooner announced than they are amended or cancelled altogether," he remarked. "It seems obvious that only a small part of the Szechwanese forces are to be sent out of the province."[4]

Eventually, Szechwanese armies got on their way. Teng Hsi-hou, Li Chia-yü, and Sun Chen, the successor to T'ien Sung-yao's command, took the Shensi road north toward Sian, then moved east to the Shansi front. From Chungking and Wanhsien, Liu Hsiang's subordinates T'ang Shih-tsun, P'an Wen-hua, and Wang Tsuan-hsü moved east into Hupei and on toward the Peiping-Hankow Railway front. These two expeditions were the first Szechwanese army ventures into the War of Resistance. Yang Sen, who had been in Kweichow when the war began, led his forces first to Hupei and then to the Shanghai area.[5] Szechwanese forces took part in the fighting at T'aiyuan, Shanghai, and Hsüchow.

The removal of large numbers of provincial troops did little to relieve existing tensions between Szechwanese militarists and the central government. The fate of provincial armies involved in actual fighting with the Japanese suggested that the war was providing Chiang Kai-shek with an excellent opportunity to reduce still further the power of Szechwanese commanders. Szechwanese armies were already renowned as China's worst.[6] In the fall of 1937 when they went off to fight the Japanese, the provincial forces lacked proper ammunition, medical facilities, maps, and even food. Provincial soldiers fighting in Shansi during the fall and winter of 1937, for example, still wore straw sandals on their feet.[7] Responsibility for providing these essentials was still disputed. As a result, when Szechwanese armies fought the enemy at all, they suffered enormous losses. By the summer of 1938 a pattern of systematic destruction seemed to have emerged. "Military circles," reported the British consul general in Chungking, "advance the stock grievance that the fighting is being done by provincial troops, who are used as cannon-fodder while the Nanking divisions are kept out of the line. Moreover, provincial forces which have suffered heavy losses are re-drafted into armies from other provinces, thus increasing the Central Government's military dominance."[8] There was serious discontent, this diplomat reported, among provincial merchants and militarists over Szechwan's suffering "in a cause which does not concern her."[9]

Regardless of the resentments and tensions engendered by this policy in Szechwan, removal of sizable provincial forces did pave the way for the transfer of central government functions to Chungking. From the start of hostilities, the tide of battle in North and East China ran against the Chinese. Tientsin fell in late July 1937. After a prolonged and heroic defense, Chinese forces abandoned Shanghai in the last week of October. Following the fall of Shanghai, Chiang Kai-shek announced that the National Government would move to Chungking, and formal notification of the government's transfer was made on November 20. Lin Sen, the titular chief of the government, arrived in Chungking on November 26, 1937 and the central government formally began to operate in its makeshift temple headquarters on December 1.

Chiang Kai-shek, however, did not go to Szechwan. After the fall of Nanking, the powerful leaders and organs of central control moved to Wuhan, where Chiang established headquarters and most of the Executive Yüan continued to work. The final transfer of central authority into Szechwan came only after Wuhan fell to the Japanese at the end of October 1938. Chiang Kai-shek finally arrived in Szechwan from Kweilin on December 8 of that year.

While his principal subordinates and other ranking Szechwanese commanders were leading their forces from Szechwan into other provinces, Liu Hsiang's own course took a different and ultimately fatal turn. In early November 1937, while it was still in control of Nanking, the central government created a Seventh War Zone under Liu Hsiang's command. The headquarters of the new organization was located in Liu Hsiang's own Nanking offices. Liu turned over control of the provincial government to his longtime associate and secretary-general, Teng Han-hsiang, and appointed his confidant and financial adviser Liu Hang-shen to aid him in his new duties.[10]

Soon after moving to Nanking, Liu's career came to an end under circumstances which bear a tinge of uncertainty even now. The standard account of Liu Hsiang's death maintains that he suffered a severe recurrence of his old abdominal problem shortly after becoming commander of the Seventh War Zone. Indeed, the British consul at Chengtu had reported in June 1936 that Liu Hsiang's illness was genuine and not politically inspired, and that it had seriously affected Liu's health.[11] When the ailment cropped up again in December 1937, Chiang Kai-shek insisted that Liu Hsiang enter a foreign-run hospital in Hankow. While Liu recuperated, Chiang appointed General Ch'en Ch'eng to act for him as commander of Liu's war zone. Liu never left the hospital; he died on January 20, 1938. As soon as Liu Hsiang was dead, the Seventh War Zone was abolished.[12]

The circumstances of Liu Hsiang's death have never been fully clarified; ritualistic eulogies telling of Liu's patriotic concern for the development of his province and the triumph of Chinese armies until the moment of his death may or may not tell the whole story. Certainly the behavior of other provincial militarists, particularly Liu's old subordinates, and the actions of the central government left room for doubt as to what had happened. Fan Shao-tseng, the former bandit who had served Liu for years, claimed that Liu had been murdered by agents of Tai Li, the head of Chiang's secret police.[13] Liu's widow, a powerful personality in her own right, also claimed that central government agents had killed her husband.[14]

Whether or not Liu died of natural causes, his removal gave the central government further, though limited, advantages in the continuing struggle for supremacy within Szechwan. By virtue of the power which he had built up over the years in his native province and the network of personal relationships which he maintained within the Szechwanese armies, Liu Hsiang had been the single most important provincial figure in Szechwanese resistance to outside intrusions. His primacy had grown stronger during the three years of direct central government activity in Szechwan; other commanders looked to Liu for cues in most areas of central–provincial relations. Liu's death removed the head from a body of military officers whose main connection with one another had been their common connection with Liu.

But the significance of Liu Hsiang's death extended only so far. As a group, the second-generation Szechwanese militarists remained. The legacy of thirty years of provincial military life did not vanish with Liu Hsiang. Liu Wen-hui, Teng Hsi-hou, P'an Wen-hua, T'ang Shih-tsun, Wang Tsuan-hsü, and dozens of other ranking Szechwanese leaders still controlled their outsized, ill-trained armies. Symbolically, perhaps, Liu Hsiang's death marked the end of an era. In concrete terms, though, Chiang Kai-shek on the day after Liu's death faced the same problems of suspicion, resentment, and outright hostility that he faced while Liu was alive. Liu's removal provoked a crisis among provincial commanders which took months to subside.[15] From the moment, a few days after Liu's death, when Szechwanese generals made it clear to Chiang that they would not accept Chang Ch'ün as Liu Hsiang's replacement in charge of the provincial government, it was evident that Liu Hsiang's death had not eliminated the sources of conflict between provincial and central government interests. Handling the Szechwanese commanders and their armies during the war against Japan was a serious problem for the Chinese Nationalists, who could ill afford to wage an all-out struggle against dissatisfied and potentially rebellious provincial forces in the heart of government-held territory.

After the war, with the departure of the National Government and the millions of wartime immigrants for their old strongholds in central and eastern China, familiar faces appeared in powerful positions within Szechwan.[16] Most of the major provincial military figures who survived through the mid-1930s still enjoyed influence in the province when the Nationalists fled from Szechwan in 1950. The same militarists who rose to provincial power in the 1920s as young men continued to play the most prominent roles in Szechwan in middle and even old age. Their continuing power testified to the strength and durability of the provincially defined power bases which they had built in the twenties and maintained against outside pressures in the thirties and forties. At the same time, it bore witness to the failure of provincial and national leadership alike to devise workable mechanisms for recruiting and advancing new political leaders. Ironically, after all the ferment, turmoil, and social upheaval of the Republican era, the passport to the most powerful positions in Szechwanese politics in 1949 was still education in a late Ch'ing military academy and early service in Ch'ing and Republican provincial armies.

The story of provincial separatism in twentieth-century Szechwan has no clear-cut ending. It certainly did not end with the Nationalist "unification" of China in 1928 or with the arrival of central government power in the province in 1935. It persisted even after the death of its principal symbol, Liu Hsiang, and the migration of the central government itself to Szechwan during the war with Japan. Evidence from the Cultural Revolution period in the 1960s suggests that the problem has recurred in other forms in the People's Republic of China.[17]

Just what constitutes the optimum relationship between national and provincial power in China has been a particularly sensitive question since the beginning of the twentieth century. The areas of conflict between province and center and the instruments available to provincial and central authorities have shifted with time. A once-and-for-all solution to the problem of provincial independence is not likely to emerge in the future. In fact, given the depth and the speed of political and social change in China since 1949, the whole idea of a permanent solution may well be a contradiction in terms.

Abbreviations

The following abbreviations are used in the Notes and in the Bibliography:

CTSTL   *Chin-tai shih tzu-liao* [Modern history materials] (Peking, 1958, 1962).

CYCL   Ssu-ch'uan sheng cheng-fu, mi-shu ch'u [Secretariat, Szechwan Provincial Government], *Ssu-ch'uan sheng hsing-cheng tu-ch'a chuan-yüan shih-cheng yen-chiu hui chi-lu* [Proceedings of the conference of Szechwan special administrative inspectors on political implementation] ([Chengtu], 1935).

F.O.   Great Britain, Foreign Office.

HHKMHIL   Chung-kuo jen-min cheng-chih hsieh-shang hui-i ch'üan-kuo wei-yüan hui, wen-shih tzu-liao yen-chiu wei-yüan hui [Historical Research Committee of the National Committee of the Chinese People's Political Consultative Conference], ed., *Hsin-hai ko-ming hui-i lu* [Memoirs of the 1911 Revolution], vol. 3 (Peking, 1962).

HWTT   *Hsin-wen t'ien-ti* [Newsdom] (Hong Kong, 1967).

HYPK   China, Chün-shih wei-yüan hui wei-yüan chang hsing-ying [Headquarters of the chairman of the Military Affairs Committee], *Chün-shih wei-yüan hui wei-yüan chang hsing-ying cheng-chih kung-tso pao-kao* [Political work report of the headquarters of the chairman of the Military Affairs Committee] (Nanking, 1935).

KWCP   *Kuo-wen chou-pao* [National news weekly] (Tientsin, 1924–37).

1936 pao-kao   Ssu-ch'uan sheng cheng-fu, mi-shu ch'u [Secretariat, Szechwan Provincial Government], *Ssu-ch'uan sheng cheng-fu erh-shih wu nien hsing-cheng tsung pao-kao* [General administrative report of the Szechwan provincial government for 1936] ([Chengtu], 1936).

143

SCWH   *Ssu-ch'uan wen-hsien* [Szechwan documents] (Taipei, 1962–72).

SCYP   *Ssu-ch'uan yüeh-pao* [Szechwan review] (Chungking, 1932–38).

S.D.   United States, Department of State.

TFTC   *Tung-fang tsa-chih* [Eastern miscellany] (Shanghai, 1904–48).

Unless otherwise indicated, the name "Washington" in citations of State Department documents denotes the destination of dispatches formally addressed to the secretary of state. The name "London" similarly refers to the destination of Foreign Office dispatches formally addressed to the secretary of state for foreign affairs. "Peking" and "Peiping" refer to the destination of American and British diplomatic correspondence formally addressed to the heads of American and British diplomatic missions to China before and after 1928.

Notes

INTRODUCTION

1 Lu Pao-ch'ien, *Chung-kuo shih-ti tsung-lun* [A general discussion of China's historical geography] (Taipei, 1962), p. 290.
2 H. G. W. Woodhead, ed., *The China Year Book, 1936* (Shanghai, 1936), p. 1.
3 Ferdinand von Richthofen, *Baron Richthofen's Letters, 1870–1872* (Shanghai, 1873), p. 129.
4 Pi Tung [pseud.], *I-pai ke jen-wu* [One hundred personalities], no. 2 (n.p., n.d.), p. 1.

CHAPTER 1

1 A recent expression of this assumption is found in Lucien Bianco, *Origins of the Chinese Revolution, 1915–1949* (Stanford, 1971), p. 24.
2 James Sheridan introduces the idea of residual warlordism after 1928 in his excellent introductory chapter (*Chinese Warlord: The Career of Feng Yü-hsiang* [Stanford, 1966], pp. 14–16).
3 Pontius (Chungking) to Washington, December 3, 1911, S.D. 893.00/979. See also Pontius (Chungking) to Washington, December 12, 1911, S.D. 893.00/983. For an analysis of the roots of revolution in Szechwan see Charles H. Hedtke, "Reluctant Revolutionaries: Szechwan and the Ch'ing Collapse, 1898–1911" (Ph.D. dissertation, University of California at Berkeley, 1968). Chou K'ai-ch'ing, ed., *Ssu-ch'uan yü hsin-hai ko-ming* [Szechwan and the Revolution of 1911] (Taipei, 1965) is an excellent combination of concise summaries and useful documents. Yang Shao-ch'uan, an important figure in the Revolution of 1911 in Szechwan, published a colorful account two decades later (see S. C. Yang, "The Revolution in Szechwan, 1911–1912," *Journal of the West China Border Research Society* 6 [1933–34]: 64–90).
4 Yang, "The Revolution in Szechwan," pp. 82–87. See also Chou, *Ssu-ch'uan yü hsin-hai ko-ming*, p. 305. The "reign of terror" in Chengtu of December 8–10, 1911 is described in Baker (Chungking) to Peking, January 13, 1912, S.D. 893.00/1158. Jerome Ch'en classifies Yin as a "revolutionary leader" (as opposed to a military leader such as T'ang Chi-yao), but I would disagree (see Ch'en, "Defining Chinese Warlords and Their Factions," *Bulletin of the School of Oriental and African Studies* 31, pt. 3 [1968]: 563). A fascinating biography of Yin appears in Chou K'ai-ch'ing, ed., *Min-kuo Ssu-ch'uan jen-wu chuan-chi* [Biographies of Szechwanese personalities of the Republican period] (Taipei, 1966), pp. 252–58.
5 Yang, "The Revolution in Szechwan," p. 88.
6 Lü P'ing-teng, *Ssu-ch'uan nung-ts'un ching-chi* [The agrarian economy of Szechwan] (Shanghai, 1936), pp. 8–9.
7 Louis M. King, *China in Turmoil: Studies in Personality* (London, 1927), pp. 20–21.
8 Yang Ch'ao-yung, "Hsin-hai hou chih Ssu-ch'uan chan-chi" [A record of the wars in Szechwan after the Revolution of 1911], *CTSTL*, 1958, no. 6, p. 56. The year 1918, when Hsiung K'o-wu issued the order to each of the Szechwan armies to seek its sustenance from the territory it occupied, is generally taken as the start of this long-lasting state of affairs.

9   See e.g. *Lu hsien chih* [Gazetteer of Lu *hsien*] (Luhsien, 1938; reprinted Taipei, 1967), *chüan* 2, pp. 63–65.

10 Shen Chien, "Hsin-hai ko-ming ch'ien-hsi wo-kuo chih lu-chün chi ch'i chün-fei" [China's armies and military budgets on the eve of the Revolution of 1911], *She-hui k'o-hsüeh* 2 (January 1937): 380.

11 Josselyn (Hankow) to Washington, May 13, 1929, S.D. 893.00/P.R. Chungking 11.

12 Feng Ho-fa, *Chung-kuo nung-ts'un ching-chi tzu-liao* [Materials on the Chinese agrarian economy] (Shanghai, 1933), p. 827.

13 The most useful source of biographical data is Chou, *Min-kuo jen-wu*, but information has been drawn in small bits from numerous sources.

14 Chang Chung-lei, "Ch'ing-mo min-ch'u Ssu-ch'uan ti chün-shih hsüeh-t'ang chi Ch'uan chün p'ai-hsi" [Szechwanese military schools of the late Ch'ing and early Republic, and Szechwanese army cliques and factions], *HHKMHIL*, pp. 346–47.

15 For Chungking, see Pontius (Chungking) to Washington, November 22, 1911, S.D. 893.00/886; and Chou, *Ssu-ch'uan yü hsin-hai ko-ming*, pp. 219–24. For Luchou, see ibid., pp. 273–74. For Kuangyüan, see P'ing Ch'ing [pseud.], "Shu-pei chün cheng-fu ch'eng-li shih-mo" [An account of the establishment of the military government of Northern Szechwan], *SCWH*, November 1965, pp. 7–9.

16 Yang Ch'ao-yung, "Chan-chi," p. 41.

17 On the war against Yüan Shih-k'ai, see Hsieh Shu, "Min-yüan i-lai Ssu-ch'uan chün-shih hsiao-shih" [A short history of Szechwanese military affairs since 1912], *Kuo-li Wu-han ta-hsüeh Ssu-ch'uan t'ung-hsüeh hui hui-k'an* 1, no. 2 (1934): 2; Yang Ch'ao-yung, "Chan-chi," p. 43; Teng Chih-ch'eng, "Hu-kuo chün chi-shih" [An account of the Army to Protect the Nation], *Shih-hsüeh nien-pao* 2, no. 2 (1935): 1–22; and Liu Ts'un-hou, *Hu-kuo Ch'uan-chün chan-chi* [The war record of the Szechwan Army to Protect the Nation] (Taipei, 1966).

18 Li P'ei-sheng, *Kuei-hsi chü-Yüeh chih yu-lai chi ch'i ching-kuo* [Origins and experiences of the Kwangsi clique's occupation of Kwangtung] ([Canton] [1921]; reprinted Taipei, n.d.), *hsü* pp. 6, 9.

19 Sheridan, *Chinese Warlord*, p. 93.

20 Winston Hsieh, "The Ideas and Ideals of a Warlord: Ch'en Chiung-ming (1878–1933)," Harvard University, East Asian Research Center, *Papers on China*, vol. 16 (Cambridge, Mass., 1962), p. 231.

21 Sheridan, *Chinese Warlord*, p. 67.

22 On the conflict with Yunnan and Kweichow, see Yang Ch'ao-yung, "Chan-chi"; Fan Ch'ung-shih, "1920–1922 nien ti Ssu-ch'uan chün-fa k'un-chan" [The chaotic warfare of the Szechwanese warlords between 1920 and 1922], *CTSTL*, 1962, no. 4, pp. 1–23; and Sir Meyrick Hewlett, *Forty Years in China* (London, 1943), pp. 92–105.

23 Hsieh, "Chün-shih hsiao-shih," p. 3.

24 Li Pai-hung, "Erh-shih nien lai chih Ch'uan-fa chan-cheng" [Szechwanese warlord wars of the last twenty years], *CTSTL*, 1962, no. 4, p. 71.

25 The Hupei expedition is well covered in Fan, "1920–1922," pp. 26–27.

26 For a treatment of this movement, see Jean Chesneaux, "The Federalist Movement in China, 1920–3," in *Modern China's Search for a Political Form*, ed. Jack Gray (London, 1969), pp. 96–137.

27 Fan, "1920–1922," p. 8. The principle of self-government at the local level as the first step in nation-building has been traced back to provincial associations among Chinese students in Japan in the early 1900s (see Robert Scalapino, "Prelude to Marxism: The Chinese Student Movement in Japan, 1900–1910," in *Approaches to Modern Chinese History*, ed. Albert Feuerwerker, Rhoads Murphey, and Mary C. Wright [Berkeley, 1967], p. 208).

28 Yang Ch'ao-yung, "Chan-chi," p. 67. See also Chesneaux, "Federalist Movement," pp. 110–12.

29 Josselyn (Chungking) to Washington, June 30, 1921, S.D. 893.00/3990.
30 Allman (Chungking) to Washington, April 7, 1922, S.D. 893.00/4405.
31 *Ssu-ch'uan sheng i hui hui-k'an*, November 14, 1926. A "Szechwan Draft Constitution" was produced by a constitutional committee in February 1923, but it was never promulgated (for the text see *Chung-kuo nien-chien* [China yearbook] [Shanghai, 1923], pp. 137–45).
32 Affleck (Chengtu) to Peking, November 18, 1925, F.O. 405/250, p. 147.
33 *Ssu-ch'uan shan-hou hui-i lu*, pt. 1, pp. 8b–9.
34 Ibid., pp. 8–12. See also Hewlett, *Forty Years in China*, pp. 100, 104, 110; and Chou, *Min-kuo jen-wu*, pp. 274–75.
35 *Ssu-ch'uan shan-hou hui-i lu*, pt. 2, shu-cheng sec., pp. 3b–7.

CHAPTER 2

1 As in the case of the first generation of militarists, Chou, *Min-kuo jen-wu*, is the most useful of many sources of biographical data.
2 See the following: *KWCP*, March 8, 1925; Chung-kung jen-ming lu pien-hsiu wei-yüan hui, ed., *Chung-kung jen-ming lu* [Roster of Chinese Communists] (Taipei, 1967), p. 607; *Who's Who In China*, 5th ed. (Shanghai, 1936), p. 226; *KWCP*, December 23, 1928; and Spiker (Chungking) to Peking, July 28, 1924, S.D. 893.00/5510.
3 Shu K'o [pseud.], "Liu Hsiang fa-ta hsiao shih" [A short history of Liu Hsiang's rise], *Chung-kuo min-chu lun-t'an pan yüeh-k'an*, November 16, 1966, p. 16.
4 Interview with a former adviser of Liu Hsiang, Taipei, April 26, 1968.
5 Spiker (Chungking) to Peking, July 28, 1924, S.D. 893.00/5510.
6 Teng's native district is mentioned in Han Min [pseud.], *Tang-tai Chung-kuo jen-wu chih* [Present-day Chinese personalities] (Shanghai, 1939). For T'ien Sung-yao, see *KWCP*, December 23, 1928.
7 Chang Chung-lei, "Ch'ing-mo hsüeh-t'ang," pp. 349–51.
8 Ibid., p. 348.
9 For an enlightening discussion of the role of personal relationships in traditional Chinese society, see Kenneth E. Folsom, *Friends, Guests, and Colleagues: The Mu-fu System in the Late Ch'ing Period* (Berkeley, 1968), pp. 16–32.
10 The names of subordinate officers in the armies of the two Lius, Teng, T'ien, and Yang can be found in different sources for different times. See *TFTC*, February 10, 1925, pp. 78–81; Toller (Chungking) to Peiping, August 29, 1930, F.O. 228/4308 Doss. 83E; Fei-chih nei-chan ta t'ung-meng, ed. *Ssu-ch'uan nei-chan hsiang chi* [The Szechwan civil war] (Shanghai, 1933), pp. 102–08; Han Shan, "Ch'uan-chün hsi-t'ung chi Ch'uan-fei wei-chih yü shih-li" [Szechwanese military systems and the location and strength of Communists in Szechwan], *Fu-hsing yüeh-k'an*, March 1935; *SCWH*, October 1965, pp. 10–14. This last item provides the names of officers after the Military Reorganization Conference of July 1937.
11 Quoted in "Szechwan Feudalism," report of Vice Consul O. Edmund Clubb (Hankow) to Washington, May 20, 1933, S.D. 893.00/12384, p. 23.
12 Ibid. See also T'ien Cho-chih, "Ssu-ch'uan wen-t'i" [The Szechwan problem], *KWCP*, July 23, 1934.
13 Sonoda Kazuki, *Hsin Chung-kuo jen-wu chih* [Men of the new China], trans. Huang Hui-ch'uan (Shanghai, 1930), p. 476.
14 Some anecdotal materials about Szechwanese militarists appear in two books by Ma Wu [Lei Hsiao-ch'en]: *Hsin shih shuo* [Stories of the new age] (Taipei, 1965), and *Wo-ti sheng-huo shih* [The story of my life] (Taipei, 1965).
15 Chang Meng-hsiu, "Hung-chün jao-Ch'uan ch'ien ti erh Liu chih chan" [The Two-Liu War which preceded Szechwan's Red Army troubles], *Pei-ching ta-hsüeh Ssu-ch'uan t'ung-hsiang hui hui-k'an*, February 10, 1934, p. 40. See also *Ssu-ch'uan nei-chan hsiang-chi*, p. 101.
16 Interview with Ho Kuo-kuang, Taipei, February 11, 1968. Also Pi, *I-pai ke jen-wu*, p. 1.

17 Hu Hsien-su, "Shu yu tsa-kan" [Random thoughts on a visit to Szechwan], *Tu-li 'ping-lun* October 1, 1933, pp. 14–20.

18 Toller (Chungking) to Peiping, July 31, 1931, F.O. 371/14748. See also *North China Herald,* January 25, 1930, p. 296.

19 *New York Times,* August 20, 1933, sec. 4, p. 3.

20 Yang Sen, "Wo-ti yang-sheng chih tao" [The way I live], *Chung-wai tsa-chih,* April 1967, pp. 4–7. See also Spiker (Chungking) to Peking, July 28, 1924, S.D. 893.00/5510. Jerome Ch'en recalls how "he encouraged football and tennis in my home town. Under him there was a large retinue of sportsmen; he played tennis himself" (letter to the author, December 3, 1968).

21 Hu, "Shu yu tsa-kan," p. 18.

22 *New York Times,* August 20, 1933, sec. 4, p. 3.

23 Yang mentions this in unpublished recollections.

24 Spiker (Chungking) to Peking, July 28, 1924, S.D. 893.00/5510.

25 Report of Ingram and Stirling, October 10, 1929, F.O. 371/13901.

26 Toller (Chungking) to Peking, January 24, 1921, F.O. 228/3273.

27 Toller (Chungking) to Peiping, April 30, 1931, F.O. 371/15473.

28 Shu, "Liu Hsiang fa-ta," p. 17.

29 Liu Hang-shen, "Jung-mu pan-sheng," (Half a lifetime in the inner circle), *HWTT,* August 19, 1967, p. 24.

30 See Haldore Hanson, "Famine Diary of a Warlord," *Democracy* (Peiping), June 22, 1937, pp. 110–12.

31 King, *China in Turmoil,* p. 81. Although the subjects of King's "studies in personality" are not identified by name, it is clear from the context here that King is writing of Liu Hsiang.

32 Hui Ying, "Feng-chien shih-li mi-man ti Ssu-ch'uan" [Szechwan, where feudal power is excessive], *Lao-tung chi-pao,* November 10, 1934, p. 170.

33 Fan, "1920–1922," p. 7.

34 Yang Ch'ao-yung, "Chan-chi," p. 64.

35 *Ssu-ch'uan sheng cheng-fu kung-pao,* March 1, 1935.

36 *Chung-kung jen-ming lu,* p. 607. See also *Shun t'ien shih pao,* October 9, 1928, in *Gendai Shina no Kiroku* [Modern China archive], comp. Hatano Ken'ichi (Tokyo, 1924–1932), October 1928 sec., p. 127.

37 For many examples of this rhetoric see Liu Hsiang, *Liu Fu-ch'eng chün-chang chiang-yen chi* [Collected speeches of General Liu Hsiang] ([Chungking] [1927]). On one occasion, Liu himself discussed his army's lack of a sense of larger purpose: "Why do we military men pursue our calling? Originally it was to protect the country and to guard the people. But now there is no ideal; this is the shame of the military" (ibid., p. 27).

38 For the extraordinary story of Liu Hsiang's infatuation with a Taoist mystic in the 1930s, see Hui, "Feng-chien," pp. 168–70; Sun Chen, "An-ch'uan yü chiao-kung" [Pacifying Szechwan and suppressing the Communists], *SCWH,* March 1966, pp. 11–13; and below, chap. 5.

39 Liu Hsiang, *Liu Fu-ch'eng,* p. 3.

40 Sheridan, *Chinese Warlord,* p. 1.

CHAPTER 3

1 For a complete list of districts in each garrison area in 1932, see Li Pai-hung, "Erh-shih nien," pp. 78–80.

2 Ibid.

3 Chung-kuo kung-ch'eng shih-hsüeh hui, ed., *Ssu-ch'uan k'ao-ch'a t'uan pao-kao* [Report of the Szechwan Investigation Commission] (n.p, 1936), *t'ieh-tao* sec., p. 23.

4 Liu Ching, *Ch'uan-K'ang i-shou ch'ien-hou* [How Szechwan and Sikang changed hands]

(Hong Kong, 1956), p. 37. See also *North China Herald*, March 15, 1930, p. 467; Toller (Chungking) to Peiping, July 1, 1930, F.O. 228/4121; and *Pai-jih hsin-wen* (Chengtu), August 1928 and April 1929.

5   See the following: Sun Chen, "Ssu-ch'uan ch'ih-huo yü an-Ch'uan" [Red predations and the pacification of Szechwan], *SCWH*, January 1966, pp. 2–11; Chang Chung-lei, "Ch'ing-mo hsüeh-t'ang," p. 358; Liu Hang-shen, "Jung-mu pan-sheng," *HWTT*, August 5, 1967, p. 24; and Lockhart (Hankow) to Washington, January 14, 1930, S.D. 893.00/P.R. Chungking 19.

6   Li Pai-hung, "Erh-shih nien," pp. 75–78. A report by the Japanese military attaché in Hankow early in 1933 placed Liu Hsiang's strength at 211,500, Liu Wen-hui's at 165,000 Teng Hsi-hou's at 88,000, T'ien Sung-yao's at 59,000, and Yang Sen's at 45,000 (see Tajiri, "Ssu-ch'uan tung-luan kai-kuan" [An overview of the disorders in Szechwan], trans. Yang Fan, *CTSTL*, 1962, no. 4, pp. 49, 61–66.)

7   Chia Wen-chin, "Sui-Hsüan chih shih-hsien chi ch'i shou-fu" [The loss and recovery of Suiting and Hsüanhan], *Tu-li p'ing-lun*, February 25, 1934, p. 13.

8   Lockhart (Hankow) to Washington, November 9, 1929, S.D. 893.00/P.R. Chungking 17.

9   Interview with a former Szechwanese military leader, Taipei, April 28, 1968. For an earlier reference, see *North China Herald*, October 4, 1919, p. 20. In 1940, an American expert on the Chinese army wrote, "Probably the least efficient of the provincial troops are those which come from Szechwan. The higher military leaders are usually opium smokers, and are correspondingly inefficient in military matters" (Evans Fordyce Carlson, *The Chinese Army: Its Organization and Military Efficiency* [New York, 1940], p. 31).

10 Lü, *Ssu-ch'uan nung-ts'un ching-chi*, p. 164. Another report on the low quality of Szechwanese army officers and the bad discipline of provincial forces is found in Shih Chin, "Ssu-ch'uan chiao-fei ti hsien-chüeh wen-t'i" [The most pressing question for bandit suppression in Szechwan], *Shih-tai kung-lun*, February 1, 1935, p. 26.

11 Toller (Chungking) to Peiping, March 31, 1931, F.O. 371/15469.

12 Graham Peck, *Through China's Wall* (Boston, 1940), pp. 170–71.

13 Chou K'ai-ch'ing, "Chien-she hsin Ssu-ch'uan ti chan-wang" [Outlook for creation of a new Szechwan], *KWCP*, May 27, 1935. See also Chang P'ei-chün, "Ssu-ch'uan cheng-ch'üan chih hsi-t'ung chi hsing-cheng hsien-chuang" [The present state of Szechwan's system of political power and administration], *Fu-hsing yüeh-k'an* 3, no. 6/7 (March 1935).

14 Kuang Wen [pseud.], "Fang-ch'ü shih-tai chih Ssu-ch'uan chün-cheng-wu hsi-t'ung" [Szechwan's military administrative systems during the garrison area period], *SCWH*, October 1966, pp. 7–8. This article is reprinted without acknowledgment from *SCYP*, August 1933, pp. 174–78.

15 Chang P'ei-chün, "Ssu-ch'uan cheng-ch'üan."

16 "Erh-shih i chün jung-ch'ü ko hsien hsien cheng kai-k'uang" [District government conditions in the Twenty-first Army garrison area], *SCYP*, September 1933, p. 148.

17 Hui, "Feng-chien," p. 164.

18 Chou, "Chien-she."

19 Chang P'ei-chün, "Ssu-ch'uan cheng-ch'üan."

20 Hu, "Shu yu tsa-kan," p. 18. Many district gazetteers provide excellent illustrations of this point; see, for example, *Mien-yang hsien chih* [Gazetteer of Mienyang *hsien*] (Mienyang, 1932; reprinted Taipei, 1967), *chüan* 4, pp. 5 ff.

21 See for example *Lu hsien chih*, *chüan* 2, pp. 63–65b.

22 T'ien, "Ssu-ch'uan wen-t'i."

23 Hua sheng [pseud.], "Min-kuo ch'u-nien chih Ssu-ch'uan ts'ai-cheng" [Szechwan's finances in the early Republic], *SCWH*, April 1966, pp. 6–7. See also Chang Hsiao-mei, *Ssu-ch'uan ching-chi ts'an-k'ao tzu-liao* [Research materials on the Szechwan economy] (Shanghai, 1939), p. C-153; and Feng Ho-fa, *Chung-kuo nung-ts'un*, p. 829.

24 Li Ming-liang, "Ssu-ch'uan nung-min ching-chi ch'iung-k'un ti yüan-yin" [Reasons for

the economic difficulties of Szechwan's peasants], *SCYP*, June 1933, pp. 1–28. Luhsien was formerly called Luchou. See also Li Pai-hung, "Erh-shih nien," p. 83.

25 *North China Herald*, January 12, 1929, p. 58.

26 Li Pai-hung, "Erh-shih nien," p. 83. Szechwan was not unique in this type of taxation. Similar cases in Amoy and Kansu are described, respectively, in O. Edmund Clubb, *Twentieth Century China* (New York, 1964), p. 187, and Sheridan, *Chinese Warlord*, p. 25.

27 Li Pai-hung, "Erh-shih nien," p. 83.

28 For an extended discussion of the role of Chungking in Liu Hsiang's garrison area, see Robert A. Kapp, "Chungking As a Center of Warlord Power," in *The Chinese City Between Two Worlds*, ed. Mark Elvin and G. William Skinner, Stanford University Press, forthcoming. See also *Pa hsien chih* [Gazetteer of Pa *hsien*] (Chungking, 1939; reprinted Taipei, 1967); Lu Ssu-hung, *Hsin Ch'ung-ch'ing* (n.p., 1939); and Wu Chi-sheng, *Hsin-tu chien-wen lu* [The story of the new capital] (Shanghai, 1940).

29 See for example Liu Hang-shen, "Jung-mu pan sheng," *HWTT*, July 29, 1967, pp. 24–25.

30 Hui, "Feng-chien," p. 163.

31 Interview with a former adviser to Liu Hsiang, Taipei, April 26, 1968.

32 See Handley-Derry (Chungking) to Peiping, July 4, 1928, F.O. 371/13184; Chang P'ei-chün, "Ssu-ch'uan cheng-ch'üan"; and Handley-Derry (Chungking) to Peiping, June 6, 1928, F.O. 371/13227.

33 Liu Hsiang, *Liu Fu-ch'eng*, p. 82.

34 Liu Hang-shen, "Fan Shao-tseng yü Lan Wen-pin" [Fan Shao-tseng and Lan Wen-pin], *Chung-wai tsa-chih*, May 1968, p. 10.

35 Hu, "Shu yu tsa-kan," p. 15.

36 This discussion of land taxation practices in Szechwan derives primarily from the following sources: Chu Hsieh, "Ssu-ch'uan t'ien-fu fu-chia shui chi nung-min ch'i-t'a fu-tan chih chen-hsiang" [Szechwanese land tax and surtaxes and other burdens of farmers], *TFTC*, July 16, 1934, p. 90; Chang Hsiao-mei, *Ching-chi tzu-liao*, p. C-113; Lü, *Ssu-ch'uan nung-ts'un ching-chi*, p. 490; China, Shih-yeh pu, comp., *Chung-kuo ching-chi nien-chien* [Chinese economic yearbook] (Shanghai, 1935), pp. F-295–97; Hui, "Feng-chien," p. 166; Feng, *Chung-kuo nung-ts'un*, p. 829.

37 On advance taxation see Chu, "Nung-min fu-tan"; Li Pai-hung, "Erh-shih nien," pp. 82–83; and Lü, *Ssu-ch'uan nung-ts'un ching chi*, pp. 486–88.

38 Chang P'ei-chün, "Ssu-ch'uan cheng-ch'üan." British observers at Wanhsien noted that "navigation taxes" collected there were not remitted to Liu Hsiang, "who is not amassing money, but are retained by the local general for the upkeep of his troops" (report of Ingram and Stirling, October 10, 1929, F.O. 371/13901).

39 *Ta kung pao* editorial, in *KWCP*, January 1, 1931. See also Hui, "Feng-chien," p. 163.

40 Toller (Chungking) to Peiping, October 9, 1930, F.O. 228/4292 mentions Fan's morphia factory. Wang Ling-chi's business appears in Liu Hang-shen, "Jung-mu pan sheng," *HWTT*, September 23, 1967, p. 23.

41 *Ssu-ch'uan k'ao-ch'a t'uan pao-kao, tien-li* sec., pp. 3, 5, 13, 16.

42 On militarist investment in banks, pawnshops, and the opium trade, see the following: Chang Hsiao-mei, *Ching-chi tzu-liao*, p. M-23; Lü, *Ssu-ch'uan nung-ts'un ching-chi*, pp. 44-45; Kuo Jung-sheng, "Ssu-ch'uan sheng ti-fang yin-hang chih yen-chin" [The evolution of Szechwanese local banks], *SCWH*, December 1967, pp. 1–9; T'ien, "Ssu-ch'uan wen-t'i"; Mei Hsin-ju, "Ssu-ch'uan chih huo-pi" [Szechwanese currency], *TFTC*, July 16, 1934.

43 Hsüeh Shao-ming, *Ch'ien-Tien-Ch'uan lü-hsing chi* [A Kweichow–Yunnan–Szechwan travelogue] (Canton, 1937), pp. 167, 207, 210. Another reference to provincial militarists' acquisition of land appears in a *Ta kung pao* editorial, *KWCP*, January 1, 1931.

44 Lü, *Ssu-ch'uan nung-ts'un ching-chi*, p. 192.

45   T'ien, "Ssu-ch'uan wen-t'i."

46   Hsüeh, *Ch'ien-Tien-Ch'uan*, p. 204. For a general discussion of militarist land ownership, see Lü, *Ssu-ch'uan nung-ts'un ching chi*, pp. 183–85.

47   See Liu Hang-shen, "Fan Shao-tseng yü Lan Wen-pin," pp. 10–13. Also Toller (Chungking) to Peiping, October 20, 1931, F.O. 371/15445; and *Ch'un-ch'iu,* January 1966, p. 21.

48   Liu Hsiang, *Liu Fu-ch'eng*, p. 67.

49   Report of Ingram and Stirling, October 10, 1929, F.O. 371/13901.

50   Liu Hang-shen, "Jung-mu pan sheng," *HWTT*, September 23, 1967, p. 20.

51   Handley-Derry (Chungking) to Peiping, June 6, 1928, F.O. 371/13227. See also Liu Ching, *Ch'uan-k'ang*, p. 10.

52   *Ssu-ch'uan nei-chan hsiang-chi*, p. 100. Fan Shao-tseng's house in Chungking boasted a glassed-in tennis court (Peck, *Through China's Wall*, p. 164).

53   Recollections of Yang Sen. See also Hu, "Shu yu tsa-kan," p. 20; and Liu Hsiang, *Liu Fu-ch'eng*, p. 78.

54   Chang Chung-lei, "Ch'ing-mo hsüeh-t'ang," p. 359. Also Liu Hang-shen, "Fan Shao-tseng yü Lan Wen-pin."

55   Recollections of Yang Sen. Yang also placed family members in high positions; two of his nephews, Yang Han-yü and Yang Han-chung, held major commands in his army during much of the period from 1927 to 1935 (letter from Chou K'ai-ch'ing to the author, April 14, 1969).

56   Toller (Chungking) to Peiping, August 29, 1930, F.O. 228/4308/Doss 83E, p. 3; and *SCWH*, October 1965, p. 10. In addition, see A. Doak Barnett, *China on the Eve of Communist Takeover* (New York, 1963), pp. 217–20.

57   *Ssu-ch'uan nung-min pu pao-kao* [Report of the Szechwan Peasant Bureau] (n.p., [1927]).

58   *Ssu-ch'uan nung-min yün-tung kai-k'uang* [Conditions in the Szechwan peasant movement] (n.p., [1927]).

59   *Nung-min pu pao-kao.*

60   *Nung-min yün-tung.*

61   For detailed accounts of rural antitax movements, see the following: China, Shih-yeh pu, comp., *Erh-shih erh nien lao-tung nien-chien* [1933 Labor yearbook] (Shanghai, 1933), pp. 69–72; *SCYP*, October 1933, pp. 155–56; *SCYP*, October 1934, p. 151.

62   Feng Ho-fa, *Chung-kuo nung-ts'un*, p. 827; also *SCYP*, June 1934, p. 177.

63   On the general problem of agrarian social change in Szechwan, the most useful sources are Lü, *Ssu-ch'uan nung-ts'un ching-chi*, pp. 170-85; Chang Hsiao-mei, *Ching-chi tzu-liao*, p. A-26; Hui, "Feng-chien"; and those portions of Hsüeh, *Ch'ien-Tien-Ch'uan* dealing with Szechwan.

64   On the organization of militia in the *chen* and *hsiang*, see for example *Lu hsien chih, chüan* 2, p. 25b; or *Ho-chiang hsien chih* [Gazetteer of Hochiang *hsien*] (Hochiang, 1929; reprinted Taipei, 1967), *chüan* 3, pp. 11b-13b. For an account of the banditry which gave rise to intensive militia development, see *Hsü-yung hsien chih, chüan* 5, pp. 18–19.

65   See *Nung-min pu pao-kao*. Also *SCYP*, June 1934, pp. 170–80; and Chang Hsiao-mei, *Ching-chi tzu-liao*, p. M-23.

66   *Nung-min pu pao-kao.*

67   Liu Hsiang, *Liu Fu-ch'eng*, p. 71.

68   Hsüeh, *Ch'ien-Tien-Ch'uan*, p. 195.

69   A very important analysis of the militia problem in Szechwan and a discussion of relations between local militia and provincial forces in various sections of Szechwan appears in *Pai-jih hsin-wen* (Chengtu), August 6, 1928, p. 6.

70   *Pa hsien chih, chüan* 17, p. 22b.

71   *West China Missionary News,* June 1927, p. 11.

72   *Asiatic* dispatch from Nanking, October 31, 1934, in unpublished papers of Norman D. Hanwell, Hoover Institution, Stanford, California.

73 *Erh-shih erh nien lao-tung nien-chien,* pp. 69–70.

74 Seizure of militia weaponry had already become a serious problem by the time of the Chengtu Conference of late 1925 (see *Ssu-ch'uan shan-hou hui-i lu,* pt. 2, *chün-cheng* sec., pp. 25, 37).

75 See *SCYP,* May 1933, pp. 166–69, and June 1934, pp. 170–80; also Chang P'ei-chün, "Ssu-ch'uan cheng-ch'üan"; and *CYCL,* pp. 110, 120–30.

76 Spiker (Chungking) to Peking, June 18, 1923, S.D. 893.00/5720; and *North China Herald,* May 26, 1923, p. 507.

77 Davidson (Chungking) to Peking, July 19, 1921, F.O. 228/3273; and *North China Herald,* April 2, 1921.

78 Blunt (Chungking) to London, December 16, 1927, F.O. 371/13183. Also *Ch'ing-nien chün-jen,* November 15, 1933, p. 11; and *Pai-jih hsin-wen,* August 7, 1928, p. 6.

79 Li Ming-liang, "Nung-min ch'iung-k'un."

80 Hui, "Feng-chien," p. 164.

81 Toller (Chungking) to Peiping, November 17, 1930, F.O. 371/17063; and Toller (Chungking) to Peiping, April 30, 1931, F.O. 371/15473.

82 Lampson (Peiping) to London, June 26, 1933, F.O. 371/17063. China, The Maritime Customs, *Decennial Reports,* Vol. 5, no. 1 (1933), p. 491, generally agrees with this assessment but notes that travel was still dangerous in parts of northern Szechwan.

83 Toller (Chungking) to Peiping, September 22, 1930, F.O. 228/4208 Doss. 32S.

84 *Ssu-ch'uan k'ao-ch'a t'uan pao-kao, kung-lu* sec., p. 6. For further information on the construction of modernized roads in Szechwan, see Chang Hsiao-mei, *Ching-chi tzu-liao,* pp. G-8–16; Lü, *Ssu-ch'uan nung-ts'un ching-chi,* pp. 57–59; *SCYP,* November 1934, pp. 159–61; and *HYPK,* pp. 120–22 and accompanying chart.

85 On the Min Sheng Company, see Min-sheng shih-yeh kung-ssu shih-i chou nien chi-nien k'an pien-chi wei-yüan hui, ed., *Min-sheng shih-yeh kung-ssu shih-i chou nien chi-nien k'an* [Commemorative volume on the eleventh anniversary of the Min Sheng Industrial Company] (Shanghai, 1937). Also of note are Shu Hsieh, "Min-sheng kung-ssu fa-chan shih" [History of the development of the Min Sheng Company], *SCWH,* May 1966, pp. 17–20; and Lu Tso-fu, "Ssu-ch'uan Chia-ling chiang san-hsia ti hsiang-ts'un yün-tung" [The rural village movement in the Three Gorges area of the Chialing River in Szechwan], *Chung-hua chiao-yü chieh* 22 (October 1934): 107–12.

86 On the West China Development Company, see Hu Kuang-piao, *Po-chu liu-shih nien* [Living in a turbulent era], 2d ed. (Hong Kong, 1964), pp. 277–310; and Liu Hang-shen, "Jung-mu pan sheng," *HWTT,* September 2, 1967, p. 25, and September 9, 1967, pp. 23–24; also "Industrial Development in West China," *China Journal* 26, no. 4 (1937): 193–95.

87 Chou, "Chien-she."

88 Hui, "Feng-chien," p. 164.

89 Ibid., p. 161. See also Min Cheng, "Ssu-ch'uan ti wei-chi yü Chung-kuo ch'ien-t'u" [Szechwan's crisis and China's future], *Kuo-li Wu-han ta-hsüeh Ssu-ch'uan t'ung-hsüeh hui hui-k'an* 1, no. 2 (1934).

90 Chou, "Chien-she."

CHAPTER 4

1 *Shih-chieh jih-pao,* August 18, 1926, in Hatano, *Gendai,* August 1926, sec., p. 245.

2 Adams (Chungking) to Peking, January 7, 1927, S.D. 893.00/8465. Liu Hsiang's former military school mentor and trusted division commander Wang Ling-chi initially opposed the collaboration with the Kuomintang. However, after an angry session with Liu Hsiang, Wang resumed his support of Liu (see Liu Hang-shen, "Jung-mu pan sheng," *HWTT,* July 15, 1967, p. 21).

3 Agnes Smedley, *The Great Road: The Life and Times of Chu Teh* (New York, 1956), p. 172.

4 Chou, *Min-kuo jen-wu*, p. 149.
5 Smedley, *The Great Road*, p. 172. See also Liu Hang-shen, "Jung-mu pan sheng," *HWTT*, July 15, 1967, p. 21.
6 Smedley, *The Great Road*, p. 179.
7 Ibid., p. 180.
8 *Ch'ing-tang shih-lu* [The record of party purification] ([Nanking], 1928), p. 341.
9 Liu Hang-shen, "Jung-mu pan sheng," *HWTT*, July 15, 1967, p. 21.
10 Liu Hsiang, *Liu Fu-ch'eng*, p. 10.
11 Ibid., p. 2
12 Ibid., p. 82. Expressions of this attitude recur often in Liu's speeches.
13 Ibid., p. 71.
14 *TFTC*, January 10, 1929, p. 205. See also Lockhart (Hankow) to Washington, December 20, 1928, S.D. 893.00/P.R. Chungking 6.
15 Lockhart (Hankow) to Washington, December 20, 1928, S.D. 893.00/P.R. Chungking 6. Also *TFTC*, January 10, 1929, p. 205.
16 The text of the General Order is found in Chou, "Chien-she."
17 Chou, "Chien-she."
18 Hu Kuang-piao, *Liu-shih nien*, p. 279.
19 Hui, "Feng-chien," p. 160.
20 This general point can be verified virtually at random. See, for example, the Peiping *Shih pao*, *KWCP*, or *TFTC*.
21 Two of the many examples of this are *Nei-cheng nien-chien* [Internal administration yearbook] (Shanghai, 1935), and *Ts'ai-cheng nien-chien* [Financial yearbook] (Shanghai, 1935). The former was compiled by the Interior Ministry of the Government of China and the latter by the Finance Ministry. The same phenomenon is evident in the privately compiled financial history by Chia Shih-i, *Min-kuo hsü ts'ai-cheng shih* [Financial history of the Republic, continued] (Shanghai, 1932–34; reprinted Taipei, 1962). Those figures concerning Szechwan that do appear in Chia Shih-i's study are hopelessly incomplete and out of date.
22 Hu Kuang-piao, *Liu-shih nien*, p. 280. See also Lockhart (Hankow) to Washington, October 11, 1929, S.D. 893.00/P.R. Chungking 16. Central government control of Szechwan's postal and telegraph systems was re-established only in 1929, after a long lapse (see China, The Maritime Customs, *Decennial Reports* 5, no. 1 [1933], p. 485).
23 Chang P'ei-chün, "Ssu-ch'uan cheng-ch'üan."
24 Lockhart (Hankow) to Washington, July 9, 1928, S.D. 893.00/P.R. Chungking 1.
25 Toller (Chungking) to Peiping, March 9, 1933, F.O. 371/17061. See also Chao T'ing-hua, *Shih-nien lai Chung-kuo hung-chün* [The Chinese Red Army over the past ten years] (Hankow, 1938), p. 33.
26 Chou, "Chien-she." Szechwan was not unique in this regard. In 1929, several provinces were "retaining" all funds. See the speech concerning financial unification of China given by Minister of Finance T.V. Soong on January 11, 1929, in Lo Chia-lun, ed., *Ko-ming wen-hsien* [Documents of the Revolution], vol. 24 (Taipei, 1961), p. 4,871.
27 Toller (Chungking) to Peiping, July 7, 1930, F.O. 228/4121. For a good account of the travails of the Salt Inspectorate officials in Szechwan and the constant negotiations with military officials over revenue remissions, see the report of F. Hussey-Freke, associate chief inspector of salt revenue, to Finance Minister T. V. Soong, enclosed in Lampson (Nanking) to London, November 20, 1930, F.O. 405/268 (Confidential Print).
28 Lockhart (Hankow) to Washington, August 7, 1929, S.D. 893.00/P.R. Chungking 14. Also Toller (Chungking) to Peiping, September 22, 1930, F.O. 228/4208 Doss. 32S.
29 *SCYP*, March 1934, p. 51. The tax was a levy on postal parcels.
30 Toller (Chungking) to Peiping, January 21, 1933, F.O. 371/17060.
31 For an account of the Reorganization Crisis see Sheridan, *Chinese Warlord*, pp. 240–67.

32 Handley-Derry (Chungking) to Peiping, January 6, 1930, F.O. 228/4116. See also Lockhart (Hankow) to Washington, April 22, 1930, S.D. 893.00/P.R. Chungking 22.
33 Toller to R. N. Maclean, August 11, 1930, encl. in Toller (Chungking) to Peiping, August 11, 1930, F.O. 228/4123.
34 *Ta kung pao,* September 14, 1930, in Hatano, *Gendai,* September 1930 sec., p. 207.
35 Liu Hang-shen, "Jung-mu pan sheng," *HWTT,* August 19, 1967, p. 24.
36 Walter Toller to Col. G. Badham-Thornhill, October 18, 1930, encl. in Toller (Chungking) to Peiping, October 18, 1930, F.O. 228/4125.
37 *Chen pao,* January 12, 1931, in Hatano, *Gendai,* January 1931 sec., p. 96. Liu declined at the last minute. Chiang was offended, and assumed that Liu's "illness" was more political than physical. See also Toller (Chungking) to Peiping, March 9, 1931, F.O. 676/81.
38 Blunt (Chungking) to London, December 16, 1927, F.O. 371/13183.
39 Sokobin (Chungking) to Peking, January 17, 1920, S.D. 893.00/3332.
40 "Chengtu Intelligence Report," March Quarter, 1922, encl. in Alston (Peking) to London, May 5, 1922, F.O. 371/8027. See also Hewlett (Chengtu) to Peking, December 5, 1921, encl. in Alston (Peking) to London, May 5, 1922, F.O. 371/8027.
41 Hewlett (Chengtu) to Peking, December 24, 1921, F.O. 371/8027; and Poincaré (Paris) to Hardinge (Paris), May 10, 1922, encl. in Hardinge (Paris) to London, May 12, 1922, F.O. 371/8027.
42 Commercial Counsellor H. H. Fox (Peking) to London, March 15, 1926, encl. in Macleay (Peking) to London, March 18, 1926, F.O. 228/3530. See also Archer (Chungking) to Peking, August 28, 1925, F.O. 228/3529.
43 Archer (Chungking) to Peking, August 19, 1924, F.O. 228/3140. There was no foreign-capitalized industry at all in the Chengtu Consular District in mid-1924 (see Ogden [Chengtu] to Peking, June 17, 1924, F.O. 228/3140).
44 *SCYP,* July 1934, p. 161.
45 Hewlett (Chengtu) to Peking, December 21, 1921, encl. in Alston (Peking) to London, May 5, 1922, F.O. 371/8027.
46 Chang Yung, "Ch'ung-ch'ing tsung kung hui ti fa-chan" [The development of the Chungking General Labor Associations], *SCWH,* June 1967, pp. 27–28.
47 Ho Ch'i-fang, *Wu Yü-chang t'ung-chih ko-ming ku-shih* [Comrade Wu Yü-chang's revolutionary story] (Hong Kong, 1949), p. 23. See also Lu Shih-t'i, "Ti-i tz'u chi-nien chou tang-wu pao-kao" [First party affairs report], *Ch'ing-tang t'e-k'an,* June 30, 1927, pp. 84–106, and especially pp. 87–90.
48 *SCYP,* July 1934, pp. 161–73.
49 Chang Yung, "Tso-yu p'ai fen-cheng yü Ch'ung-ch'ing kung-yün ti yin-hsiang" [Strife between left and right and its influence on the Chungking labor movement], *SCWH,* July 1967, pp. 26–28. See also Chou K'ai-ch'ing, "Ssu-ch'uan tang-wu chih hui-ku" [A review of Party affairs in Szechwan], *SCWH,* July 1964, p. 9.
50 Chang Yung, "Tso-yu p'ai," p. 27.
51 *Ch'ing-tang shih-lu,* p. 342.
52 Lu Shih-t'i, "Pao-kao," p. 91. See also *SCWH,* November 1967, pp. 11–13; and Chang Yung, "Tso-yu p'ai," pp. 26–28. For a good contemporary account of Liu Hsiang's assault on the Kuomintang Right, see "Ssu-ch'uan sheng tang-pu chih-yüan pao-kao" [Report by members of the Szechwan party bureau], *Ch'ing-tang shih-lu,* p. 341.
53 *Ch'ing-tang shih-lu,* pp. 342, 346.
54 Ibid., p. 475.
55 See the following dispatches: Pratt (Chungking) to Peking, March 11, 1927, F.O. 228/3273; MacMurray (Peking) to Washington, March 31, 1927, S.D. 893.00/8589; Scott (Hankow) to Peking, April 7, 1927, F.O. 228/3433. While the British consulate in Chungking was reopened in November 1927, the American consulate remained closed for years, its duties partially absorbed by the consulate general in Hankow.

56 Scott (Hankow) to Peking, April 7, 1927, F.O. 228/3433.
57 A good account of this critical incident is found in *Chen pao*, May 14, 1927, in Hatano, *Gendai*, May 1927 sec., p. 212. Also see Lu Shih-t'i, "Pao-kao," p. 93.
58 Li Yün-han, *Jung-kung*, p. 667.
59 *Chen pao*, May 14, 1927, in Hatano, *Gendai*, May 1927 sec., p. 212.
60 For examples of militarist assaults on suspected subversives in Chungking and Chengtu schools, see *Chiao-yü tsa-chih*, September 1930, p. 119, and December 1930, p. 126. See also *Huang Pao*, March 21, 1928, in Hatano, *Gendai*, March 1928 sec., p. 296.
61 Lu Shih-t'i, "Pao-kao," p. 93.
62 *Ch'ing-tang t'e-k'an*, June 10, 1927, pp. 5–6.
63 *Ssu-ch'uan tang-wu chou-pao* [Szechwan party affairs weekly], December 22, 1927.
64 Lu Shih-t'i, "Pao-kao," p. 96. See also Chou, "Tang-wu hui-ku," p. 9.
65 Chung-kuo kuo-min tang chung-yang chih-hsing wei-yüan hui, tang-shih shih-liao pien-tsuan wei-yüan hui, comp., *Min-kuo shih-pa nien Chung-kuo kuo-min tang nien-chien* [1929 Kuomintang yearbook] (Nanking, 1929), p. 630. The present account of Kuomintang development in Szechwan follows the information in this yearbook and in the 1934 Kuomintang Yearbook. Minor variations in chronology and terminology appear in Chou, "Tang-wu hui-ku." See also Lu Shih-t'i, "Pao-kao," pp. 84–106.
66 *Min-kuo shih-pa nien Chung-kuo kuo-min tang nien-chien*, pp. 630–31, 739.
67 For a biography of Tseng K'uo-ch'ing, see Chung-kuo kuo-min tang chung-yang chih-hsing wei-yüan hui, tang-shih shih-liao pien-tsuan wei-yüan hui, comp., *Min-kuo erh-shih san nien Chung-kuo kuo-min tang nien-chien* [1934 Kuomintang yearbook] (Nanking, 1934), *ping* section, pp. 102–03.
68 Chou, "Tang-wu hui-ku," pp. 6–11. For a similarly dismal tale of Party failure in an important Yangtze district, see *Lu hsien chih, chüan* 2, pp. 23 ff.
69 Lockhart (Hankow) to Washington, September 9, 1929, S.D. 893.00/P.R. Chungking 15. The Szechwanese sent no delegates to the conference (see Lo, *Ko-ming wen-hsien*, vol. 24, p. 4,863).
70 Toller (Chungking) to Peiping, March 31, 1931, F.O. 371/15469.
71 Chou, "Chien-she." See also *KWCP*, March 11, 1935.
72 Toller (Chungking) to Peiping, February 11, 1933, F.O. 371/17061. Also *KWCP*, March 11, 1935.
73 H. G. W. Woodhead, ed., *The China year Book, 1932* (Shanghai, 1932), p. 542; and *KWCP*, April 6, 1931.
74 Liu Hang-shen, "Jung-mu pan sheng," *HWTT*, August 26, 1967, p. 24. For terms of the loan and the critical reaction of one of China's most respected newspapers, see *KWCP*, August 3, 1931 and August 10, 1931. In concluding its criticism of the loan, the Tientsin *Ta kung pao* said, "The garrison areas of Szechwan have always been beyond the reach of the central government's law and order. Of all the provinces, the central government is most impotent in Szechwan. What 'rehabilitation' is there to speak of in places like this? How could the Finance Ministry make a case for this loan, and how could it be approved?" (*KWCP*, August 3, 1931).
75 Liu Hang-shen, "Jung-mu pan sheng," *HWTT*, August 26, 1967, pp. 24–25.
76 Recollections of Liu Hang-shen.
77 Kan Chi-yung, "Ju-ho kai-chin chin-jih Ssu-ch'uan" [How to improve today's Szechwan], *SCYP*, February 1933, pp. 1–16.
78 Chou K'ai-ch'ing, ed., *Chiao-fei yü ch'iu-Ch'uan* [Bandit-suppression and the salvation of Szechwan] (n.p., 1933), unpaginated. The quotations are from two speeches entitled "Ch'iu-Ch'uan chih tse tsai yü Ch'uan-jen" [Responsibility for saving Szechwan rests with the Szechwanese] and "Chung-yang tui Liu Hsiang chih tse-wang" [The Responsibilities which the central government has placed on Liu Hsiang].

CHAPTER 5

1 Huang Chü, "Ch'uan-chün chiao-fei chih ching-kuo" [Bandit-suppression experiences of the Szechwan armies], *Fu-hsing yüeh-k'an* 3, no. 6/7 (March 1935). A thorough treatment of the Two-Liu War is found in *Ssu-ch'uan nei-chan hsiang-chi.*

2 Wang Chien-min, *Chung-kuo kung-ch'an tang shih-kao* [Draft history of the Chinese Communist Party] (Taipei, 1965), p. 218.

3 Chou K'ai-ch'ing, "Ch'uan-pei chiao-fei chün-shih chih kai-kuan" [Views of bandit suppression in northern Szechwan], *KWCP*, April 30, 1935.

4 Wang, *Kung-ch'an tang*, p. 218.

5 Chang Kuo-t'ao, "Hui-i," *Ming-pao yüeh-k'an*, September 1969, p. 74.

6 Ibid., p. 73.

7 Huang Tzu-ching, ed., "Ch'uan-Shan ch'ü ko-ming ken-chü-ti tzu-liao hsüan-chi" [Selected materials on the Szechwan–Shensi revolutionary base], *CTSTL*, 1958, no. 3, p. 105. See also B. Perlin, "Struggle for Soviets in Szechwan," *China Today*, February 1936, pp. 94–95; and Nym Wales [Helen Foster Snow], *Inside Red China* (New York, 1939), p. 139.

8 Tung Ming [pseud.], "Ch'uan-sheng ch'ih-huo chi Ch'uan-chün chiao-fei chih ching-kuo" [Red predations in Szechwan and the Szechwanese armies' bandit-suppression experiences], *KWCP*, November 5, 1934.

9 Chou, "Ch'uan-pei chiao-fei."

10 Huang Tzu-ching, ed., "Ch'uan-Shan ch'ü," p. 105. Chang Kuo-t'ao has revealed that the Communists originally intended to hold only the T'ung-Nan-Pa districts (see "Hui-i," *Ming-pao yüeh-k'an*, September 1969, p. 75).

11 Hsün Shih [pseud.], "Ch'uan tung-pei chiao-ch'ih yin-hsiang chi" [Impressions of Red-suppression in northeastern Szechwan], *KWCP*, May 20, 1935.

12 Wales, *Inside Red China*, p. 59. Tung Ming estimated Hsü's strength in late 1933 at about 40,000 ("Ch'uan-sheng ch'ih-huo"). The maximum figure of 80,000 appears in Wales, *Inside Red China*, p. 61. Wang Chien-min cites the 100,000 figure, but this may include "Red Guards" and other ill-armed secondary defense forces (see *Kung-ch'an tang*, p. 219). The figure of 200,000 regular Red Army troops mentioned in *Tou-cheng*, June 30, 1934, p. 21, is undoubtedly inflated.

13 To Chang Kuo-t'ao, the natives of northeastern Szechwan seemed monumentally backward and ignorant (see "Hui-i," *Ming-pao yüeh-k'an*, November 1969, pp. 98–99).

14 The best account of developments in the Communist areas of northern Szechwan is the series of articles by Hsün Shih in *KWCP*, collectively called "Yin-hsiang chi," published between March 11 and May 20, 1935. Also useful is Feng Shao-lieh, *Shih-nien hung-chün* [Ten years of the Red Army] (Shanghai, 1938), pp. 24–25; and Norman D. Hanwell, "The Chinese Red Army," *Asia* 36 (May 1936): 317–22.

15 Feng Shao-lieh, *Shih-nien hung-chün*, pp. 39–43. See also *Tou-cheng*, June 30, 1934, p. 21.

16 Feng Shao-lieh, *Shih-nien hung-chün*, p. 41. Also Hsün Shih, "Yin-hsiang chi," *KWCP*, May 20, 1935.

17 Chang Kuo-t'ao, "Hui-i," *Ming-pao yüeh-k'an*, September 1969, p. 75.

18 Tung, "Ch'uan-sheng ch'ih-huo." See also Huang Tzu-ching, ed., "Ch'uan-Shan ch'ü," pp. 105–06; and Chang Kuo-t'ao, "Hui-i," *Ming-pao yüeh-k'an*, November 1969, pp. 97–98.

19 Tung, "Ch'uan-sheng ch'ih-huo."

20 Wales, *Inside Red China*, pp. 139, 59.

21 *KWCP*, March 11, 1935, and Huang Chü, "Chiao-fei ching-kuo." Later, T'ien made much of his army's solitary struggle against the Communists in 1933 while other provincial armies were resting and fortifying themselves (see *Chiao-fei t'e-k'an*, July 21, 1934, p. 8).

22 Sun, "Ch'ih-huo yü an-Ch'uan," p. 8.

23 *Tu-li p'ing-lun,* November 5, 1933, p. 3.
24 This is taken from a translation by Norman Hanwell from the Tientsin *Yung pao,* the date of which Hanwell calls "late October 1933." It is part of an unpublished compilation of Chinese news coverage of Communism in Szechwan by Hanwell. *KWCP,* March 11, 1935, contains the assertion that Hsüanhan was taken by eleven Communist soldiers.
25 *KWCP,* March 11, 1935.
26 *Ch'ing-nien chün-jen,* December 31, 1934, pp. 12–13. See also Wallis (Chungking) to Peiping, April 6, 1934, F.O. 371/18081.
27 *KWCP,* March 11, 1935, and Chou, "Ch'uan-pei chiao-fei." It was rumored that during the brief period when Chungking was threatened, 150 million *yüan* was remitted to banks in Shanghai (*KWCP,* March 11, 1935).
28 Tung, "Ch'uan-sheng ch'ih-huo."
29 Huang Chü, "Chiao-fei ching-kuo."
30 Details of some of these exaggerated claims appear in *Ch'ing-nien chün-jen,* December 31, 1934, p. 12.
31 See *KWCP,* April 23, 1934, September 3, 1934, and April 8, 1935. Also *Ch'ing-nien chün-jen,* November 15, 1933, p. 10.
32 Sun, "An-Ch'uan yü chiao-kung," p. 12. See also Hui, "Feng-chien," pp. 168–70.
33 *KWCP,* April 8, 1935. Wang was also said to have alarmed Liu Hsiang by amassing unauthorized power and by attempting to gain control of the remnants of Liu Ts'un-hou's Twenty-third Army (see Liu Hang-shen, "Jung-mu pan sheng," *HWTT,* September 23, 1967, pp. 20–21).
34 *KWCP,* May 20, 1935.
35 T'ien, "Ssu-ch'uan wen-t'i."
36 The best account of the financial crisis of 1934 is Chang Yü-chiu, "Ssu-ch'uan chih chin-yung k'ung-pu yü Liu Hsiang tung-hsia" [Szechwan's currency panic and Liu Hsiang's eastward journey], *Yin-hang chou-k'an,* December 4, 1934, pp. 11–20. See also Lin I-ts'ai, "Fei-huan chung Ch'uan Ch'ien ts'ai-cheng chih nan-kuan" [Financial crisis in Szechwan and Kweichow in the midst of Communist disturbances], *KWCP,* June 3, 1935.
37 Lin, "Fei-huan nan-kuan."
38 Hua Sheng, "Min-ch'u ts'ai-cheng," pp. 8–9. This article details the bond issues and their amounts.
39 T'ien, "Ssu-ch'uan wen-t'i." Decline of the opium export trade is also mentioned in Hsüeh, *Ch'ien-Tien-Ch'uan,* p. 171.
40 T'ien, "Ssu-ch'uan wen-t'i."
41 China, Ch'uan-kuo ching-chi wei-yüan hui, ed., *Ssu-ch'uan k'ao-ch'a pao-kao shu* [Report on Szechwan] (Shanghai, 1935), p. 57.
42 Hsüeh, *Ch'ien-Tien-Ch'uan,* p. 186. A similar picture of depression and decline in T'ien Sung-yao's headquarters city of T'ungch'uan appears in ibid., p. 195.
43 See T'ien, "Ssu-ch'uan wen-t'i," and Chou, "Ch'uan-pei chiao-fei." Lin I-ts'ai, "Fei-huan nan-kuan," numbers the refugees in the affected districts of northern Szechwan at 300,000.
44 Tung, "Ch'uan-sheng ch'ih-huo." See also Huang Tzu-ching, ed., "Ch'uan-Shan ch'ü," p. 107.
45 *KWCP,* September 3, 1934, and May 20, 1935.
46 *KWCP,* September 10, 1934.
47 *KWCP,* September 17, 1934.
48 Chou, "Ch'uan-pei chiao-fei."
49 Liu Hang-shen, "Jung-mu pan sheng," *HWTT,* September 30, 1967, p. 23.
50 *KWCP,* October 22, 1934.
51 *KWCP,* November 19, 1934.

52 Szechwan's emergence to prominence in the press is clearly illustrated in such publications as *KWCP, TFTC,* the Tientsin *Ta kung pao,* and the *North China Herald.*
53 *KWCP,* December 2, 1934. The full name of the staff corps was *Kuo-min cheng-fu chün-shih wei-yüan hui wei-yüan chang hsing-ying ts'an-mou t'uan* [Staff corps of the headquarters of the chairman of the military affairs committee of the National Government].
54 Ho Kuo-kuang, *Pa-shih tzu-shu* [Recollections at eighty] (Taipei, 1964), p. 26.
55 *KWCP,* November 26, 1934, and ibid., December 2, 1934.
56 Unpublished recollections of Liu Hang-shen. See *SCYP,* January 1935, p. 42.
57 Perlin, "Soviets," (continued), *China Today,* March 1936, p. 115. See also Hu Yü-kao, *Kung-fei hsi-ts'uan chi* [Record of the Communists' westward trek] (Kweiyang, 1946), p. 302.

CHAPTER 6

1   *KWCP,* November 26, 1934. See also ibid., January 21, 1935, for another early expression of this sentiment.
2   *KWCP,* January 21, 1935.
3   *SCYP,* January 1935, p. 221.
4   Ho Kuo-kuang, *Pa-shih tzu-shu,* p. 26.
5   *SCYP,* January 1935, p. 42.
6   Davidson (Chungking) to London, April 30, 1935, F.O. 371/19303.
7   Anthony Garavente, "The Long March," *China Quarterly* 22 (April–June 1965): 117.
8   Edgar Snow, *Red Star Over China* (New York, 1938), pp. 180–81.
9   Hu Yü-kao, *Kung-fei hsi-ts'uan chi,* p. 607.
10 *SCYP,* January 1935, p. 226. Hu Yü-kao states that in January and February Hsü made a feint into Shensi and was repulsed (*Kung-fei hsi-ts'uan chi,* p. 583).
11 Ibid., pp. 583, 586.
12 Ibid., p. 592.
13 Ibid., p. 607. This date is also used by Ho Kan-chih in *A History of the Modern Chinese Revolution* (Peking, 1959), p. 207. In *Chung-kuo kung-ch'an tang shih-kao,* vol. 2, Wang Chien-min dates the meeting of the two forces June 14 (p. 647) and June 15 (p. 727). Jerome Ch'en uses June 12 in *Mao and the Chinese Revolution* (London, 1965), p. 192. Neither Stuart Schram, in his biography of Mao, nor Anthony Garavente in his article on the Long March, nor Dick Wilson in *The Long March 1935: The Epic of Chinese Communism's Survival* (London, 1971) specifies the date of first contact between the two armies, though Wilson discloses that the main forces of the First and Fourth Front armies met near Moukung on July 20 (p. 189).
14 Stuart Schram, *Mao Tse-tung* (Harmondsworth, Middlesex, 1967), pp. 187–88. Ho Lung and Hsiao K'o went from Hupei through Kweichow and Yunnan into Sikang in 1936, and Szechwanese armies moved to fend off their advance. But Ho Lung never created the crisis in Szechwan that Chu Te and Mao Tse-tung had caused (see Ho Kuo-kuang, *Pa-shih tzu-shu,* p. 22).
15 *Ch'ing-nien chün-jen,* April 30, 1935, p. 3.
16 Berger (Tientsin) to Washington, August 15, 1935, S.D. 893.00/P.R. Tientsin 86. See also E. R. Leach to I. Kinloch, August 5, 1935, encl. in Butterfield and Swire (London) to Foreign Office (received September 16, 1935), F.O. 371/19307.
17 Liu Hang-shen, "Jung-mu pan sheng," *HWTT,* October 21, 1967, p. 24.
18 For discussion of troop movements in western Szechwan, see China, Kuo-fang pu shih-cheng chü [History Bureau, Ministry of Defense], *Chiao-fei chan-shih* [History of the bandit suppression wars], vol. 10 (Taipei, 1962), pp. 899–958 and accompanying maps.
19 Davidson (Chungking) to London, April 30, 1935, F.O. 371/19303. These forces were commanded by Hsü Yüan-ch'üan and Shang-kuan Yün-hsiang. See *SCYP,* January 1935, p. 226.

20 Ho Kuo-kuang, *Pa-shih tzu-shu*, p. 24.
21 Sun Chen, "Chiao-kung yü t'ao-ni" [Suppressing Communists and punishing rebels], *SCWH*, June 1966, pp. 1–13. T'ien's dismissal at this time marked the end of his career as a militarist.
22 Interview of Gen. Chou Hua-nan with Col. William Whitson. I am grateful to Lt. Col. Harry Collier for the opportunity to read the text of this interview in Taipei in 1968.
23 *KWCP*, January 1, 1935.
24 A report on the ceremonies at the formal establishment of the provincial government will be found in Davidson (Chungking) to Peiping, February 11, 1935; F.O. 371/19307. See also *KWCP*, February 18, 1935. The provincial government moved from Chungking to Chengtu, the traditional provincial capital, in July 1935 (see Berger [Tientsin] to Washington, August 15, 1935, S.D. 893.00/13213).
25 Chou, "Chien-she." See also *KWCP*, January 1, 1935.
26 For the text of these regulations, see Ch'eng Mou-hsing, *Chiao-fei ti-fang hsing-cheng chih-tu* [Bandit suppression local administrative systems] (Shanghai, 1936), pp. 30–34.
27 Liu Hang-shen, "Jung-mu pan sheng," *HWTT*, October 21, 1967, p. 23. See also *CYCL*, p. 23; and Teng Han-hsiang, *Teng Ming-chieh hsien-sheng yen-lun chi* [Collected speeches of Teng Han-hsiang] ([Chengtu], 1937), p. 90.
28 Ho Kuo-kuang, *Pa-shih tzu-shu*, pp. 34–35.
29 Sun, "Chiao-kung yü t'ao-ni," pp. 10–11.
30 Letter of E. R. Leach to the *Times* of London, October 31, 1935, printed in the *Times* of London, December 3, 1935.
31 Yang Yung-t'ai, *Yang Yung-t'ai hsien-sheng yen-lun chi* [Collected addresses of Yang Yung-t'ai] (Jesselton, Sabah, 1965), p. 46. The texts of most of the central government's local administrative reform measures are reproduced in Ch'eng, *Ti-fang*.
32 Chou K'ai-ch'ing, "Ts'e-ting Ssu-ch'uan wei k'ang-Jih ken-chü-ti chih ching-kuo" [Experiences in making Szechwan a base for anti-Japanese resistance], *SCWH*, August 1969, p. 4. Yang's influence on Chiang Kai-shek was very strong in 1935 and 1936. This is widely believed to have been a factor in Yang's assassination in 1936, while he was governor of Hupei. See also Li Huang, "Chi-ch'i hsi-cheng pin wei shuang" [An account of the anticommunist campaign in 1933] (cont.), *Chuan-chi wen-hsüeh*, September 1968, p. 18.
33 The special inspectorate system is thoroughly treated, with documentation, in Ch'eng *Ti-fang*, pp. 48–78. See also *HYPK*, pp. 4–5.
34 Chou, "Chien-she."
35 *Chün-cheng hsün-k'an*, June 10, 1935, p. 102.
36 *SCYP*, May 1935, pp. 211–12; and *HYPK*, p. 116.
37 Yang Yung-t'ai, *Yen-lun chi*, p. 47.
38 *CYCL*, pp. 5, 20. For another discussion of the duties of the special administrative inspectors, see Teng Han-hsiang, *Teng Ming-chieh*, pp. 3–4.
39 The position of the special administrative inspectors relative to the provincial government is discussed by Yang Yung-t'ai (see *Yen-lun chi*, pp. 13–14).
40 *CYCL*, p. 80.
41 For an excellent description of district government reorganization in Szechwan in 1935, see Mi Ch'ing-yün, "Chiang-fei huo-Ch'uan chi" [The record of the bandit Chiang's predations in Szechwan], *CTSTL*, 1962, no. 4, pp. 85–86. See also *HYPK*, p. 13.
42 *SCYP*, September 1936, p. 52. See also Ssu-ch'uan sheng cheng-fu [Szechwan Provincial Government], ed., *Ssu-ch'uan sheng kai-k'uang* [Conditions in Szechwan] (Chengtu, 1939), p. 15.
43 Mi, "Chiang-fei," pp. 87–88.
44 *CYCL*, p. 14.
45 Mi, "Chiang-fei," p. 89.
46 *SCYP*, June 1935, pp. 212–14. Also *CYCL*, p. 14.

47 *1936 pao-kao*, p. 2.
48 *CYCL*, p. 20. See also Teng Han-hsiang, *Teng Ming-chieh*, p. 12. For an example of the regulations, see *CYCL*, pp. 124–30.
49 Hua Sheng [pseud.], "Ssu-ch'uan chih hsien ti-fang ts'ai-cheng" [Szechwan's district and local finance], *SCWH*, September 1966, p. 9. See also *HYPK*, p. 117.
50 *Chung-yang yin-hang chou-k'an*, August 1935, pp. 1730–31. Also *HYPK*, p. 118.
51 Lü, *Ssu-ch'uan nung-ts'un ching-chi*, p. 25.
52 Chang Hsiao-mei, *Ching-chi tzu-liao*, pp. C–8–12.
53 Hua, "Ti-fang ts'ai-cheng," pp. 1–9. See also *KWCP*, April 30, 1935.
54 *Ssu-ch'uan sheng kai-k'uang*, p. 68.
55 *CYCL*, p. 45. The speech is dated May 18, 1935.
56 *SCYP*, June, 1935, p. 161. See also *HYPK*, p. 124. With the exception of the Kweichow highway, the portions of the interprovincial highways listed as completed in 1935 were actually already-existing roads between various points in Szechwan, such as Chengtu and Mienyang to the northeast or Chengtu and Yaan to the west.
57 *Ssu-ch'uan sheng kai-k'uang*, pp. 26–27.
58 A competent discussion of the New Life Movement is Samuel Chu, "The New Life Movement, 1934–1937," in *Researches in the Social Sciences on China,* ed. John E. Lane (New York, 1957). The Confucian revival in Nationalist China is well treated in Mary C. Wright, *The Last Stand of Chinese Conservatism: The T'ung-Chih Restoration, 1862–1874* (Stanford, 1962), pp. 300–12.
59 Chou, "K'ang-jih ken-chü-ti," p. 2.
60 *KWCP*, March 25, 1935.
61 Chiang Chung-cheng [Chiang Kai-shek], *Chiang Tsung-t'ung yen-lun hui-pien, ti i ch'i* [Speeches of President Chiang, first period] (Taipei, 1956), p. 133. See also idem, *O-mei hsün-lien chi,* [Collected remarks made at the Omei Training Center] (Nanking, 1947), p. 484.
62 Norman D. Hanwell to Professor Malbone Graham, May 2, 1935.
63 Joseph Beech, president of West China Union University, Chengtu, to Consul General Paul Josselyn at Hankow, March 25, 1935, in Josselyn (Hankow) to Peiping, April 11, 1935, encl. in Lockhart (Peiping) to Washington, April 19, 1935, S.D. 893.00/13085. In his letter. Dr. Beech gave several reasons for the strength of Chiang's position in Szechwan early in his visit to the province: (1) The mass of the people were sick of the plight to which the competing provincial militarists had brought them; (2) large financial interests in the province looked to the central government for desperately needed economic regulation; (3) business elements had been hurt by militarist taxes and sought relief from Chiang; (4) elements of the Szechwan military establishment, hopelessly enmeshed with the Chinese Communists, felt that there were worse things that could happen than the arrival of Chiang Kai-shek.
64 This passage is quoted by Dryden Linsley Phelps in "Chiang Kai-shek Cleans Up in Szechwan," *Asia* 36 (July 1936): 441. See also excerpts of an address by Chiang Kai-shek (*KWCP*, June 3, 1935), in which Chiang said, "It is important to know the quality of the men being used. The success or failure of government depends on the selection of the right men through careful examination." Of course, this emphasis on the quality and training of the Nationalists' leadership personnel is not so very far removed from the Chinese Communists' emphasis on the role of the party member or cadre. The difference in the two approaches lay in the question of where the "revolution" ought to root its strength—at the top or at the bottom.

CHAPTER 7

1 Teng Han-hsiang, *Teng Ming-chieh*, pp. 57–59.
2 Ibid., pp. 41, 29.

3 *SCYP*, September 1936, p. 426.

4 *1936 pao-kao*, p. 2. See also *SCYP*, September 1936, p. 485.

5 This is part of a letter by Sherwood Eddy to *The Chinese Recorder*, as quoted by J. O. P. Bland in a letter to the *Times* of London (see the *Times* of London, October 22, 1935).

6 Mills (Chungking) to London, May 7, 1937, F.O. 371/20984. See also Chang Hsiao-mei, *Ching-chi tzu-liao*, pp. C-136–138.

7 Huang Yen-p'ei, *Shu-tao* [The road to Shu] (Shanghai, 1936), p. 86. See also *Ta kung pao*, May 20, 1935, for the anguished reaction of several districts to the imposition of the new "peace preservation fee."

8 Huang Yen-p'ei, *Shu tao*, p. 88. Some districts ware granted partial pax remissions because of natural disasters or Communist predations (see ibid., p. 87; and *1936 pao-kao*, p. 10).

9 See *Ta kung pao*, March 31, 1935, for some early cases of this. This general observation is corroborated by Lü P'ing-teng in *Ssu-ch'uan nung-ts'un ching-chi*, p. 476.

10 Quoted from the Chungking *Shang-wu jih-pao*, February 16, 1936, encl. in a letter from Norman D. Hanwell to Richard Walsh, June 29, 1936. The translation is by Hanwell. See also Sun, "Chiao-kung yü t'ao-ni," p. 11.

11 Norman D. Hanwell, probably to his family, from Mienchou, Szechwan, October 5, 1935.

12 The abuses connected with central government-inspired construction projects are well documented. Mi, "Chiang-fei," pp. 101–07, details a single instance very well. See also Pai Yua-yüan, "Labor Tax in the Building of the Szechwan–Hunan Highway," in *Agrarian China*, edited by the Institute of Pacific Relations (London, 1939), pp. 110–12. Labor taxation and the taxation picture in general are discussed in Ju Sheng, "Ssu-ch'uan Kuan-hsien ti nung-ts'un" [The farm villages of Kuanhsien, Szechwan], *TFTC*, January 16, 1936, pp. 110–12. An official in Huayang district adjacent to Chengtu reported that out of eight thousand men impressed for labor by the central government's army and its provincial allies, one quarter died (Hsiang Shang, *Hsi-nan lü-hsing tsa-hsieh* [Travels in the southwest] [Shanghai, 1937], p. 292).

13 Huang Yen-p'ei, *Shu tao*, p. 100. Norman Hanwell, in a letter from Mienchou dated October 4, 1935, elaborates at length on the problems of peasants forced to labor on construction projects or to carry supplies for central government army units in Szechwan. In one case, conscripted laborers had to sell the clothes they wore in order to return to their homes from the place where their work ended.

14 Teng Han-hsiang, *Teng Ming-chieh*, p. 71. See also *HYPK*, p. 116.

15 Mi, "Chiang-fei," p. 90. See the speech by Teng Han-hsiang in *SCYP*, September 1936, p. 485.

16 *Ssu-ch'uan sheng kai-k'uang*, p. 16.

17 *Ssu-ch'uan hsien-hsün*, May 10, 1936, p. 56. This source was the journal of the District Government Personnel Training Institute.

18 Ma, *Wo-ti sheng-huo shih*, p. 67. See also idem, *Hsin shih shuo*, p. 137. Mi Ch'ing-yün states that the "Director of Education" at the Institute was Wang Yu-yung, a political Science Clique member who later served briefly as chief of the administrative section of the provincial government. But the post of "head" of the institute and that of "Director of Education" were presumably separate, so there is no conflict between the two informants.

19 Ma, *Hsin shih shuo*, p. 137. See also Mi, "Chiang-fei," p. 90.

20 Mi, "Chiang-fei," p. 90; and Chou "K'ang-Jih ken-chü ti," p. 2.

21 Phelps, "Chiang Cleans Up," p. 442.

22 See the following: Mi, "Chiang-fei," p. 91; Teng Han-hsiang, *Teng Ming-chieh*, p. 90; and *Chün-cheng hsün-k'an*, July 10, 1935, p. 112. The organization and training of *pao-chia* units and peace preservation forces ran into serious early difficulties as a result of jurisdictional confusions and the lack of commitment among those selected to head the *pao* and *chia* (see Teng Han-hsiang, *Teng Ming-chieh*, p. 96).

23 Teng Han-hsiang, *Teng Ming-Chieh,* p, 69.

24 Ibid., pp. 84–85. Emphasis added.

25 For a slanted discussion of the *pieh-tung tui,* see Chiang, Mayling Soong, *War Messages and Other Selections* (Hankow, 1938), pp. 308–10. In his informative study of political processes and factions in the Nationalist party-state, Hung-mao Tien makes clear the link between the *pieh-tung tui,* the so-called Blue Shirts, *(lan-i she),* and the Whampoa Clique, one of the major contending factions in the central power structure (see Hung-mao Tien, *Government and Politics in Kuomintang China, 1927–1937* [Stanford, 1972]).

26 Liu Hang-shen, "Jung-mu pan sheng," *HWTT,* October 21, 1967, p. 24. See also Ma, *Wo-ti sheng-huo shih,* p. 108; and Li Huang, "Hsi-cheng" (continued.), *Chuan-chi wen-hsüeh,* September 1968, p. 17. K'ang Tse was a native of Szechwan.

27 Ho Kuo-kuang, *Pa-shih tzu-shu,* pp. 29–30.

28 For this unsavory episode, see Ma, *Wo-ti sheng-huo shih,* pp. 108–09; and idem, *Hsin shih shuo,* p. 194. These anecdotal accounts have been corroborated in personal interviews conducted in Taiwan.

29 See *SCYP,* March 1936, pp. 264–68; and ibid., May 1936, p. 283, For Liu's remarks, see *Ssu-ch'uan hsien-hsün,* May 10, 1936, pp. 62–68. For indications of the high turnover rate among special inspectors, see *CYCL,* pp. 135–37; and *Ssu-ch'uan sheng cheng-fu chao-chi ko-ch'ü chuan-yüan hui-i chi-lu* [Record of the conference of all special inspectors convened by the provincial government] ([Chengtu], 1937).

30 See the "Daily Events" sections of *SCYP,* March–June 1936; and Liu Hang-shen, "Jung-mu pan sheng," *HWTT,* October 28, 1967, p. 24.

31 Peck, *Through China's Wall,* p. 244. See also Mills (Chungking) to London, May 7, 1937, F.O. 371/20984.

32 *Yüeh-pao,* May 1937, p. 1,064; and Peck, *Through China's Wall,* p. 244.

33 See the following: Pai Yua-yüan, "Labor Tax," p. 112; Mi, "Chiang-fei," pp. 101–07; Huang Yen-p'ei, *Shu tao,* pp. 102–04; and Ch'ang Yü, "P'o-sui chih Ssu-ch'uan nung-ts'un" [Szechwan's bankrupt agrarian villages], *KWCP,* July 20, 1936.

34 Mills (Chungking) to London, May 7, 1937, F.O. 371/20984.

35 *Democracy* (Peiping), June 22, 1937, pp. 110–11.

36 Mills (Chungking) to London, October 4, 1937, F.O. 371/20985.

37 Peck (Nanking) to Washington, May 27, 1937, S.D. 893.00/14137.

38 See Huang Hsü-ch'u, "Ju-Kuei i-wang lu" [Kwangsi reminiscences], *Ch'un-ch'iu,* July 16, 1965, p. 18; Peck (Nanking) to Washington, May 27, 1937, S.D. 893.00/14137; *China Weekly Review,* June 13, 1936, pp. 45, 50, 56; *KWCP,* April 12, 1937, p. 57.

39 Teng Han-hsiang, *Teng Ming-chieh,* p. 69.

40 Peck (Nanking) to Washington, May 27, 1937, S.D. 893.00/14137. *KWCP,* April 12, 1937, p. 57, alludes to a circular telegram by Liu Hsiang during the Sian Crisis which further aggravated tensions between Chiang and himself. Another source reported that Liu issued a proclamation supporting Chiang's captors on the day Chiang was released (see *New York Times,* June 2, 1937, p. 4).

41 Teng Han-hsiang, *Teng Ming-chieh,* p. 103. This speech, one of several with similar themes, was made on December 21, 1936.

42 Peck (Nanking) to Washington, May 27, 1937, S.D. 893.00/14137. Peck mentions ten divisions as the size of the National Government reinforcements. See also Josselyn (Hankow) to Washington, May 20, 1937, S.D. 893.00/14132, for evidence of troop movements up the Yangtze.

43 Peck, *Through China's Wall,* p. 185.

44 Josselyn (Hankow) to Washington, May 25, 1937, S.D. 893.00/14138.

45 *Fortnightly Survey of Current Events* (Nanking), June 2, 1937. See also Josselyn (Hankow) to Washington, May 20, 1937, S.D. 893.00/14132. Nanking's chief aim was to move

Liu's forces out of Chungking to Yungch'uan (Mills [Chungking] to Peiping, May 22, 1937, F.O. 371/20970). See also *Cheng-feng tsa-chih pan-yüeh-k'an,* June 16, 1937, p. 793.

46 Peck (Nanking) to Washington, May 27, 1937, S.D. 893.00/14137; and Josselyn (Hankow) to Washington, June 24, 1937, S.D. 893.00/14152. Most revealing of all are the "major events" sections of *SCWH* for the spring of 1937 (see *SCWH,* January 1968, pp. 27–30, February 1968, pp. 28–31, March 1968, pp. 26–31, and April 1968, pp. 28–32).

47 Ho Kuo-kuang, *Pa-shih tzu-shu,* p. 30.

48 Translated from *SCWH,* May 1968, p. 27.

49 Mills (Chungking) to Nanking, June 25, 1937, F.O. 371/20970. The same materials are found, in Chinese, in *SCWH,* June 1968, pp. 29–30.

50 Ho Kuo-Kuang, *Pa-shih tzu-shu,* p. 31.

51 *SCWH,* July 1968, pp. 28–29. See also Sun Chen, "Ssu-ch'uan chin i-pu t'ung-i yü k'ang-chan" [Szechwan's progress toward unification and the War of Resistance], *SCWH,* October 1966, p. 2.

52 Knatchbull-Hugessen (Peiping) to London, June 7, 1937, F.O. 371/20970.

53 This point was raised by a former provncial official during an interview with the author on Taiwan in 1968. For comments on the composition and purposes of new administrative units, see Chang Hsiao-mei, *Ching-chi tzu-liao,* p. M-41, and the speech by Yang Yung-t'ai in *CYCL,* p. 14.

54 *Yüeh pao,* May 1937, p. 1,064.

55 For one of many indications of this, see Chang Hsiao-mei, *Ching-chi tzu-liao,* p. C-5. Evidence that this problem continued during the War of Resistance appears frequently in *Kuo-min ts'an-cheng hui Ch'uan-K'ang shih-ch'a t'uan pao-kao shu* [Report of the Szechwan-Sikang Investigation Committee of the People's Political Council] (n.p., 1938; reprinted Taipei, 1971).

CHAPTER 8

1 "Observations and Impressions During a Trip Up the Yangtze River to Chungking," by E. R. Rickover, (Tokyo), November 18, 1935, S.D. 123 D 562/281.

2 See the speech by Teng Han-hsiang on October 4, 1937 in *SCWH,* November 1968, p. 27.

3 *SCWH,* May 1970, p. 5.

4 Mills (Chungking) to London, October 4, 1937, F.O. 371/20985.

5 Chou K'ai-ch'ing, *Ssu-ch'uan yü tui-Jih k'ang-chan* [Szechwan and the Anti-Japanese War of Resistance] (Taipei, 1970), pp. 169–73.

6 See, for example, Carlson, *The Chinese Army,* p. 31.

7 Chou, *Ssu-ch'uan yü tui-Jih k'ang-chan,* p. 171.

8 Toller (Chungking) to London, August 29, 1938, F.O. 371/22082.

9 Toller (Chungking) to London, September 27, 1938, F.O. 371/22131.

10 *SCWH,* March 1968, p. 13.

11 Mills (Chungking) to London, June 20, 1936, F.O. 371/20255.

12 *SCWH,* March 1968, p. 13.

13 Chiang Shang-ch'ing, *Cheng-hai mi-wen,* p. 97.

14 Interview with Ho Kuo-kuang, Taipei, February 11, 1968.

15 For evidence of the upheaval among provincial militarists after the death of Liu Hsiang, and of the ensuing maneuvering by provincial and central government officials alike, see Chou, *Ssu-ch'uan yü tui-Jih k'ang-chan,* pp. 121–36. See also *Hsin Shu pao,* a Chungking newspaper, for the early months of 1938. Among the useful diplomatic dispatches are Mills (Chungking) to Shanghai, April 1, 1938, F.O. 371/22129; Toller (Chungking) to Shanghai, August 3, 1938, F.O. 371/22082; and Toller (Chungking) to Shanghai, October 5, 1938, F.O. 371/22131. It is interesting to note the textual variations in the same article concerning Liu Hsiang's last weeks, as it appeared in different Chinese

magazines. See Tai Kao-hsiang, "Liu Hsiang chin-ching huan-ping ching-kuo chui-i" [Recollections of Liu Hsiang's visit to the capital and his illness], *Ch'un-ch'iu,* January 1968, p. 8; and idem, "Chui-i Liu Hsiang tao-ching huan-ping ch'ing-hsing" [Recollections of the circumstances surrounding Liu Hsiang's illness and visit to the capital], *SCWH,* February 1968, pp. 12–13.

16 Barnett, *China on the Eve of Communist Takeover,* p. 107.

17 Thomas Jay Mathews, "The Cultural Revolution in Szechwan," in *The Cultural Revolution in the Provinces* (Cambridge, Mass.: East Asian Research Center, 1971), pp. 94–146. See in particular pp. 130–33, 143–46.

Glossary

An-Ch'uan chan　安川戰

Chang Ching-yao　張敬堯

Chang Ch'ün　張羣

Chang Hsien-chung　張獻忠

Chang Hsüeh-liang　張學良

Chang Kuo-t'ao　張國燾

Chang Lan　張瀾

Chang Tso-lin　張作林

Chao Erh-sun　趙爾巽

Chao Heng-t'i　趙恆惕

chen　鎮

Ch'en Ch'eng　陳誠

Ch'en Chi-t'ang　陳濟棠

Ch'en Chiung-ming　陳炯明

Ch'en I　陳宧

Ch'en Shao-kuei　陳紹媯

Cheng-wu ch'u　政務處

Cheng-wu wei-yüan hui　政務委員會

chia　甲

Chialing (River)　嘉陵

chiao-fei　教匪

Ch'ien (River)　黔

Chienko　劍閣

Chienyang　簡陽

Chou Chun　周駿

Chou Tao-kang　周道剛

chü　局

Chü (River)　渠

ch'ü　區

ch'u-cheng　出征

Chühsien　渠縣

Chu-ko Liang　諸葛亮

Chu Te　朱德

chün-chang　軍長

chün-fa　軍閥

fa-t'uan　法團

Fan Shao-tseng　范紹增

fang-ch'ü　防區

fen-kuei　分攤

Feng Yü-hsiang　馮玉祥

Fengchieh　奉節

Fou (River)　涪

Fouling　涪陵

fu-chia　附加

fu-hsing min-tsu chih ken-chü ti　復興民族之根據地

Hanchung　漢中

Ho Kuo-kuang　賀國光

Ho Lung　賀龍

Ho Ying-ch'in　何應欽

Hochiang　合江

Hsi-liang　錫良

hsiang　鄉

Hsiang Ch'uan-i　向傳義

Hsiao K'o　蕭克

Hsich'ang　西昌

Hsieh P'ei-chün　謝培均

Hsien-cheng jen-yüan hsün-lien so　縣政人員訓練所

Hsinching　新津

Hsing-cheng tu-ch'a chuan-yüan ch'ü　行政督察專員區

hsiu-ts'ai　秀才

Hsiung K'o-wu　熊克武

Hsü Hsiang-ch'ien　徐向前

Hsü Yüan-ch'uan　徐源泉

Hsüanhan　宣漢

Hsüchow　徐州

Hsüeh Yüeh　薛岳

Hu Ching-i　胡景伊

Hu Tsung-nan　胡宗南

Huang Fu-sheng　黃復生

Huang Yen-p'ei　黃炎培

Huili　會理

Ipin　宜賓

K'aichiang　開江

K'aihsien　開縣

Kan Chi-yung　甘績鏞

K'ang Tse　康澤

k'o　科

Ko-lao hui　哥老會

kua　剮

Kuangan　廣安

Kuangyüan　廣元

Kuanhsien　灌縣

165

kung-lu 公路

Kuo Ch'ang-ming 郭昌明

Kuo-min cheng-fu wei-yüan hui 國民政府委員會

Kweilin 桂林

Lai Hsin-hui 賴心輝

lan-i she 藍衣社

Lan Wen-pin 藍文彬

Langchung 閬中

Li Chia-yü 李家鈺

Li Lei-fu 李雷夫

Li Po 李白

Li Tsung-jen 李宗仁

lien-pao 聯保

lin 臨

Liu Chang 劉璋

Liu Ch'eng-hsün 劉成勳

Liu Hang-shen 劉航琛

Liu Hsiang 劉湘

Liu Pang-chun 劉邦俊

Liu Pei 劉備

Liu Ts'un-hou 劉存厚

Liu Ts'ung-yün 劉從雲

Liu Wen-hui 劉文輝

Liu Yüan-t'ang 劉元唐

Liu Yüan-tsung 劉元宗

Lo Lun 羅倫

Lo Tse-chou 羅澤州

Loshan 樂山

lü 閭

Lu-chün pien-mu tui 陸軍弁目隊

Lu Shih-t'i 盧師諦

Luchou 瀘州

Luting 瀘定

Maoerhkai 毛兒蓋

Maohsien 茂縣

Mapien 馬邊

Meishan 眉山

Mienyang 綿陽

Min (River) 岷

Min Sheng 民生

min-t'uan 民團

Moukung 懋功

Nanchang 南昌

Nanchiang 南江

Nanch'ung 南充

Nanpu 南部

Nihon Shikan Gakko 日本士官學校

Omei 峨眉

Pa 巴

Pachung 巴中

Pahsien 巴縣

P'an Wen-hua 潘文華

pao-an ch'u 保安處

pao-an tui 保安隊

pao chia 保甲

Pao-lu t'ung-chih hui 保路同志會

Paoning 保寧

Paoting 保定

Peip'ei 北碚

piao-shih chiao-huan i-ch'ieh cheng-ch'üan
    表示交還一切政權

pieh-tung tui 別動隊

Pihsien 郫縣

P'u Tien-chün 蒲殿俊

Sant'ai 三臺

Shang-kuan Yün-hsiang 上官雲相

Shao Ming-shu 邵明叔

Shen-ping 神兵

Shih Ch'ing-yang 石青陽

Shu 蜀

shu-cheng 庶政

Shui-ching hou-tzu 水晶猴子

Sian 西安

Ssu-ch'uan lu-chün hsiao-hsüeh 四川陸軍小學

Ssu-ch'uan lu-chün su-ch'eng hsüeh-hsiao
    四川陸軍速成學校

Ssu-ch'uan shan-hou hui-i 四川善後會議

Ssu-ch'uan shih chung-yang chih Ssu-ch'uan
    四川是中央之四川

Ssu-ch'uan wu-pei hsüeh-t'ang 四川武備學堂

Ssu-ma Hsiang-ju 司馬相如

ssu-shu 私塾

Su Tung-p'o 蘇東坡

Suining 綏寧

Suiting 綏定

Sun Chen 孫震

Ta kung pao 大公報

Ta Pa Shan 大巴山

Tachu 大竹

Tahsien 達縣

Tai Chi-t'ao 戴季陶

Tai Li 戴笠

T'aiyüan 太原

Tan Mou-hsin 但懋辛

T'ang Chi-yao 唐繼堯

T'ang Sheng-chih 唐生智

T'ang Shih-tsun 唐式遵

tao 道

Tatu (River) 大渡

Tayi 大邑

Teng Han-hsiang 鄧漢祥

Teng Hsi-hou 鄧錫侯

Teyang 德陽

T'ien-fu chih kuo 天府之國

T'ien Sung-yao　田頌堯
T'o (River)　沱
Ts'ai-cheng t'e-p'ai yüan　財政特派員
Ts'ai O　蔡鍔
Ts'ao K'un　曹錕
Tseng K'uo-ch'ing　曾擴情
Tsou Lu　鄒魯
t'u-fei　土匪
t'uan　團
Tuan Ch'i-jui　段祺瑞
t'uan-fa　團閥
T'ungchiang　通江
T'ungch'uan　潼川
T'ung-meng hui　同盟會
tzu-chih chi-kuan　自治機關
Tzuchung　資中
Tzuliuching　自流井
Wang Ling-chi　王陵基
Wang Tsuan-hsü　王纘緒
Wang Yu-yung　王又鏞
Wanhsien　萬縣

Wanyüan　萬源
Wu P'ei-fu　吳佩孚
Wu Yü-chang　吳玉章
Wut'ungch'iao　五通橋
Yaan　雅安
Yang Ch'uan-yü　楊全宇
yang-feng yin-wei　楊奉陰違
Yang Hu-ch'eng　楊虎成
Yang Sen　楊森
Yang Shu-k'an　楊庶堪
Yang Yung-t'ai　楊永泰
Yen Hsi-shan　閻錫山
Yin Ch'ang-heng　尹昌衡
Yin Ch'ang-ling　尹昌齡
Yingshan　營山
Yüan Shih-k'ai　袁世凱
Yüan Tsu-ming　袁祖銘
Yünan ch'ang　雲安場
Yungch'uan　永川
Yuyang　酉陽

Bibliography

Afanas'yeskiy, Ye. A. *Szechwan, Communist China.* Moscow: Publishing House of Oriental Literature, 1962. Washington, D.C.: Joint Publications Research Service Publication no. 15,308, 1962.

Asia, 1918–37. New York.

Asian Survey, 1965, 1968. Berkeley, Calif.

Barnett, A. Doak. *China on the Eve of Communist Takeover.* New York: Frederick A. Praeger, 1963.

Beech, Joseph. "University Beginnings: A Story of the West China Union University." *Journal of the West China Border Research Society* 6 (1933–34): 91–104.

Bianco, Lucien. *Origins of the Chinese Revolution, 1915–1949.* Stanford, Calif.: Stanford University Press, 1971.

Bloch, Kurt. "Warlordism: A Transitory Stage in Chinese Government." *American Journal of Sociology* 43 (March 1938): 691–703.

Brace, A. J. "Some Secret Societies in Szechwan." *Journal of the West China Border Research Society* 8 (1936): 177–80.

Broomhall, Marshall. *W. W. Cassels: First Bishop in Western China.* London: China Inland Mission Press, 1926.

Brown, H. D., and Li Min-liang. "A Survey of Fifty Farms on the Chengtu Plain, Szechwan, China." *Chinese Economic Journal* 2 (January 1928): 44–73.

Bulletin of the Diocese of Western China, 1911–38. Chengtu.

Burton, Wilbur. "Tug of War in Central Asia—II." *Asia* 35 (October 1935): 610–13.

Carlson, Evans Fordyce. *The Chinese Army: Its Organization and Military Efficiency.* New York: Institute of Pacific Relations, 1940.

Chang Ai-p'ing 張愛萍. *Ts'ung Tsun-i tao Ta-tu ho* 從遵義到大渡河 [From Tsun-i to the Tatu River]. Hong Kong, 1960.

[Chang] Chi-luan 張季鸞. "Ju-Shu chi" 入蜀記 [Into Szechwan]. *KWCP,* May 20, 1935.

Chang Chung-lei 張仲雷. "Ch'ing-mo min-ch'u Ssu-ch'uan ti chün-shih hsüeh-t'ang chi Ch'uan-chün p'ai-hsi" 清末民初四川軍事學堂及川軍派系 [Szechwanese military schools of the late Ch'ing and early Republic, and Szechwanese army cliques and factions]. *HHKMHIL,* pp. 345–64.

Chang Hsiao-mei 張肖梅. *Ssu-ch'uan ching-chi ts'an-k'ao tzu-liao* 四川經濟參考資料 [Research materials on the Szechwan economy]. Shanghai, 1939.

Chang Hua-kuei 張華貴. "Min-sheng kung-ssu kai-k'uang" 民生公司概況 [Condition of the Min Sheng Company]. *Fu-hsing yüeh-k'an* 3, no. 6/7 (March 1935).

Chang Jen-min 張任民. "Ts'e-tung Ch'uan-Ch'ien liang sheng ts'an-chia pei-fa chih hui-i" 策動川黔兩省參加北伐之回憶 [Reminiscences of pressuring Szechwan and Kweichow to join the Northern Expedition]. *Ch'un-ch'iu*, August, 1961, pp. 2–5, 8.

Chang Kuo-t'ao 張國燾. "Wo-ti hui-i" 我的回憶 [Reminiscences]. *Ming-pao yüeh-k'an*, September 1969, pp. 72–77; October 1969, pp. 95–99; November 1969, pp. 96–99; December 1969, pp. 79–85.

Chang Meng-chiu 張夢九. "Fan Shao-tseng jen sha hsin pu-sha" 范紹增人傻心不傻 [Fan Shao-tseng, a stupid man with a smart heart]. *Ch'un-ch'iu*, March 1968, p. 38.

Chang Meng-hsiu 張孟休. "Hung-chün jao-Ch'uan ch'ien ti erh-Liu chih chan" 紅軍擾川前的二劉之戰 [The Two Liu War which preceded Szechwan's Red Army troubles]. *Pei-ching ta-hsüeh Ssu-ch'uan t'ung-hsiang hui hui-k'an*, February 10, 1934, pp. 38–53.

Chang P'ei-chün 張培均. "Ssu-ch'uan cheng-ch'üan chih hsi-t'ung chi hsing-cheng hsien-chuang" 四川政權之系統及行政現狀 [The present state of Szechwan's system of political power and administration]. *Fu-hsing yüeh-k'an* 3, no. 6/7 (March 1935).

Ch'ang Yü 昌裕. "P'o-sui chih Ssu-ch'uan nung-ts'un" 破碎之四川農村 [Szechwan's bankrupt agrarian villages]. *KWCP*, July 20, 1936.

Chang Yü-chiu 張禹九. "Ssu-ch'uan chih chin-yung k'ung-pu yü Liu Hsiang tung-hsia" 四川之金融恐怖與劉湘東下 [Szechwan's currency panic and Liu Hsiang's eastward journey]. *Yin-hang chou-k'an*, December 4, 1934, pp. 11–20.

Chang Yu-i 章有義, comp. *Chung-kuo chin-tai nung-yeh shih tzu-liao* 中國近代農業史資料 [Historical materials on modern Chinese agriculture]. Vol. 2, 1912–27; vol. 3, 1927–37. Peking, 1957.

Chang Yung 張鏞. "Ch'ung-ch'ing tsung kung hui ti fa-chan" 重慶總工會的發展 [The development of the Chungking General Labor Associations]. *SCWH*, June 1967, pp. 27–28.

————. "Tso-yu p'ai fen-cheng yü Ch'ung-ch'ing kung-yün ti ying-hsiang" 左右派紛爭與重慶工運的影響 [Strife between left and right and its influence on the Chungking labor movement]. *SCWH*, July 1967, pp. 26–28.

Ch'ao Fan 超凡 [pseud.]. "Ssu-ch'uan 'p'ao-ko' ta-yeh Wen Ho-sheng chuan-ch'i" 四川袍哥大爺文和笙傳奇 [The story of Szechwan Elder Brother Society leader Wen Ho-sheng]. *Ch'un-ch'iu*, March 1968, pp. 19–21.

Chao T'ing-hua 趙廷華. *Shih-nien lai Chung-kuo ti hung-chün* 十年來中國的紅軍 [The Chinese Red Army over the past ten years]. Hankow, 1938.

Ch'en, Jerome. "Defining Chinese Warlords and Their Factions." *Bulletin of the School of Oriental and African Studies* 31, pt. 3 (1968): 563–600.

_____. "Historical Background." *Modern China's Search for a Political Form.* Edited by Jack Gray. London: Oxford University Press, 1969.

_____. *Mao and the Chinese Revolution.* London: Oxford University Press, 1965.

Cheng-feng tsa-chih pan-yüeh-k'an 正風雜誌半月刊 [Cheng-feng bi-weekly]. 1937.

Cheng Li-chien 鄭勵儉. *Ssu-ch'uan hsin ti-chih* 四川新地誌 [New geography of Szechwan]. N.p., 1946.

Ch'eng Mou-hsing 程懋型. *Chiao-fei ti-fang hsing-cheng chih-tu* 剿匪地方行政制度 [Bandit suppression local administrative systems]. Shanghai, 1936.

Chesneaux, Jean, "The Federalist Movement in China, 1920–3." *Modern China's Search for a Political Form.* Edited by Jack Gray. London: Oxford University Press, 1969.

Chia Shih-i 賈士毅. *Min-kuo hsü ts'ai-cheng shih* 民國續財政史 [Financial history of the Republic, continued]. Shanghai, 1934; reprinted Taipei, 1962.

Chia Wen-chin 賈問津. "Sui-Hsüan chih shih-hsien chi ch'i shou-fu" 綏宣之失陷及其收復 [The loss and recovery of Suiting and Hsüanhan]. *Tu-li p'ing-lun,* February 25, 1934, pp. 12–20.

Chiang Chung-cheng 蔣中正 [Chiang Kai-shek]. *Chiang tsung-t'ung yen-lun hui-pien, ti-i ch'i* 蔣總統言論彙編, 第一期 [Speeches of President Chiang, first period]. Taipei, 1956.

_____. *O-mei hsün-lien chi* 峨帽訓練集 [Collected remarks made at the Omei Training Center]. Nanking, 1947.

Chiang Shang-ch'ing 江上清 [pseud.]. *Cheng-hai mi-wen* 政海秘聞 [Inside stories of politics]. Hong Kong, 1966.

Chiao-fei t'e-k'an 剿匪特刊 [Bandit suppression special journal], 1934. Luhsien, Szechwan.

Chiao-yü tsa-chih 教育雜誌 [The educational review], 1930–32. Shanghai.

Chin-tai shih tzu-liao 近代史資料 [Modern history materials]. 1958, 1962. Peking.

China, Ch'üan-kuo ching-chi wei-yüan hui 全國經濟委員會 [All-China Economic Committee]. *Ssu-ch'uan k'ao-ch'a pao-kao shu* 四川考察報告書 [Report on Szechwan]. Shanghai, 1935.

_____, Chün-shih wei-yüan hui wei-yüan chang hsing-ying 軍事委員會委員長行營. *Chün-shih wei-yüan hui wei-yüan chang hsing-ying cheng-chih kung-tso pao-kao* 軍事委員會委員長行營政治工作報告 [Political work report of the headquarters of the chairman of the Military Affairs Committee]. Nanking, 1935.

_____, Kuo-fang pu shih-cheng chü 國防部史政局 [History Bureau, Ministry of Defense], comp. *Chiao-fei chan-shih* 剿匪戰史 [History of the bandit-suppression wars]. Vol. 10. Taipei, 1962.

———, The Maritime Customs. *Decennial Reports on the Trade, Industries, etc., of the Ports Open to Foreign Commerce, and on the Condition and Development of the Treaty Port Provinces.* Vols. 4, 5. Shanghai: The Maritime Customs, 1924, 1933.

———, Nei-cheng pu 內政部 [Interior Ministry]. *Nei-cheng nien-chien* 內政年鑑 [Internal administration annual]. Nanking, 1935.

———, Shih-yeh pu 實業部 [Ministry of Industry]. *Chung-kuo ching-chi nien-chien* 中國經濟年鑑 [Chinese economic yearbook]. Nanking, 1935.

———, Shih-yeh pu 實業部 [Ministry of Industry], comp. *Erh-shih erh nien lao-tung nien-chien* 二十二年勞動年鑑 [1933 Labor yearbook]. Shanghai, 1933.

The China Quarterly, 1965, 1968. London.

China Today, 1936–37. New York.

China Weekly Review, 1920–37. Shanghai.

Chinese Economic Journal, 1928, 1934. Peiping.

Chinese Social and Political Science Review, 1927. Peking.

Ch'ing-nien chün-jen 青年軍人 [Young soldier], 1933–36. Tientsin and Canton.

Ch'ing-tang shih-lu 清黨實錄 [The record of party purification]. [Nanking], 1928.

Ch'ing-tang t'e-k'an 清黨特刊 [Party purification special journal], 1927. Chungking.

Ch'iu Chu-shuang 邱翥雙. "Lun Ssu-ch'uan chün-t'uan chih ping-min" 論四川軍團之病民 [The harm which the armies and militia of Szechwan do to the people]. *Fu-hsing yüeh-k'an* 3, no. 6/7 (March 1935).

Chou Ch'uan-ju 周傳儒. *Ssu-ch'uan sheng i-p'ieh* 四川省一瞥 [A glance at Szechwan]. Shanghai, 1926.

Chou Hsing 周行. "Ssu-ch'uan Pi-hsien ti nung-ts'un" 四川郫縣的農村 [Agriculture in Pihsien, Szechwan]. *TFTC,* November 16, 1935, pp. 100–02.

Chou K'ai-ch'ing 周開慶, ed. *Chiao-fei yü ch'iu-Ch'uan* 剿匪與救川 [Bandit suppression and the salvation of Szechwan]. N.p., 1933.

———. "Chien-she hsin Ssu-ch'uan ti chan-wang" 建設新四川的展望 [Outlook for the creation of a new Szechwan]. *KWCP,* May 27, 1935.

———. "Ch'uan-pei chiao-fei chün-shih chih kai-kuan" 川北剿匪軍事之概觀 [Views of bandit suppression in northern Szechwan]. *KWCP,* April 30, 1935.

———, ed. *Min-kuo Ssu-ch'uan jen-wu chuan-chi* 民國四川人物傳記 [Biographies of Szechwanese personalities of the republican period]. Taipei, 1966.

———. "Ssu-ch'uan tang-wu chih hui-ku" 四川黨務之回顧 [A review of Party affairs in Szechwan]. *SCWH,* July 1964, pp. 6–11.

———, ed. *Ssu-ch'uan yü hsin-hai ko-ming* 四川與辛亥革命 [Szechwan and the Revolution of 1911]. Taipei, 1965.

———. *Ssu-ch'uan yü tui-Jih k'ang-chan* 四川與對日抗戰 [Szechwan and the Anti-Japanese War of Resistance]. Taipei, 1970.

_____. "Ts'e-ting Ssu-ch'uan wei k'ang-Jih ken-chü-ti chih ching-kuo" 策定四川為抗日根據地之經過 [Experiences in making Szechwan a base for anti-Japanese resistance]. *SCWH*, August 1969, pp. 1–6.

Chou Li-san 周立三, Hou Hsüeh-t'ao 候學燾, and Ch'en Ssu-ch'iao 陳泗橋, comps. *Ssu-ch'uan ching-chi ti-t'u chi* 四川經濟地圖集 [Economic atlas of Szechwan]. Nanking, 1946.

_____. *Ssu-ch'uan ching-chi ti-t'u chi shuo-ming* 四川經濟地圖集說明 [Explanation of the economic atlas of Szechwan]. Nanking, 1946.

Chu Hsieh 朱偰. "Ssu-ch'uan t'ien-fu fu-chia shui chi nung-min ch'i-t'a fu-tan chih chen-hsiang" 四川田賦附加稅及農民其他負擔之眞相 [Szechwanese land tax and surtaxes and other burdens of farmers]. *TFTC*, July 16, 1934. pp. 87–93.

Chu, Samuel C. "The New Life Movement, 1934–1937." *Researches in the Social Sciences on China.* Edited by John E. Lane. Columbia University East Asian Institute Studies, no. 3. New York, 1957.

Chuan-chi wen-hsüeh 傳記文學 [Biography], 1962–69. Taipei.

Ch'uan Han-sheng 全漢昇 and Wang Yeh-chien 王業鍵. "Chin-tai Ssu-ch'uan Ho-chiang hsien wu-chia yü kung-tzu ti pien-tung ch'ü-shih" 近代四川合江縣物價與工資的變動趨勢 [Fluctuation trends of prices and wages in Hochiang, Szechwan, 1875–1925]. *Bulletin of the Institute of History and Philology, Academia Sinica* (Taiwan) 34 (1962): 265–74.

Chuang Tse-hsüan 莊澤宣. *Lung Shu chih yu* 隴蜀之游 [Travels in Shensi and Szechwan]. N.p., 1941.

Chün-cheng hsün-k'an 軍政旬刊 [Military administration magazine], 1935–36. Nanking.

Ch'un-ch'iu 春秋 [Spring and autumn], 1957–69. Hong Kong.

Chung-hua chiao-yü chieh 中華教育界 [Chinese education world], 1934. Shanghai.

Chung-hua chien-she hsüeh-hui 中華建設學會 [China Reconstruction Study Association]. *Chung-hua chien-she hsüeh-hui tui mu-ch'ien Ch'uan-chü chih chien-i* 中華建設學會對目前川局之建議 [Recommendations of the China Reconstruction Study Association concerning present conditions in Szechwan]. Shanghai, 1933.

Chung-kung jen-ming lu pien-hsiu wei-yüan hui 中共人名錄編修委員會 [Editorial Committee for Roster of Chinese Communists], ed. *Chung-kung jen-ming lu* 中共人名錄 [Roster of Chinese Communists]. Taipei, 1967.

Chung-kuo jen-min cheng-chih hsieh-shang hui-i ch'uan-kuo wei-yüan hui, wen-shih tzu-liao yen-chiu wei-yüan hui 中國人民政治協商會議全國委員會文史資料研究委員會 [Research Committee on Literary and Historical Materials, National Committee of the Chinese People's Political Consultative Conference]. *Hsin-hai ko-ming hui-i lu* 辛亥革命回憶錄 [Recollections of the Revolution of 1911]. Vol. 3. Peking, 1962.

Chung-kuo kung-ch'eng shih-hsüeh hui 中國工程師學會 [China Engineering

Study Association], ed. *Ssu-ch'uan k'ao-ch'a t'uan pao-kao* 四川考察團報告 [Report of the Szechwan Investigation Commission]. N. p., 1936.

Chung-kuo kuo-min tang chung-yang chih-hsing wei-yüan hui, tang-shih shih-liao pien-tsuan wei-yüan hui 中國國民黨中央執行委員會黨史史料編纂委員會 [Kuomintang Archives], comp. *Min-kuo erh-shih san nien Chung-kuo kuo-min tang nien-chien* 民國二十三年中國國民黨年鑑 [1934 Kuomintang yearbook]. Nanking, 1934.

———. *Min-kuo shih-pa nien Chung-kuo kuo-min tang nien-chien* 民國十八年中國國民黨年鑑 [1929 Kuomintang yearbook]. Nanking, 1929.

Chung-kuo kuo-min tang Ssu-ch'uan tang-shih ts'ai-liao 中國國民黨四川黨史材料 [Materials on the history of the Kuomintang in Szechwan]. Pts. 1 and 2. N.p., 1940, 1945.

Chung-kuo nien-chien 中國年鑑 [China yearbook]. Shanghai, 1923.

Chung-wai tsa-chih 中外雜誌 [Kaleidoscope], 1967–69. Taipei.

Chung-yang yin-hang yüeh-k'an 中央銀行月刊 [Monthly Magazine of the Central Bank of China], 1934–37. Shanghai.

Clubb, O. Edmund. *Twentieth Century China.* New York: Columbia University Press, 1964.

Cressey, George B. *China's Geographic Foundations.* New York: McGraw-Hill Book Co., 1934.

David, Norman. "Ping Ts'ai in Szechwan." *China Weekly Review,* October 26, 1935, p. 268.

Decker, J. W. "Report on a Visit to West China." Submitted to the Board of Managers of the American Baptist Foreign Mission Society, 1930. Divinity Library, Yale University, New Haven, Conn.

Dye, D. S. "The Szechwanese Use of Their Water Resources for Agriculture." *Journal of the West China Border Research Society* 3 (1926–29): 40–54.

Eberhard, Wolfram. "Chinese Regional Stereotypes." *Asian Survey* 5 (1965): 596–608.

"Exchange of Notes between the British and Chinese Governments Relative to the Bombardment of Wanhsien (Szechwan)." *Chinese Social and Political Science Review* 11 (1927), Public Documents section, pp. 68–78.

Fan Ch'ung-shih 范崇實. "1920–1922 nien ti Ssu-ch'uan chün-fa k'un-chan" 1920–1922 年的四川軍閥混戰 [The chaotic warfare of the Szechwanese warlords between 1920 and 1922]. *CTSTL,* 1962, no. 4, pp. 1–23.

Fan Yin-nan 樊蔭南. *Tang-tai Chung-kuo ming-jen lu* 當代中國名人錄 [Modern Chinese famous men]. Shanghai, 1931.

Fei-chih nei-chan ta t'ung-meng 廢止內戰大同盟 [Great Alliance for the Abolition of Civil War], ed. *Ssu-ch'uan nei-chan hsiang-chi* 四川內戰祥記 [The Szechwan civil war]. Shanghai, 1933.

Feng Ho-fa 馮和法. *Chung-kuo nung-ts'un ching-chi tzu-liao* 中國農村經濟資料 [Materials on the Chinese agrarian economy]. Shanghai, 1933.

Feng Shao-lieh 馮紹烈. *Shih-nien hung-chün* 十年紅軍 [Ten years of the Red Army]. Shanghai, 1938.

Feuerwerker, Albert, Rhoads Murphey, and Mary C. Wright, eds. *Approaches to Modern Chinese History.* Berkeley and Los Angeles: University of California Press, 1967.

"First Trains in Szechwan." *China Reconstructs,* March-April 1952, pp. 32–34.

Folsom, Kenneth E. *Friends, Guests, and Colleagues: The Mu-fu System in the Late Ch'ing Period.* Berkeley and Los Angeles: University of California Press, 1968.

Fortnightly Review of Current Events, 1937. Nanking.

Fu-hsing yüeh-k'an 復興月刊 [Regeneration monthly], 1935. Shanghai.

Fu Jun-hua 傅潤華. *Chung-kuo tang-tai ming-jen chuan* 中國當代名人傳 [Biographies of present-day Chinese notables]. Shanghai, 1948.

Garavente, Anthony. "The Long March." *China Quarterly* 22 (April-June 1965): 89–124.

Gillin, Donald G. *Warlord: Yen Hsi-shan in Shansi Province.* Princeton, N. J.: Princeton University Press, 1967.

————. "Warlordism in Modern China." *Journal of Asian Studies* 26 (May 1967): 469–74.

Gilman, William. "Liu Hsiang—The Szechwan War Lord." *China Today,* June 1935, p. 167.

Han Min 厂民 [pseud.]. *Tang-tai Chung-kuo jen-wu chih* 當代中國人物誌 [Present-day Chinese personalities]. Shanghai, 1939.

Han Shan 寒蟬 [pseud.]. "Ch'uan-chün hsi-t'ung chi Ch'uan-fei wei-chih yü shih-li" 川軍系統及川匪位置與實力 [Szechwanese military systems and the location and strength of Communists in Szechwan]. *Fu-hsing yüeh-k'an* 3, no. 6/7 (March 1935).

Hanson, Haldore. "Famine Diary of a Warlord." *Democracy* (Peiping), June 22, 1937, pp. 110–12.

Hanwell, Norman D. "The Chinese Red Army." *Asia* 36 (May 1936): 317–22.

Hatano Ken'ichi 波多野乾一, comp. *Gendai shina no kiroku* 現代支那之紀錄 [Modern China archive]. Tokyo, 1924–32.

Hatano, Yoshihiro. "The New Armies." *China in Revolution: The First Phase, 1900–1913.* Edited by Mary Clabaugh Wright. New Haven: Yale University Press, 1968.

Hedtke, Charles H. "Reluctant Revolutionaries: Szechwan and the Ch'ing Collapse, 1898–1911." Ph.D. dissertation, University of California at Berkeley, 1968.

Hewlett, Sir Meyrick. *Forty Years in China.* London: Macmillan & Co., 1943.

Ho-chiang hsien chih 合江縣志 [Gazetteer of Hochiang *hsien*]. Hochiang, 1929; reprinted Taipei, 1967.

Ho Ch'i-fang 何其芳. Wu Yü-chang t'ung-chih ko-ming ku-shih 吳玉章同志革命故事 [Comrade Wu Yü-chang's revolutionary story]. Hong Kong, 1949.

Ho Hsi-ya 何西亞. "Chia-tzu ta chan hou ch'üan-kuo chün-tui chih tiao-ch'a" 甲子大戰後全國軍隊之調查 [An investigation of the entire country's armed forces after the recent war]. *TFTC*, January 10, 1925, pp. 103–12; January 25, 1925, pp. 34–57; February 10, 1925, pp. 69–83.

Ho Kan-chih. *A History of the Modern Chinese Revolution.* Peking: Foreign Languages Press, 1959.

Ho Kuo-kuang 賀國光. "Chiao-fei yü an-Ch'uan chih ching-kuo" 剿匪與安川之經過 [Experiences in bandit suppression and the pacification of Szechwan]. *SCWH*, January 1965, pp. 8–13.

_____. *Pa-shih tzu-shu* 八十自述 [Recollections at eighty]. Taipei, 1964.

Hosie, Alexander. *Szechwan: Its Products, Industries, and Resources.* Shanghai: Kelly and Walsh, 1922.

Hsiang, C. Y. "Mountain Economy in Szechwan." *Pacific Affairs* 14 (December 1941): 448–62.

Hsiang Shang 向尚 et al. *Hsi-nan lü-hsing tsa-hsieh* 西南旅行雜寫 [Travels in the southwest]. Shanghai, 1937.

Hsiang-tao chou-pao 嚮導週報 [The guide weekly], 1923. Shanghai.

Hsieh Chih-yün. "Szechwan: A Second Kiangsi?" *China Weekly Review*, October 27, 1934, p. 288.

Hsieh Shu 謝樹. "Min yüan i-lai Ssu-ch'uan chün-shih hsiao-shih" 民元以來四川軍事小史 [A short history of Szechwanese military affairs since 1912]. *Kuo-li Wu-han ta-hsüeh Ssu-ch'uan t'ung-hsüeh hui hui-k'an* 1, no. 2 (1934).

Hsieh, Winston. "The Ideas and Ideals of a Warlord: Ch'en Chiung-ming (1878–1933)." Harvard University, East Asian Research Center, *Papers on China*. Vol. 16. Cambridge, Mass., 1962.

Hsien-fa yao-lan 憲法要覽 [A look at constitutions]. Peking, 1922.

Hsin shih-chieh pan-yüeh-k'an 新世界半月刊 [New world bi-weekly], 1937. Peip'ei, Szechwan.

Hsin Shu pao 新蜀報 [The new Szechwan paper], 1938. Chungking.

Hsin-wen t'ien-ti 新聞天地 [Newsdom], 1967. Hong Kong.

Hsü Chih-tao 徐志道. "Ch'uan-chün chiang-ling hsing-hsing se-se" 川軍將領形形色色 [The many varieties of Szechwanese generals]. *Chung-wai tsa-chih*, February 1972, pp. 28–35.

Hsü Ya-ming 徐亞明. "Ssu-ch'uan hsin chien-she chung chih hsiao san-hsia" 四川新建設中之小三峽 [The Three Little Gorges area in the midst of Szechwan's new reconstruction]. *Fu-hsing yüeh-k'an* 3, no. 6/7 (March 1935).

Hsü Ying 徐盈. *Tang-tai chung-kuo shih-yeh jen-wu chih* 當代中國實業人物誌 [Modern Chinese industrialists]. Shanghai, 1948.

Hsü-yung hsien chih 叙永縣志 [Gazetteer of Hsüyung *hsien*]. Hsüyung, 1933; reprinted Taipei, 1967.

Hsüeh Shao-ming 薛紹銘. *Ch'ien-Tien-Ch'uan lü-hsing chi* 黔滇川旅行記 [A Kweichow-Yunnan-Szechwan travelogue]. Canton, 1937.

Hsün Shih 循實 [pseud.]. "Ch'uan tung-pei chiao-ch'ih yin-hsiang chi" 川東北剿赤印象記 [Impressions of Red-suppression in northeastern Szechwan]. *KWCP*, March 11, March 18, April 8, April 15, April 22, May 6, May 13, and May 20, 1935.

Hu Hsien-su 胡先驌. "Shu yu tsa-kan" 蜀遊雜感 [Random thoughts on a visit to Szechwan]. *Tu-li p'ing-lun*, October 1, 1933, pp. 14–20.

Hu Huan-yung 胡煥庸. *Ssu-ch'uan ti-li* 四川地理 [Geography of Szechwan]. N.p., 1938.

Hu Kuang-piao 胡光麃. *Po-chu liu-shih nien* 波逐六十年 [Living in a turbulent era]. 2d ed. Hong Kong, 1964.

Hu Shu-hua 胡庶華. "Ssu-ch'uan ti kung-yeh" 四川的工業 [Szechwan's industry]. *Shih-shih yüeh-pao*, September 1934, pp. 159–64.

Hu Yü-kao 胡羽高. Kung-fei hsi-ts'uan chi 共匪西竄記 [Record of the Communists' westward trek]. Kweiyang, 1946.

Hua Sheng 華生 [pseud.]. "Min-kuo ch'u-nien chih Ssu-ch'uan ts'ai-cheng 民國初年之四川財政 [Szechwan's finances in the early Republic]. *SCWH*, April 1966, pp. 1–9.

_____. "Ssu-ch'uan chih hsien ti-fang ts'ai-cheng" 四川之縣地方財政 [Szechwan's district and local finance]. *SCWH*, September 1966, pp. 1–12.

Huai Ping 懷冰 [pseud.]. "Shih Liu Hsiang t'ung-i Ssu-ch'uan hai-shih hung-chün lai chien-she Ssu-ch'uan su-wei-ai." 是劉湘統一四川還是紅軍來建設四川蘇維埃 [Is Liu Hsiang unifying Szechwan or is the Red Army building a Szechwan soviet?]. *Hung-ch'i chou-pao* 63 (n.d.).

Huang Chü 黃渠. "Ch'uan-chün chiao-fei chih ching-kuo" 川軍剿匪之經過 [Bandit suppression experiences of the Szechwan armies]. *Fu-hsing yüeh-k'an* 3, no. 6/7 (March 1935).

Huang Chu-i 黃主一. "Ch'uan-pei nung-min hsien-k'uang chih i-pan" 川北農民現況之一斑 [Present conditions among farmers of northern Szechwan]. *TFTC*, August 25, 1927, pp. 33–39.

Huang Hsü-ch'u 黃旭初. "Ju-Kuei i-wang lu" 入桂憶往錄 [Kwangsi reminiscences]. *Ch'un-ch'iu*, July 16, 1965, pp. 15–18.

Huang Kung-wei 黃公偉. *Chung-kuo chin-tai jen-wu i-hua* 中國近代人物逸話 [Casual talk about modern Chinese personalities]. Taipei, 1949.

Huang Tzu-ching 黃自敬, ed. "Ch'uan-Shan ch'ü ko-ming ken-chü-ti tzu-liao hsüan-chi 川陝區革命根據地資料選輯 [Selected materials on the Szechwan-Shensi revolutionary base]. *CTSTL*, 1958, no. 3, pp. 105–41.

Huang Yen-p'ei 黃炎培. *Shu tao* 蜀道 [The road to Shu]. Shanghai, 1936.

Hua-yang hsien chih 華陽縣志 [Gazetteer of Huayang *hsien*]. Chengtu, 1934; reprinted Taipei, 1967.

Hui Ying 惠英 [pseud.]. "Feng-chien shih-li mi-man ti Ssu-ch'uan" 封建

勢力瀰漫的四川 [Szechwan, where feudal power is excessive]. *Lao-tung chi-pao*, November 10, 1934, pp. 160–72.

Hung-ch'i chou-pao 紅旗週報 [Red Flag weekly], 1933. Shanghai.

Hung-chün chieh-pao 紅軍捷報 [Red Army victory report], 1933. [Juichin].

Hutson, James. "Chinese Secret Societies." *China Journal* 9 (1928): 164–70, 215–21, 276–82; 10 (1929): 12–16.

Institute of Pacific Relations, ed. *Agrarian China: Selected Source Materials from Chinese Authors*. London: G. Allen, 1939.

Israel, John. *Student Nationalism in China, 1927–1937*. Stanford, Calif.: Stanford University Press, 1966.

Jen-wu tsa-chih 人物雜誌 [Personalities magazine], 1946–47. Chungking and Shanghai.

Journal of the West China Border Research Society, 1926–36. Chengtu.

Ju Sheng 如生. "Ssu-ch'uan Kuan-hsien ti nung-ts'un" 四川灌縣的農村 [The farm villages of Kuanhsien, Szechwan]. *TFTC*, January 16, 1936, pp. 110–12.

Kan Chi-yung 甘績鏞. "Ju-ho kai-chin chih-jih Ssu-ch'uan" 如何改進今日四川 [How to improve today's Szechwan]. *SCYP*, February 1933, pp. 1–16.

K'ang Hsüan-i 康選宜. "Ch'uan-chan chien-shih" 川戰簡史 [A brief history of Szechwan's wars]. *Fu-hsing yüeh-k'an* 3, no. 6/7 (March 1935).

King, Louis M. *China in Turomoil: Studies in Personality*. London: Heath Cranton, 1927.

Ko Sui-ch'eng 葛綏成. Ssu-ch'uan chih hsing. 四川之行 [Szechwan journey]. Shanghai, 1934.

Kuang Wen 廣文 [pseud.]. "Fang-ch'ü shih-tai chih Ssu-ch'uan chün-cheng wu hsi-t'ung" 防區時代之四川軍政務系統 [Szechwan's military administrative systems during the garrison area period]. *SCWH*, October 1966, pp. 7–8.

Kuhn, Philip. *Rebellion and Its Enemies in Late Imperial China: Militarization and Social Structure, 1796–1864*. Cambridge, Mass.: Harvard University Press, 1970.

Kuo Jung-sheng 郭榮生. "Ssu-ch'uan sheng ti-fang yin-hang chih yen-chin" 四川省地方銀行之演進 [The evolution of Szechwanese local banks]. *SCWH*, December 1967, pp. 1–9.

Kuo-li Wu-han ta-hsüeh Ssu-ch'uan t'ung-hsüeh hui hui-k'an 國立武漢大學四川同學會會刊 [Magazine of the National Wuhan University Szechwanese Students' Association], 1934. Wuhan.

Kuo-wen chou-pao 國聞週報 [National news weekly], 1924–37. Tientsin.

Lang, Olga. *Pa Chin and His Writings*. Cambridge, Mass.: Harvard University Press, 1967.

Li Huan 李寰. "Wu P'ei-fu ping-pai ju-Ch'uan chi" 吳佩孚兵敗入川記 [The story of Wu P'ei-fu's entry into Szechwan after his defeat]. *Chung-wai tsa-chih*, June 1967, pp. 35–36.

Li Huang 李璜. "Chi-ch'i hsi-cheng pin wei shuang" 記起西征鬢未霜 [An account of the anti-Communist campaign in Szechwan in 1933]. *Chuan-chi wen-hsüeh,* August 1968, pp. 6–13, and September 1968, pp. 11–18.

Li Kuo-chen 李國楨. "Ssu-ch'uan ti nung-ts'un kao li tai" 四川的農村高利貸 [Agrarian usury in Szechwan]. *Chung-kuo nung-ts'un* 2 (November 1936): 67–72.

Li Ming-liang 李明良. "Ssu-ch'uan nung-min ching-chi ch'iung-k'un ti yüan-yin 四川農民經濟窮困的原因 [Reasons for the economic difficulties of Szechwan's peasants]. *SCYP,* June 1933, pp. 1–28.

Li Pai-hung 李白虹. "Erh-shih nien lai chih Ch'uan-fa chan-cheng" 二十年來之川閥戰爭 [Szechwanese warlord wars of the last twenty years]. *CTSTL,* 1962, no. 4, pp. 67–84.

_____. "Ssu-ch'uan min-chung yün-tung chih fa-chan chieh-tuan" 四川民眾運動之發展階段 [Stages in the development of the mass movement in Szechwan]. *Pei-ching ta-hsüeh Ssu-ch'uan t'ung-hsiang hui hui-k'an,* February 10, 1934, pp. 55–59.

Li P'ei-sheng 李培生. *Kuei-hsi chü-Yüeh chih yu-lai chi ch'i ching-kuo* 桂系據粵之由來及其經過 [Origins and experiences of the Kwangsi clique's occupation of Kwangtung]. [Canton], [1921]; reprinted Taipei, n.d.

Li Yün-han 李雲漢. *Ts'ung jung-kung tao ch'ing-tang* 從容共到清黨 [From admission of the Communists to party purification]. Taipei, 1966.

Liao T'ai-ch'u. "The Ko-Lao Hui in Szechwan." *Pacific Affairs,* June 1947, pp. 161–73.

_____. "Rural Education in Transition: A Study of Old-Fashioned Chinese Schools *(Ssu-shu)* in Shantung and Szechwan." *Yenching Jorunal of Social Studies* 4 (February 1949): 19–68.

Lin Chao. "The Tsinling and Tapashan as a Barrier to Communications between Szechwan and the Northwestern Provinces." *Ti-li hsüeh-pao* 14 (December 1947): 5–14.

Lin I-ts'ai 林驥材. "Ch'ien-Ch'uan fei-fen wei-mieh chih yüan-yin" 黔川匪氛未滅之原因 [Reasons for the failure to eradicate the bandit poison in Kweichow and Szechwan]. *KWCP,* March 25, 1935.

_____. "Fei-huan chung Ch'uan-Ch'ien ts'ai-cheng chih nan-kuan" 匪患中川黔財政之難關 [Financial crisis in Szechwan and Kweichow in the midst of Communist disturbances]. *KWCP,* June 3, 1935.

Lin, P. S. "Regional Independence and Predatory Militarism." *People's Tribune,* n.s. 3 (1932–33): 101–06.

Liu Ching 劉錦. *Ch'uan-K'ang i-shou ch'ien-hou* 川康易守前後 [How Szechwan and Sikang changed hands]. Hong Kong, 1956.

Liu Hang-shen 劉航琛. "Fan Shao-tseng yü Lan Wen-pin" 范紹增與藍文彬 [Fan Shao-tseng and Lan Wen-pin]. *Chung-wai tsa-chih,* May 1968, pp. 10–13.

_____. "Jung-mu pan sheng" 戎幕半生 [Half a lifetime in the inner circle]. *HWTT*, July 8–November 25, 1967.

Liu Hsiang 劉湘. *Liu Fu-ch'eng chün-chang chiang-yen chi* 劉甫澄軍長講演集 [Collected speeches of General Liu Hsiang]. [Chungking], [1927].

_____. *Ssu-ch'uan sheng k'ang-chan shih-ch'i chung-hsin kung-tso* 四川省抗戰時期中心工作 [Szechwan's central tasks during the resistance war]. Chengtu, 1937.

Liu Ts'un-hou 劉存厚. *Hu-kuo Ch'uan-chün chan-chi* 護國川軍戰記 [The war record of the Szechwan Army to Protect the Nation]. Taipei, 1966.

Lo Chia-lun 羅家倫, ed. *Ko-ming wen-hsien* 革命文獻 [Documents of the Revolution]. Vol. 24. Taipei, 1961.

Lu hsien chih 瀘縣志 [Gazetteer of Lu *hsien*]. Luhsien, 1938; reprinted Taipei, 1967.

Lu Pao-ch'ien 陸寶千. *Chung-kuo shih-ti tsung lun* 中國史地綜論 [A general discussion of China's historical georgraphy]. Taipei, 1962.

Lü P'ing-teng 呂平等. *Ssu-ch'uan nung-ts'un ching-chi* 四川農村經濟 [The economy of Szechwanese farm villages]. Shanghai, 1936.

Lu Shih-t'i 盧師諦. "Ti-i tz'u chi-nien chou tang-wu pao-kao" 第一次紀念週黨務報告 [First party affairs report]. *Ch'ing-tang t'e-k'an*, June 30, 1927, pp. 84–106.

Lu Ssu-hung 陸思紅. *Hsin Ch'ung-ch'ing* 新重慶 [New Chungking]. Shanghai, 1939.

Lu Tso-fu 盧作孚. *Chung-kuo ti chien-she wen-t'i yü jen ti hsün-lien* 中國的建設問題與人的訓練 [The question of reconstruction in China and the training of the people]. Shanghai, 1934.

_____. "Ssu-ch'uan Chia-ling chiang san-hsia ti hsiang-ts'un yün-tung" 四川嘉陵江三峽的鄉村運動 [The rural village movement in the Three Gorges area of the Chialing River in Szechwan]. *Chung-hua chiao-yü chieh* 22 (October 1934): 107–12.

_____. "Ssu-ch'uan sheng tsui-chin ching-chi chien-she hsing-cheng" 四川省最近經濟建設行政 [Latest economic reconstruction in Szechwan]. *Shih-yeh pu yüeh-k'an*, February 10, 1937, pp. 149–53.

Ma Wu 馬五 [Lei Hsiao-ch'en, 雷嘯岑]. *Hsin shih shuo* 新世說 [Stories of the new age]. Taipei, 1965.

_____. *Wo-ti sheng-huo shih* 我的生活史 [The story of my life]. Taipei, 1965.

Mei Hsin-ju 梅心如. "Ssu-ch'uan chih huo-pi" 四川之貨幣 [Szechwan's currency]. *TFTC*, July 16, 1934, pp. 189–98.

Meng, C. Y. W. "Whither Szechwan?" *China Weekly Review*, October 20, 1934, pp. 262–63.

Mi Ch'ing-yün 米慶云. "Chiang-fei huo-Ch'uan chi" 蔣匪禍川記 [The record of the bandit Chiang's predations in Szechwan]. *CTSTL*, 1962, no. 4, pp. 85–135.

Mien-yang hsien chih 綿陽縣志 [Gazetteer of Mienyang *hsien*]. Mienyang, 1932; reprinted Taipei, 1967.

Min Cheng 敏政 [pseud.]. "Ssu-ch'uan ti wei-chi yü Chung-kuo ch'ien-t'u" 四川的危機與中國前途 [Szechwan's crisis and China's future]. *Kuo-li Wu-han ta-hsüeh Ssu-ch'uan t'ung-hsüeh hui hui-k'an* 1, no. 2 (1934).

Min-sheng shih-yeh kung-ssu shih-i chou nien chi-nien k'an pien-chi wei-yüan hui 民生實業公司十一週年紀年刊編輯委員會, comp. *Min-sheng shih-yeh kung-ssu shih-i chou nien chi-nien k'an* 民生實業公司十一週年紀年刊 [Commemorative volume on the eleventh anniversary of the Min Sheng Industrial Company]. Shanghai, 1937.

Ming-pao yüeh-k'an 明報月刊 [Ming Pao monthly], 1968–69. Hong Kong.

Myers, Ramon. "The Usefulness of Local Gazetteers for the Study of Modern Chinese Economic History: Szechwan Province during the Ch'ing and Republican Periods." *Tsing Hua Journal of Chinese Studies*, n.s. 6 (December 1967): 72–104.

New York Times, 1910–38.

North China Herald, 1911–37. Shanghai.

Oksenberg, Michel. "The Institutionalisation of the Chinese Communist Revolution: The Ladder of Success on the Eve of the Cultural Revolution." *China Quarterly* 36 (October–December 1968): 61–92.

Oriental Affairs, 1935–38. Shanghai.

Pa hsien chih 巴縣志 [Gazetteer of Pa *hsien*]. Chungking, 1939; reprinted Taipei, 1967.

Pai-jih hsin-wen 白日新聞 [White sun news], August 1928 and April 1929. Chengtu.

Pai Yua-yuan. "Labor Tax in the Building of the Szechwan–Hunan Highway." *Agrarian China*. Edited by the Institute of Pacific Relations. London, 1939.

Pai Yun 白云 [pseud.]. "Ssu-ch'uan chih ko-tang ko-p'ai" 四川之各黨各派 [Szechwan's cliques and factions]. *She-hui hsin-wen*, November 15, 1932, p. 326.

Peck, Graham. *Through China's Wall*. Boston: Houghton Mifflin, 1940.

Pei-ching ta-hsüeh Ssu-ch'uan t'ung-hsiang hui hui-k'an 北京大學四川同鄉會會刊 [Magazine of the Association of Szechwanese at Peking University], 1934. Peiping.

Perleberg, Max. *Who's Who in Modern China*. Hong Kong: Ye Olde Printerie, 1954.

Perlin, B. "Struggle for Soviets in Szechwan." *China Today*, February 1936, pp. 93–96, and March 1936, pp. 114–17.

Petro, W. *Triple Commission*. London: John Murray, 1968.

Phelps, Dryden Linsley. "Chiang Kai-shek Cleans Up in Szechwan." *Asia* 36 (July 1936): 438–42.

Pi Tung 筆董 [pseud.]. *I-pai ke jen-wu* 一百個人物 [One hundred personalities]. N.p., n.d.

Pien-shih yen-chiu 邊事研究 [Border affairs research], 1936. Chungking.

P'ing Ch'ing 平青 [pseud.]. "Shu-pei chün cheng-fu ch'eng-li shih-mo" 蜀北軍政府成立始末 [An account of the establishment of the military government of northern Szechwan]. *SCWH*, November 1965, pp. 7–9.

R.T. "One Night in Chunking." *Blackwood's Magazine*, May 1934, pp. 581–602.

Richardson, H. K. "Face to Face with Business in Szechwan." *Asia* 20 (May 1920): 426–34.

Richthofen, Ferdinand von. *Baron Richtohfen's Letters, 1870–1872*. Shanghai: North China Herald, 1873.

Scalapino, Robert A. "Prelude to Marxism: The Chinese Student Movement in Japan, 1900–1910." *Approaches to Modern Chinese History*. Edited by Albert Feuerwerker, Rhoads Murphey, and Mary C. Wright. Berkeley and Los Angeles: University of California Press, 1967.

Schram, Stuart. *Mao Tse-tung*. Harmondsworth, Middlesex.: Penguin Books, 1967.

———. *The Political Thought of Mao Tse-tung*. New York: Frederick A. Praeger, 1963.

She-hui hsin-wen 社會新聞 [News of the society], 1932–33. Shanghai.

Shen Chien 沈鑑. "Hsin-hai ko-ming ch'ien-hsi wo-kuo chih lu-chün chi ch'i chün-fei" 辛亥革命前夕我國之陸軍及其軍費 [China's armies and military budgets on the eve of the 1911 Revolution]. *She-hui k'o-hsüeh* 2 (January 1937): 343–408.

Shen Mo-shih 沈默士. *Liu Hsiang t'ung-i Ssu-ch'uan nei-mo* 劉湘統一四川內幕 [The inside story of Liu Hsiang's unification of Szechwan]. Hong Kong, 1968.

Sheng-huo 生活 [Life], 1933. Shanghai.

Sheridan, James E. *Chinese Warlord: The Career of Feng Yü-hsiang*. Stanford, Calif.: Stanford University Press, 1966.

Shih Chin 師進 [pseud.]. "Ssu-ch'uan chiao-fei ti hsien-chüeh wen-t'i" 四川剿匪的先決問題 [The most pressing question for bandit suppression in Szechwan]. *Shih-tai kung-lun*, February 1, 1935. p. 26.

Shih pao 實報 [Truth post], 1928–38. Peiping.

Shih-shih yüeh-pao 時事月報 [Current events monthly], 1929–38. Nanking, Hankow.

Shih-tai kung-lun 時代公論 [Timely debate], 1932–35. Nanking.

Shih-yeh pu yüeh-k'an 實業部月刊 [Industry ministry monthly], 1937. Nanking.

Shu Hsieh 蜀俠 "Min-sheng kung-ssu fa-chan shih" 民生公司發展史 [History of the development of the Min Sheng Company]. *SCWH*, May 1966, pp. 17–20.

Shu K'o 蜀客 [pseud.]. "Liu Hsiang fa-ta hsiao shih" 劉湘發達小史 [A short history of Liu Hsiang's rise]. *Chung-kuo min-chu lun-t'an pan-yüeh-k'an*, November 16, 1966, pp. 16–18.

Smedley, Agnes. *The Great Road: The Life and Times of Chu Teh*. New York: Monthly Review Press, 1956.

Snow, Edgar. *Red Star over China*. New York: Random House, 1938.

Sonoda Kazuki 園田一龜. *Hsin Chung-kuo jen-wu chih* 新中國人物誌 [Men of the new China]. Translated by Huang Hui-ch'uan 黃惠泉. Shanghai, 1930.

Spencer, J. E. "On Regionalism in China." *Journal of Geography* 46 (April 1947): 123–36.

Ssu-ch'uan chiao-yü 四川教育 [Szechwan education], 1937. Chengtu.

Ssu-ch'uan chin-yen yüeh-k'an 四川禁烟月刊 [Szechwan opium suppression monthly], 1938. Chengtu.

Ssu-ch'uan ching-chi chi-k'an 四川經濟季刊 [Szechwan economic quarterly], 1943–45. Chungking.

Ssu-ch'uan ching-chi yüeh-k'an 四川經濟月刊 [Szechwan economic monthly], 1934–36. Chungking.

Ssu-ch'uan ch'ou-pei sheng-hsien chou-k'an 四川籌備省憲週刊 [Szechwan constitutional preparation weekly], 1922. N.p.

Ssu-ch'uan hsien-hsün 四川縣訓 [Journal of the Szechwan District Government Personnel Training Institute], 1936. N.p.

Ssu-ch'uan kung-lu yüeh-k'an 四川公路月刊 [Szechwan highways monthly], 1936–37. Chengtu.

Ssu-ch'uan nei-wu t'ung-chi pao-kao shu 四川內務統計報告書 [Szechwan internal statistics report]. Chengtu, 1920.

Ssu-ch'uan nung-min pu pao-kao 四川農民部報告 [Report of the Szechwan Peasant Bureau]. N.p., [1927].

Ssu-ch'uan nung-min yün-tung kai-k'uang 四川農民運動概況 [Conditions in the Szechwan peasant movement]. N.p., [1927].

Ssu-ch'uan pao-an chi-k'an 四川保安季刊 [Szechwan peace preservation quarterly], 1936. Chengtu.

Ssu-ch'uan shan-hou hui-i lu 四川善後會議錄 [Proceedings of the Szechwan Rehabilitation Conference]. [Chengtu], 1926.

Ssu-ch'uan sheng cheng-fu mi-shu ch'u 四川省政府秘書處 [Secretariat, Szechwan provincial government]. *Ssu-ch'uan sheng cheng-fu erh-shih ssu nien-tu min-cheng chi-hua kang-yao* 四川省政府二十四年度民政計畫綱要 [Outline of the 1935 Szechwan provincial government civil administrative plan]. [Chengtu], 1935.

———. *Ssu-ch'uan sheng cheng-fu erh-shih ssu nien-tu shih-cheng kang-yao* 四川省政府二十四年度施政綱要 [Outline of the Szechwan provincial government 1935 implementation plan]. [Chengtu], 1935.

———. *Ssu-ch'uan sheng cheng-fu erh-shih wu nien hsing-cheng tsung pao-kao*

四川省政府二十五年行政總報告 [General administrative report of the Szechwan provincial government for 1936]. [Chengtu], 1937.

―――. *Ssu-ch'uan sheng hsing-cheng tu-ch'a chuan-yüan shih-cheng yen-chiu hui chi-lu* 四川省行政督察專員施政研究會紀錄 [Proceedings of the conference of Szechwan special administrative inspectors on political implementation]. [Chengtu], 1935.

―――. *Ssu-ch'uan sheng kai-k'uang* 四川省概況 [Conditions in Szechwan]. Chengtu, 1939.

Ssu-ch'uan sheng cheng-fu, mi-shu ch'u, kung-pao shih 四川省政府秘書處公報室 [Office of the Government Gazette, Szechwan Provincial Government Secretariat]. *Ssu-ch'uan sheng cheng-fu chao-chi ko-ch'ü chuan-yüan hui-i chi-lu* 四川省政府召集各區專員會議紀錄 [Record of the conference of special administrative inspectors convened by the Szechwan provincial government]. [Chengtu], 1937.

―――. *Ssu-ch'uan sheng cheng-fu kung-pao* 四川省政府公報 [Szechwan Provincial Government Gazette]. Chungking and Chengtu, 1935–37.

Ssu-ch'uan sheng i hui hui-k'an 四川省議會會刊 [Magazine of the Szechwan Provincial Assembly], 1926. Chengtu.

Ssu-ch'uan tang-wu chou-pao 四川黨務週報 [Szechwan party affairs weekly], 1927. Chungking.

Ssu-ch'uan wen-hsien 四川文獻 [Szechwan documents], 1962–72. Taipei.

Ssu-ch'uan yüeh-pao 四川月報 [Szechwan review], 1932–38. Chungking.

Sun Chen 孫震. "An-Ch'uan yü chiao-kung" 安川與剿共 [Pacifying Szechwan and suppressing the Communists]. *SCWH*, March 1966, pp. 6–14.

―――. "Chiao-kung yü t'ao-ni" 剿共與討逆 [Suppressing Communists and punishing rebels]. *SCWH*, June 1966, pp. 1–13.

―――. "Ssu-ch'uan ch'ih-huo yü an-Ch'uan" 四川赤禍與安川 [Red predations and the pacification of Szechwan]. *SCWH*, January 1966, pp. 2–11.

―――. "Ssu-ch'uan chin i-pu t'ung-i yü k'ang-chan" 四川進一步統一與抗戰 [Szechwan's progress toward unification and the War of Resistance]. *SCWH*, October 1966, pp. 1–7

Sun Ching-shih. *Economic Geography of Southwestern China.* Peking, 1962. Washington D.C.: Joint Publications Research Service, Publication no. 15,069, 1962.

Sung Chung-k'an 宋仲堪 and Fu K'uang-lin 傅況鱗. *Ssu-ch'uan ko-lao hui kai-shan chih shang-chüeh* 四川哥老會改善之商榷 [A viewpoint on the reform of the Elder Brother Society in Szechwan]. Chengtu, 1940.

Tai Kao-hsiang 戴高翔. "Liu Hsiang chin-ching huan-ping ching-kuo chui-i" 劉湘晋京患病經過追憶 [Recollections of Liu Hsiang's visit to the capital and his illness]. *Ch'un-ch'iu*, January 1968, p. 8.

―――. "Chui-i Liu Hsiang tao-ching huan-ping ch'ing-hsing" 追憶劉湘

到京患病情形 [Recollections of the circumstances surrounding Liu Hsiang's illness and visit to the capital]. *SCWH*, February 1968, pp. 12–13.

Tajiri 田尻. "Ssu-ch'uan tung-luan kai-kuan" 四川動亂概觀 [An overview of the disorders in Szechwan], trans. Yang Fan 楊凡. *CTSTL*, 1962, no. 4, pp. 49, 61–66.

Tan Shih-hua. *A Chinese Testament: The Autobiography of Tan Shih-hua, As Told to S. Tretiakov.* New York: Simon and Schuster, 1934.

T'ao K'ang-te 陶亢德, ed. *Ya-p'ien chih chin-hsi* 鴉片之今昔 [Opium yesterday and today]. Shanghai, 1937.

Ta-yi hsien chih 大邑縣志 [Gazetteer of Tayi *hsien*]. Tayi, 1930; reprinted Taipei, 1967.

Teng Chih-ch'eng 鄧之誠. "Hu-kuo chün chi-shih" 護國軍紀實 [An account of the Army to Protect the Nation]. *Shih-hsüeh nien-pao* 2, no. 2(1935): 1–22.

Teng Han-hsiang 鄧漢祥. *Teng Ming-chieh hsien-sheng yen-lun chi* 鄧鳴階先生言論集 [Collected speeches of Teng Han-hsiang]. [Chengtu], 1937.

T'ien Cho-chih 田倬之. "Ssu-ch'uan wen-t'i" 四川問題 [The Szechwan problem]. *KWCP*, July 23, 1934.

Tien, Hung-mao. *Government and Politics in Kuomintang China, 1927-1937.* Stanford, Calif.: Stanford University Press, 1972.

Tou-cheng 鬪爭 [Struggle], 1932–34. Juichin.

Trans-Pacific, 1919–38. Tokyo.

Ts'ao Kang-chieh 曹剛傑. "Ts'ung Ssu-ch'uan ti ts'ai-cheng ching-chi shuo tao chiao-fei" 從四川的財政經濟說到剿匪 [Bandit suppression from the financial and economic standpoint in Szechwan]. *Kuo-li Wu-han ta-hsüeh Ssü-ch'uan t'ung-hsüeh-hui hui-k'an* 2, no. 1 (1934).

Tu-li p'ing-lun 獨立評論 [Independent critic], 1933–36. Peiping.

Tung-fang tsa-chih 東方雜誌 [Eastern miscellany], 1912–37. Shanghai.

Tung Ming 東明 [pseud.]. "Ch'uan-sheng ch'ih-huo chi Ch'uan-chün chiao-fei chih ching-kuo" 川省赤禍及川軍剿匪之經過 [Red predations in Szechwan and the Szechwan armies' bandit suppression experiences]. *KWCP*, November 5, 1934.

Wales, Nym [Helen Foster Snow]. *Inside Red China.* New York: Doubleday, Doran & Co., 1939.

Wan, K. "Industrial Development in Szechwan." *Chinese Economic Journal* 15 (December 1934): 609–20.

Wang Chien-min 王健民. *Chung-kuo kung-ch'an tang shih-kao* 中國共產黨史稿 [Draft history of the Chinese Communist Party]. Taipei, 1965.

Wang Ming [Ch'en Shao-yü] and Kan Sing. *Revolutionary China Today.* Moscow: Cooperative Publishing Society of Foreign Workers in the USSR, 1934.

Wei-ta fa-shih 衛大法師 [pseud.]. *Chung-kuo ti pang-hui* 中國的幫會 [Chinese secret societies]. Chungking, 1949.

Wen Hsiu 文修. "Liu-lo Wu-han ti Liu Ts'ung-yün" 流落武漢的劉從雲

[The visitor to Wuhan—Liu Ts'ung-yün]. *Kuo-li Wu-han ta-hsüeh Ssu-ch'uan t'ung-hsüeh hui hui-k'an* 1, no. 2 (1934).

Wen Kung-chih 文公直. *Tsui-chin san-shih nien Chung-kuo chün-shih shih* 最近三十年中國軍事史 [The military history of China over the last thirty years]. Shanghai, 1930; reprinted Taipei, 1962.

West China Missionary News, 1899–1950. Chengtu.

Whang, Paul K. "Szechwan: The Hotbed of Civil Wars." *China Weekly Review,* October 22, 1932, pp. 344–45.

Whitson, William. "The Concept of Military Generation: The Chinese Communist Case." *Asian Survey* 8 (November 1968): 921–48.

Who's Who in China, Fifth Edition. Shanghai: The China Weekly Review, 1936.

Widler, Elly. *Six Months Prisoner of the Szechwan Military.* Shanghai: China Press, 1924.

Wiens, Herold. "The 'Shu Tao' or Road to Szechwan." *Geographical Review* 39 (1949): 584–604.

Wilbur, C. Martin. "Military Separatism and the Process of Reunification under the Nationalist Regime." *China in Crisis.* Edited by Ping-ti Ho and Tang Tsou. Chicago: University of Chicago Press, 1968.

Wilson, Dick. *The Long March: The Epic of Chinese Communism's Survival.* London: Hamish Hamilton, 1971.

Wo-ch'iu chung-tzu 沃丘仲子 [Fei Hsing-chien, 費行簡]. *Tang-tai ming-jen hsiao-chuan* 當代名人小傳 [Short biographies of modern famous men]. Shanghai, 1920.

Wo Yü 握瑜 [pseud.]. "Ssu-ch'uan nung-ts'un ching-chi chih chien-t'ao" 四川農村經濟之檢討 [Investigation of the Szechwanese farm village economy]. *Kuo-li Wu-han ta-hsüeh Ssu-ch'uan t'ung-hsüeh hui hui-k'an* 1, no. 2 (1934).

Woodhead, H. G. W., ed. *The China Year Book, 1932, 1936.* Shanghai: North-China Daily News & Herald, 1932, 1936.

_____. *The Yangtze and Its Problems.* Shanghai: Mercury Press, 1931.

Wou, Odoric Y. K. "A Chinese 'Warlord' Faction: The Chihli Clique, 1918–1924." Columbia Essays in International Affairs. *The Dean's Papers,* 3 (1967): 249–73.

Wright, Mary Clabaugh, ed. *China in Revolution: The First Phase, 1900–1913.* New Haven: Yale University Press, 1968.

_____. *The Last Stand of Chinese Conservatism: The T'ung-Chih Restoration, 1862–1874.* Stanford, Calif.: Stanford University Press, 1957.

Wu Chi-sheng 吳濟生. *Hsin-tu chien-wen lu* 新都見聞錄 [The story of the new capital]. Shanghai, 1940.

Wu-sheng hsien chih 武勝縣志 [Gazetteer of Wusheng *hsien*]. Wusheng, 1931; reprinted Taipei, 1968.

Yang Ch'ao-yung 楊兆容. "Hsin-hai hou chih Ssu-ch'uan chan-chi" 辛亥後之

四川戰記 [A record of the wars in Szechwan after the Revolution of 1911]. *CTSTL*, 1958, no. 6, pp. 39–92.

Yang, S. C. "The Revolution in Szechwan, 1911–1912." *Journal of the West China Border Research Society* 6 (1933–34): 64–90.

Yang Sen 楊森. "Wo-ti yang-sheng chih tao" 我的養生之道 [The way I live]. *Chung-wai tsa-chih,* April 1967, pp. 4–7.

————. "Wu Tzu-yü hsien-sheng yu Ssu-ch'uan hui-i lu" 吳子玉先生游四川回憶錄 [Reminiscences of Wu P'ei-fu's sojourn in Szechwan]. *Chuan-chi wen-hsüeh,* April 1966, pp. 7–10.

Yang Ting-sheng 柳定生, ed. *Ssu-ch'uan li-shih* 四川歷史 [The history of Szechwan]. Chengtu, 1942.

Yang Yung-t'ai 楊永泰. *Yang Yung-t'ai hsien-sheng yen-lun chi* 楊永泰先生言論集 [Collected addresses of Yang Yung-t'ai]. Jesselton, Sabah, 1965.

Yin-hang chou-k'an 銀行週刊 [Banker's weekly], 1934–1937. Shanghai.

Yü Nung 與農 [pseud.]. "Ssu-ch'uan chih k'o-chüan tsa-shui yü chiao-ch'ih ch'ien-t'u" 四川之苛捐雜稅與剿赤前途 [Szechwan's burdensome taxes and miscellaneous levies and the future of bandit suppression]. *Kuo-li Wu-han ta-hsüeh Ssu-ch'uan t'ung-hsüeh hui hui-k'an* 1, no. 2 (1934).

Yüeh pao 月報 [The monthly report], 1937. Shanghai.

Government Archives

F.O. Great Britain, Foreign Office. Embassy and Consular Archives (File F.O. 228).

Great Britain, Foreign Office. Foreign Office Correspondence (Files F.O. 371 and F.O. 676).

S.D. United States Department of State. General Records of the Department of State. Record Group 59, "China: Internal Affairs, 1910–1938."

Index